A Time to Build Anew

*How to Find the True,
Good, and Beautiful
in America*

TODD HARTCH

A Time
to
Build Anew

*How to Find the
True, Good, and Beautiful
in America*

 Angelico Press

First published in the USA
by Angelico Press 2021
© Todd Hartch 2021

For information, address:
Angelico Press
169 Monitor St.
Brooklyn, NY 11222
angelicopress.com
info@angelicopress.com

ISBN 978-1-62138-711-4 pb
ISBN 978-1-62138-712-1 cloth
ISBN 978-1-62138-713-8 ebook

Cover design: Michael Schrauzer

CONTENTS

Introduction

THIS BOOK is a response to the sad, silly America of 2020, and now 2021, but it is not about politics, at least not as usually understood. It is not primarily a diagnosis of cultural malaise. And it is not a theoretical proposal or a plan. This is a book of examples, a book of models, a book about how to live in America.

Almost 2000 years ago, in a society as divided and confusing as our own, the apostle Paul told his friends in Philippi, "Join with others in being imitators of me, brothers and sisters, and observe those who thus conduct themselves according to the model you have in us."[1] Paul's letters make clear that he was happy to advise, teach, and rebuke the early Christians in his orbit, but in this instance he demonstrated that his words were not enough. His flock also needed flesh and blood examples of how to live. Theological and moral advice, as essential as it is, can become dry and abstract if not coupled with living models.

Saint Pius X, after his withering denunciation of the heresy of modernism in *Pascendi dominici gregis*, wrote his next two encyclicals on Saint Anselm and Saint Charles Borromeo. "We are of the opinion," he said, "that the shining example of Christ's soldiers has far greater value in the winning and sanctifying of souls than the words of profound treatises."[2] He pointed to the example of Anselm, who wanted to live a quiet life of study and prayer, but "was forced, out of love for sound doctrine and for the sanctity of the Church, to give up a life of peace, the friendship of the great ones of the world, the favors of the powerful, the united affection, which he at first enjoyed, of his very brethren in troubles of all kinds."[3] As necessary as was the analysis and condemnation of modernism in *Pascendi*, by

---

1. Philippians 3:17.
2. Pius X, *Editae saepe*, 1910.
3. Pius X, *Communium rerum*, 1909.

1

itself it was a largely negative project; Anselm and Charles Borromeo provided the positive alternative. Their lives showed Catholics how to live.

The two great questions for Catholics and other orthodox Christians in America today are "what is wrong?" and "what should we do?" As far as trying to understand our circumstances, we have a rich array of resources as the heirs of the Second Vatican Council and the rich papal magisteria of John XXIII, Paul VI, John Paul II, and Benedict XVI, all of which is available for free on the Internet. Published in 1992, the *Catechism of the Catholic Church*—the first new general catechism since the Council of Trent—synthesizes Catholic doctrine in a clear and even beautiful manner. Popular media, including the EWTN television and radio networks, Bishop Robert Barron's Word on Fire ministries, and the apologists at Catholic Answers, have made orthodox Catholic teaching more accessible than ever before. Catholic books and magazines for every reading and educational level, from kindergarten to post-graduate, are being published by serious Catholic publishers. For many Catholics, the first step should be to read, first, what the Church teaches, and then to investigate how wise Catholics have applied those truths to the specific circumstances of our day.

Yet many of the most committed Catholics are still at a loss. They know what books to read. They know what television shows to watch. They do not know what to do. They do not know how to live. They need models and examples and this is what this book seeks to provide. To paraphrase Paul, my purpose is to identify those who have lived well so that twenty-first-century American Catholics can follow their example. Of course, your own gifts and talents are unique, as is your specific situation, so you should not copy them blindly or mechanistically. Rather, study them, take inspiration from them, and adapt their insights and methods to your circumstances.

The rest of this introduction provides the historical background for today's situation and lays out the problems, ranging from annoyances to life-threatening issues, that American Catholics face in the early twenty-first century. It then offers a historical and theological justification for not giving up hope and revisits the role of models and examples in our life of faith. The chapters that follow provide seven different examples of ways to live in beauty, goodness, and truth, despite the ugliness, meanness, and pervasive falsehoods of our age.

Where We Stand

Although this book is not primarily a diagnosis of cultural malaise, a certain amount of explanation is necessary to set the stage for the examples that make up the bulk of this book. We need to have some idea about the nature of the crisis we are in before we can see the relevance of the examples in the rest of the book. For the purposes of a brief and necessarily simplified introduction, I will focus on three related issues that together help to explain the contemporary Catholic situation: first and most important, the challenges posed by modernity; second, Vatican II and the flawed Catholic response to modernity; and, third, the nature of social and cultural change in the past century.[4] Modernity receives the bulk of my attention because it is the root issue.

The heart of the problem is not, as many Catholics believe, Vatican II, but rather modernity itself. As important as the Second Vatican Council (1962–1965) was, both for good and for ill, it was itself a *response* to larger problems, which we could describe broadly as modernity, and the closely associated processes of industrialization and urbanization. These large-scale developments, far more than the Second Vatican Council's suggested reforms, represent the biggest challenge faced by Catholicism since the Reformation, and possibly since the Muslim invasions of the seventh and eighth centuries. Taking modernity not in the chronological sense but as the progressive disenchantment of the world, often characterized by secular forms of political power, flattening of social hierarchies, market economies, individualism, and the nation state, it is clear why its

---

4. For an extended analysis of modernity and religion, see Brad Gregory's *The Unintended Reformation: How a Religious Revolution Secularized Society* (Cambridge: Belknap Press, 2012) and Thomas Pfau's *Minding the Modern: Human Agency, Intellectual Traditions, and Responsible Knowledge* (Notre Dame: University of Notre Dame Press, 2013).

rise posed a challenge to Catholicism. Since the Catholic Church had worked hand-in-hand with political authorities throughout the Middle Ages and the early modern period, the development of the anticlerical secular state, exemplified by the French Revolution (1789–1799) and its successor states, came as a particular shock. No longer the honored partner of European monarchies, even in predominantly Catholic countries, the nineteenth-century Catholic Church found itself disenfranchised, dispossessed, and persecuted. Even the more religiously friendly Constitution of the United States of America, which permitted Catholicism but gave it no special place in society, raised new questions about the Catholic role in a pluralistic society. Modernity's attack on authority undermined not only the Church's political and public role, but also, and what is ultimately more important, its moral and philosophical influence. It was not merely its power that became suspect, but its claims to truth.

Modernity's flattening effect on social hierarchies, which shifted power from royals and nobles to merchants and bureaucrats and away from monarchy to representative forms of government, was not *per se* incompatible with the Church, for there was no definitive reason why the Church could not work as well with one class as with another, and it had existed under all sorts of political systems in its long history. However, this social flattening implicitly and sometimes explicitly critiqued the Church, which stood out more and more as a hierarchical institution. What gave the Church the right to stand against the flattening forces of modernity? In many countries of the world, such as post-revolutionary Mexico in the period from 1917 to 1930, Catholicism came to be identified by the secular elite as the principal enemy of progress, a redoubt of fanatical oppressors who took advantage of the weak by keeping them ignorant and submissive. The pope and the bishops, in particular, had an air of medieval pomp and authority that could not help but attract attention. Although there was no necessary reason why Catholics could not participate in a democratic society or cooperate with a democratic government, to outsiders (and, it must be said, to some traditional Catholics) the papacy, the traditional dress of clerics, and a host of other ties to the medieval past suggested an

4

uncompromising institution that had no place in a modern nation. Individual Catholics struggled to find their place and role in democratic mass societies.

Economic and social change made the crisis for Catholicism even more acute. Industrialization, starting about 1760 in Britain and spreading throughout western Europe and North America in the nineteenth and twentieth centuries, destroyed traditional ways of life that had fit well with Catholicism. Men, women, and children moved to cities, worked in dangerous and repetitive jobs, and lived in ugly, crowded conditions. It was not just the physical and emotional stress of the new environment that threatened the Catholic faith of the new industrial workers; it was also their uprooting from community, extended family, and local church, and their anonymous existence in a mass of other uprooted and stressed workers. Even as the Catholic Church tried to respond with new parishes and new methods of ministry (such as the many lay movements of Catholic Action), other political and social actors offered alternative solutions to urban difficulties. Diametrically opposed to Catholicism were Marxism and other atheistic socialist movements, and these rivals the Church confronted directly in its emerging social teaching, most notably by Leo XIII in *Rerum novarum* of 1891.

Perhaps even more challenging than socialism was simple complacency. Many members of the new mass societies felt detached from Catholicism and from religion in general. They often focused more on material comfort than on spiritual issues. Educated in state schools, informed by secular newspapers, separated from the natural world, they increasingly accepted a functionally agnostic or deist perspective in which God, if he existed at all, was not a matter of great importance. As industrialization deepened and the logic of the market permeated more and more institutions, many Europeans and North Americans came to see themselves primarily as individuals and consumers and attempted to maximize their happiness through consumption and leisure, with little thought for moral and religious goods.

The Catholic Church in the United States had to confront the same issues of urbanization and industrialization, and, as in Europe, many Catholics were lost to radicalization, drink, secularism, and the other pathologies of modernity, but it was in some respects more successful than the churches of Europe in attracting and integrating urban Catholics into parish life. European migration in the nineteenth century turned what had been a small and marginal institution into one of the major players in urban America. Often located in ethnic neighborhoods, parishes became focal points of culture as well as religion. Catholic schools, lay organizations, festivals, and devotional traditions imported from the old country made it possible for millions of immigrant Catholics and their children to live in what is now often termed "the Catholic ghetto" but is probably better understood as a network of Catholic subcultures. Poverty characterized the lives of many, and deep intellectual life was rare, to name just two obvious pitfalls of pre-Vatican II American Catholicism, but the achievements of the Church in the era from 1850 to 1960 were also obvious. Most impressively, a poor Church of immigrants fashioned a comprehensive system of Catholic life in an often hostile land. Generations of Catholics lived the faith and passed it on to their children. Large families were happy to send a daughter to a religious order or a son to the priesthood, and the same generosity enabled the building of a vast system of parochial schools, with religious sisters as the primary teachers.

The system started to break down, however, before the Second Vatican Council. There were many reasons, some cultural, some economic, but one of the most important was a specifically American form of modernity: suburbanization. After World War II, industrial methods were applied to the building of millions of new single family homes in growing rings around the nation's cities. The novelty of the post-war building pattern was its separation of large tracts of homes from agricultural, commercial, and industrial zones and its radical dependence on the private automobile. The problem for the Catholic Church was not simply that urban churches were losing members to the suburbs. It was that, even when new Catholic churches were built in the suburbs, the automobile-dependent suburban lifestyle tended to marginalize the Church. The new suburban churches were places to drive to once or twice a week, not centers of spiritual, cultural, and social life for large ethnic communities. The surviving urban churches were also no longer the spiritual, cultural, and social centers of large ethnic communities that they once had been—because the surviving ethnic communities were no longer large and because other groups, often not Catholic, moved in to replace those who moved out of the suburbs. If Europeans lost their Catholic faith in the cities, Americans lost it in the suburbs.

In a nutshell, the American Catholic struggle since 1950 was how to avoid closing urban churches and how to make suburban Catholicism vital. That struggle was exacerbated by cultural and economic changes of the 1960s that made religious life and the priesthood less appealing to young Catholics. At exactly the time when the Catholic Church in the United States needed an infusion of committed young nuns and priests to deal with the twin challenges of suburbanization and urban recomposition, it instead lost many of those it already had and saw the number of new recruits slow to a trickle. Catholics of all sorts, from the most recent immigrant to the prosperous suburban housewife, were having a difficult time figuring out how to live a Catholic life in modern America.

The second major issue that explains the contemporary Catholic situation in the United States is the flawed Catholic response to modernity. This flawed response is related to the Second Vatican Council, but not in the way many believe. To the extent that Vatican II is a source of difficulties for today's Catholics, it is largely a problem caused by ignorance of the texts of the council and the failure to carry out its directives, although the ambiguity of some passages does bear some of the blame.

The council was an attempt by the Catholic Church to come to terms with modernity. Unlike nineteenth- and early twentieth-century popes who confronted the errors of modernism—the religious relativism that is associated with but not identical to modernity—head on, the council fathers took a more positive approach, emphasizing areas of common interest rather than denouncing errors:

> The joys and the hopes, the griefs and the anxieties of the men of this age, especially those who are poor or in any way afflicted, these are the joys and hopes, the griefs and anxieties of the followers of Christ. Indeed, nothing genuinely human fails to raise

an echo in their hearts. For theirs is a community composed of men. United in Christ, they are led by the Holy Spirit in their journey to the Kingdom of their Father and they have welcomed the news of salvation which is meant for every man. That is why this community realizes that it is truly linked with mankind and its history by the deepest of bonds.[5]

These opening lines of the council's statement on the place of the Church in the modern world signal not a new teaching—for Catholic doctrine cannot reverse itself or contradict previous teachings—but a new approach.

Perhaps, however, the council fathers went too far. So different was the tone of the Second Vatican Council, so far was it from the "anathemas" in the *Syllabus of Errors* of Pope Pius IX, for example, that many Catholics concluded that Catholic *doctrines* had changed and that those that had not yet changed could be changed in the future. Had they taken the time to read the texts of the council they would have noticed a recurrent theme of continuity with previous councils and magisterial teachings and an all-embracing reliance on the Scriptures.[6] But few lay Catholics did read the documents and the bishops and priests who brought the teachings of Vatican II back to Catholics in the pews did a remarkably poor job of explaining what was happening and why it was happening.

In contrast to the Catholics of Poland, where Karol Wojtyła, the future pope John Paul II, started 500 small groups that studied the council documents for decades, American Catholics experienced Vatican II principally in severe but largely unexplained liturgical changes (a simplified liturgy in the vernacular, rather than the traditional Latin) and then in a growing sense that almost everything Catholic was "up for grabs."[7] Each one of the council's sixteen docu-

---

5. *Gaudium et spes* 1.

6. For example, the council's most important document, *Lumen gentium*, says clearly in its first paragraph that it is "following faithfully the teaching of previous councils," while *Sacrosanctum concilium*, the document that reformed the liturgy, said it was in "faithful obedience to tradition."

7. George Weigel, *Witness to Hope: The Biography of Pope John Paul II* (New York: Harper Collins, 1999), 204–5.

ments had much to say that could have been helpful to American Catholics, but most believers seem to have internalized ideas that were not in the documents themselves, or to have focused on the least important elements of the texts, or to have ignored the most important directives. For instance, lay people became more involved in the formal liturgy, taking to heart the council's call for "active participation" by all the faithful. They became lectors, ushers, cantors, and extraordinary ministers of Holy Communion. All these activities were in keeping with new lay roles allowed by the council, but the major point of the council was not to make lay people into mini-clerics. The main call of the council was for lay people to "seek the kingdom of God by engaging in temporal affairs and by ordering them according to the plan of God." They should do this "in the world, that is, in each and in all of the secular professions and occupations" and "in the ordinary circumstances of family and social life, from which the very web of their existence is woven." They should "work for the sanctification of the world from within as a leaven" and "make Christ known to others, especially by the testimony of a life resplendent in faith, hope and charity."[8]

In other words, Vatican II emphasized the special vocation of lay Catholics, not to the ambo or the head of the communion line, but to the worlds of family, commerce, politics, culture, and all the many forms of human life *outside* of the doors of a church. They were supposed to transform their environments and to be witnesses of Christ to all those around them. After the Second Vatican Council this worldly lay vocation was exactly what American Catholics failed at most dramatically, with Catholics conforming to the culture of modernity much more than they transformed it. In fact, they did *much worse* in this area than the generations before Vatican II, who created vibrant Catholic subcultures. The "crisis of Vatican II" is thus less a crisis of the council's teachings, than a crisis of faulty explanation by the hierarchy and faulty implementation by the laity. The most neglected aspect of Vatican II is the mission of the laity, which is a key theme of this book.

The third issue that explains the contemporary Catholic situation

8. *Lumen gentium* 31.

is the rapidity of change that has characterized the industrial era. One part of the issue is that scientific discoveries build on each other and that one new technology leads to another. For instance, the integrated circuit and the continuous improvements in new generations of microchips have led to rapid improvements in the memory and function of computers even as they have facilitated the rapid shrinkage of computer size. Another part of the issue is that new technologies are not neutral additions to a way of life, but, to the extent that they are adopted, alter that way of life. For instance, the addition of digital cameras, video recorders, text, and Internet access to cell phones has led to new practices, including "selfies," the now ubiquitous videos of police violence, "sexting," and the inability of some unfortunates to spend more than five minutes without fiddling with their phones. When you put these two aspects of technological development together, you see that a society characterized by continuous scientific discoveries and continuous technological developments will also be a society characterized by rapid social, economic, and cultural change. A society without technological development *might* change socially, economically, or culturally, but it might not. A society with technological development *will* change socially, economically, or culturally. As entire professions disappear, new ones emerge. Shepherds, so fundamental to biblical society, now seem quaint, while "information technology" specialists are now common enough to warrant their own abbreviations and television shows. Once-important customs vanish, while new ones, unimaginable to previous generations, come to seem normal, even natural.

In reality, a new technology takes generations to evaluate. What does it do to family life? What are its political implications? How, then, should it be limited? But in industrial society over the last 200 years technological change has come so quickly and so persistently that little such evaluation has taken place. Parents at any given time have not understood the full implications of the newest technologies, meaning that they cannot prudently advise and care for their own children. Should a child work in a factory? Should a child drive a car? Should a child have a smart phone? These and a multitude of other questions were new to succeeding generations of Americans faced with unfamiliar technologies. The answers, especially to the first two questions, might seem obvious today, but that is only because enough time has passed that the impact and implications of the technologies have become more evident.

However, parents, teachers, lawmakers, pastors, and other leaders do not have a hundred years; they have to make decisions about new technologies in the present. They must decide yea or nay, when, at what age, and how each technology should be used. The default decision in the last century has been to accept almost every technological innovation with minimal limitations. This is not as crazy as it sounds, because, as is evident from extended life spans and improved standards of living, many new technologies have had obvious and extensive positive impacts on human life, but it is still not the best policy. Technologies must be tested and evaluated. People know this principle in their hearts and actually apply it when a new technology is obviously dangerous, but we all find it harder to do when a technology has some obviously positive results or promises positive results.

To take just two technologies where the evaluation process never happened or was short-circuited by economic pressures, we shall look briefly at the automobile and the contraceptive pill. Although the noise, speed, and danger of the automobile were obvious in its early years, many Americans overcame their early objections because of the new technology's benefits: quicker and more convenient travel and thus the ability to live further from work. The auto industry's efficient attacks on its rivals, including campaigns to punish the newly invented "crime" of jaywalking and lobbying for government support of roads and highways, paved the way for increasing American reliance on private automobiles as the normal and "natural" mode of travel.[9] But few Americans examined the implications of relying on this mode of transportation: longer and longer commutes as one ring of suburbs expanded beyond the last, increasing isolation of Americans in their moving metal boxes and cul-de-sacs, massive consumption of fossil fuels, forms of settle-

---

9. Peter D. Norton, "Street Rivals: Jaywalking and the Invention of the Motor Age Street," *Technology and Culture* 48, no. 2 (April 2007): 331–59; James J. Flink, *The Automobile Age* (Cambridge, MA: MIT Press, 1990), 369–73.

ment designed more for cars than humans, roadways that made fewer and fewer concessions to pedestrians and bicycles, and a noticeable pull-back from the public sphere.[10]

The contraceptive pill had, if possible, an even more radical cultural impact than the automobile. Although contraception was rejected by all Christian denominations until 1930 and was then only permitted by Anglicans in exceptional circumstances, in the following decades it slowly became acceptable in Protestant denominations.[11] What really turned on the floodgates of acceptance was the approval of the birth control pill (a combination of estrogen and progestogen hormones) by the US Food and Drug Administration in 1960. The pill's effectiveness at preventing pregnancy and ready availability gradually overcame moral objections, so that by the 1990s it was rare to find an American Protestant who had moral objections to contraception. In 1968, Pope Paul VI reaffirmed the Catholic Church's rejection of contraception in *Humanae vitae*, but with less effect than he had hoped. Catholics were soon contracepting at the same high rates as other Americans.

The results were far-reaching. Sex was transformed from a procreative and unitive act into a form of pleasure-seeking and amusement. Detached from reproduction, it lost both its sacred and mysterious allure and its marital context. Just as Paul VI had predicted, divorce and promiscuity plagued the lands that adopted the pill. When what was intended to be commitment-free unreproductive sex nevertheless led to pregnancies (when the pill failed or was used sporadically) the solution was not to examine the logical fallacy of "safe sex" or to interrogate the promises of the pill, but to call for abortion as a necessary backup strategy. The combination of a pill-fueled sexual free-for-all with the more than fifty million abortions committed in the United States since the Supreme Court identified abortion as a constitutional right in 1973 has fostered a selfish

---

10. Andres Duany, Elizabeth Plater-Zyberk, and Jeff Speck, *Suburban Nation: The Rise of Sprawl and the Decline of the American Dream* (New York: North Point Press, 2000), 5–12.

11. Mary Eberstadt, *How the West Really Lost God: A New Theory of Secularization* (West Conshohocken, PA: Templeton Press, 2013), 144–47.

and utilitarian culture in which confused victims of the sexual revolution assert their "pride" at having taken the lives of their own children so that they could stay in college or complete a project at work.

In short, the Catholic Church's long encounter with modernity has been difficult. In the United States, the Catholic response to urbanization and industrialization succeeded more than its later attempts to deal with the post-industrial challenges of suburbanization, technological change, and material prosperity. Although the texts of the Second Vatican Council do in fact offer both real insight into the modern world and specific guidelines about what the faithful should be doing, they were not explained in a deep or ongoing way in the immediate aftermath of the council. Catholics, adrift like the rest of America, have struggled to evaluate the new technologies that emerge from Detroit, Hollywood, and Silicon Valley, and have felt themselves buffeted by the rapid cultural changes that inevitably follow. In today's ugly America, it is difficult to know what is true and it is hard to be good.

What Hope Do We Have?

Is there any hope? Of course there is. As Christ promised Peter, the gates of Hell will never prevail against the Church. The Church is more beloved of Christ than we can imagine. The graces that he has bestowed on it cannot be conceived. And as individuals we also have hope because he has promised that, whatever our circumstance, he will always provide a way for us. Although there is no guarantee of peace or prosperity—God does have a wonderful plan for your life, but it might be martyrdom—there is a promise of his constant presence and faithfulness.[12]

There is also hope because we have models from the past and present who show us how to live. They are of inestimable worth to us because they "put flesh on the bones" of our ideas. As Jody Bottum has pointed out in his meditation on "Post-Protestant America," many Catholics have no idea how to live out their faith because they are converts or "reverts" who have read their way into the

---

12. Matthew 16:18; 1 Corinthians 10:13; Hebrews 13:5.

Church.[13] They know the Catechism and Scott Hahn or Joseph Ratzinger, but they do not know how to spend their time. The culture is declining noticeably, their local church offers little of interest, and the world of politics seems crass and unchangeable, so they work and read and pray and attend Mass but make no difference to the world around them. They know they should be doing something, but they do not know what to do or how to do it. They might know what is true, but they do not know how to communicate or teach truth. They might know what is good, but they do not know how to do good, or are afraid to start. The ugliness and banality of their world drives them to despair, but they do not know how to beautify it.

American history should give us hope. From Plymouth Rock to Pennsylvania, from Cotton Mather to Jonathan Edwards, from Harvard to the College of William and Mary, recent immigrants and established residents devoted themselves to religiously informed renewal and reformation. If countries have a sort of cultural DNA—and I believe they do—America's genetic code includes a profound openness to the religious reform of culture, to moral reform movements, and to the physical organization and reorganization of cities on the basis of moral and religious visions. In fact, most of the great reform movements in American history—the anti-slavery movement, the women's movement, the modern civil rights movement, the farmworkers movement, and the anti-abortion movement—are infused with a fervent, practical piety that seems particularly American.

To give a famous example, the Puritans of Massachusetts Bay, trying to escape from persecution and what they perceived as the decadence and irreligion of England, sought to build a new Christian society in the wilderness. The continuing vitality of Harvard University and the beauty of the Beacon Hill neighborhood are ongoing legacies of that Puritan experiment. William Penn's colony in Pennsylvania had a far different vision, but it too was fundamentally religious, attempting to foster freedom of religion and pacifism

13. Joseph Bottum, *An Anxious Age: The Post-Protestant Ethic and the Spirit of America* (New York: Image, 2014).

in keeping with the founder's Quaker faith. The unpretentious but graceful colonial architecture of Elspreth's Alley and Society Hill in Philadelphia are witnesses to the success of Penn's vision of creating a welcoming, prosperous, and lasting society in the New World.

Of course, the Catholic presence on the East Coast was small until the middle of the nineteenth century. But on the other side of the continent, the string of settlements from San Diego to San Francisco, including San Luis Obispo, Carmel, Santa Barbara, and sixteen other missions started by Spanish and Mexican Franciscans between 1769 and 1823 point to the Catholic visionaries who risked their lives to build a Catholic society in the New World. At the heart of each mission were a church, a central plaza, and other important buildings; in many cases these missions evolved into the modern cities of California. The former missions' names and those of the cities named after angels (Los Angeles), the Eucharist (Sacramento), and mercy (Merced) are so familiar that it is often possible to ignore the sacred geography of America's most populous state.

In other words, although the United States cannot be characterized in the strict sense as a Christian nation, much less a Catholic one, it has a strong tradition of public religious activism, including specifically Catholic mission and reform. Religious believers have carved out new communities, built institutions, and made cultures of moral and aesthetic beauty. Christians, including Catholics, have started new cities, built new churches, and crafted beautiful places in the wilderness.

The American present also should give us hope. The seven examples from the twentieth and twenty-first centuries that make up the chapters of this book are just the tip of the iceberg. America today teems with Catholics and other people of good will who are creating luminous beauty, doing good works in the city, and teaching the truth to those who are hungering for it.

The True, the Good, and Beautiful

The examples that follow are all, in one way or another, related to the "three things that will never die: truth, goodness and beauty." As Peter Kreeft explains,

These are the three things we all need, and need absolutely, and know we need, and know we need absolutely. Our minds want not only some truth and some falsehood, but all truth, without limit. Our wills want not only some good and some evil, but all good, without limit. Our desires, imaginations, feelings or hearts want not just some beauty and some ugliness, but all beauty without limit. For these are the only three things that we never get bored with, and never will, because they are three attributes of God, and therefore of all God's creation: three transcendental or absolutely universal properties of all reality. All that exists is true, the proper object of mind. All that exists is good, the proper object of the will. All that exists is beautiful, the proper object of the heart, or feelings, or desires, or sensibilities, or imagination.[14]

So important, nay, essential, are these three transcendentals, argues Kreeft, that all cultures strive for them in some way, often focusing on one, but always giving at least some attention to the others. Their philosophers seek and teach truth; their prophets proclaim the principles of goodness and justice; their artists produce works of beauty.[15] In fact, it is impossible for even the smallest, seemingly most insignificant aspect of creation, merely because it exists, not to reflect truth, goodness, and beauty in some way; but human beings have a unique superabundance of truth, goodness, and beauty, because they are made in the image and likeness of God, and because of the works of culture that they are able to create. As rational creatures, human beings have the god-like ability to know the truth, to magnify goodness, and to let beauty shine.

At the heart of our cultural malaise are failures to seek the true, the good, and the beautiful, due largely to modernity's insistence that reality is simply "neutral," rather than full of truth, goodness, and beauty. Modernity deprives us of our birthright by giving us a cosmos of neutral space and meaningless material objects. Since

14. Peter Kreeft, "Lewis's Philosophy of Truth, Goodness and Beauty," in *C.S. Lewis as Philosopher: Truth, Goodness and Beauty*, ed. David Baggett, Gary Habermas, and Jerry Walls (Downers Grove, IL: InterVarsity Press), 23.

15. Ibid., 24.

human happiness is found "in the contemplation of the three realities that modernity has tried to conceal, namely, those of truth, goodness, and beauty," it is no surprise that the modern world is so gloomy.[16] We live in physically ugly cities whose inhabitants increasingly do evil and believe lies.

To give just one example, a man whom we shall call Sam drives home alone from work on a busy four-lane road, past stores with large signs and enormous parking lots, fast-food places, chain stores, big boxes. After arriving at his home, which is not exactly beautiful but is much more attractive than anything on the strip he just drove down, he microwaves some food while watching pornography on his tablet. Sam feels a bit uncomfortable with his growing use of those images, but he tells himself that there is no need to worry, since he is not hurting anyone.

Sam's city has been constructed without thought for beauty in public places because beauty is not seen as practical or efficient, although it is valued in the private realm, particularly by the wealthy. He lacks close relationships with other people and tries to use electronic images as a substitute for human intimacy. He has qualms about pornography but has no coherent moral framework that would enable him to analyze exactly what is wrong with his actions. In fact, Sam's actions are objectively sinful and, although only God can judge his heart, it is probable that they are mortal sins for which he merits eternal damnation.[17] Sadly, his moral code is so truncated, so devoid of depth and substance, that it offers him no clarity about the status of his acts or about the necessity and possibility of repentance and change of life. Sadly also, most of the built environment where Sam lives and works is ugly and dehumanizing; there is little in it to point him away from his acedia, only invitations to consumption and subtle reminders of his aloneness. The problem is not that this is a poor or unimaginative society; it is that

16. James Matthew Wilson, *The Vision of the Soul: Truth, Goodness, and Beauty in the Western Tradition* (Washington, DC: Catholic University of America Press, 2017), 43.

17. *The Catechism of the Catholic Church* (CCC) defines use of pornography as a grave sin and says that those who die in a state of mortal sin will be consigned to hell: CCC 1035, 2354.

this society's thought and resources have been devoted more to selling Sam gadgets he does not need and to building an infrastructure designed to whisk him, sitting alone in his car, quickly from work to home, than to teaching him the truth, or helping him do the good, or inspiring him with beauty.

The thesis of this book is that Americans do not have to live this way. Two great lessons of classical and Christian thought are that "reality is ordered to beauty" and that "human dignity specifically consists in our capacity to perceive and contemplate that splendorous order."[18] The despair and ugliness of today's America is actually unrealistic because it is based on faulty understandings of reality and the human person. The true, the good, and the beautiful are available to all. The examples that follow include a sculptor, two religious orders, a university, an architecture school, a trio of professors, and a politician. Even now Americans from different walks of life are seeking and finding the truths that could set Sam free. They are doing works of mercy and love. And they are creating art, music, and architecture whose beauty points beyond itself, giving witness to a better way.

18. Wilson, *Vision of the Soul*, 26, 89.

1

Beauty and Tradition
The Sculpture of Frederick Hart

I n 1989, JAMES F. COOPER, the editor of a traditional arts journal, read a piece in the *Washington Post* by a sculptor he had never heard of. Unlike many of his fellow artists, Frederick Hart sympathized with complaints about the way in which the National Endowment for the Arts was spending taxpayers' money. "Once, art served society rather than biting at its heels," said Hart. "Once, under the banner of beauty and order, art was a rich and meaningful embellishment of life, embracing—not desecrating—its ideals." Good public art, he argued, should be ennobling, not denigrating. "If art is to flourish in the 21st century," he said, "it must renew its moral authority by . . . rededicating itself to life rather than art. Works of art achieve greatness by embodying great ideas, as well as by sheer mastery of the medium."[1] Cooper was so impressed by Hart's words that he traveled to meet him in Washington, DC. As they ate lunch, Hart asked if his visitor had ever seen his sculpture at Washington National Cathedral. Cooper had never heard of it.

"We went there on a Friday afternoon. There were workmen still working on the façade. And I recall that they started to descend, climbed down the scaffolding as we were approaching. It was almost like a movie. And I recall being amazed," Cooper says.[2] "I had almost given up on finding a contemporary artist whose work

1. Frederick Hart, "Contemporary Art Is Perverted Art," *Washington Post*, 22 August 1989.
2. "Art Under the Radar," *Think Tank with Ben Wattenberg*, PBS, 23 August 2001, http://www.pbs.org/thinktank/arts_transcript.html.

could be measured against the Old Masters. . . . The setting sun illu-minated with breathtaking clarity the details of one of the most beautiful works of art I have ever encountered. . . . Then I realized that the man standing beside me, singlehandedly, beginning at age twenty-six in 1969, had conceived and brought to fruition a work of art that successfully challenges the combined artistic vision of the last half century."[3] Cooper said, "I'm really delighted to meet you, because if I hadn't found you, I would have had to invent you."[4]

Frederick Hart's early life offered little promise of the great talent that he ultimately manifested. After a difficult childhood that included the death of his mother, many years living with an aunt in South Carolina, dropping out of high school, and being kicked out of college, Hart moved to Washington, DC, in 1961 with the vague idea of studying art. After brief stints at the Corcoran School of Art and American University, he decided that he wanted to sculpt. In search of a teacher, he apprenticed himself to Felix de Weldon, sculptor of the Iwo Jima memorial, and worked in 1966 as an orna-mentalist, doing decorative plaster work. "The world of art that I had suddenly found myself in, in 1961, was just not what I had dreamed of living," Hart said. "So I rebelled completely against the whole modern establishment, or the modern academy, if you will, and just went off completely on my own, seeking, you know, a com-pletely traditional or classically-oriented artistic endeavor."[5] Soon he realized that the national center of traditional stone carving was across town at the National Cathedral, an Episcopal cathedral that was being built in the Gothic style, with flying buttresses, gargoyles, and all the other fine stonework of a traditional European cathe-dral. Since Roger Morigi, the head stone carver, had plenty of Italian assistants and saw no reason to hire an inexperienced Amer-ican apprentice, in 1967 Hart took the only job he could find at the cathedral, as a mail clerk. He approached Morigi repeatedly, but

---

3. James F. Cooper, "The Reënchantment of Public Art," in *Frederick Hart: Sculptor*, ed. Marshall Lee (New York: Hudson Hills Press, 1994), 59.
4. "Art Under the Radar."
5. Ibid.

could not convince him to take a chance. It was only after Hart's experiments on small pieces of limestone exposed his obvious flare for sculpture that Morigi accepted him as an apprentice.[6]

If he had been anywhere else in America, Hart might not even have known about the stone carving going on at the cathedral, and if he had been less bullish in his pursuit of an apprenticeship, he might have remained a mere amateur and enthusiast, but the providential combination of circumstance and Hart's drive to learn put him in exactly the right place—perhaps the only appropriate place in the entire world—to learn and hone the skills of traditional sculpture at the hands of a master carver and in the context of a team of experienced craftsmen working on "the last great Gothic cathedral ever built."[7]

"Roger Morigi taught me what truly makes sculpture work. He was basically a stone carver but he had the soul of an artist—a meticulous craftsman," said Hart. "The cathedral became a magical place for me, a place outside this century. The wonderful Italian stone carvers who worked there were the last sliver of a generation, a link back to the major American architectural world of the early 1900s as well as to the great American sculptors Augustus Saint-Gaudens and Daniel Chester French. Working at the cathedral was the best experience of my life. It taught me how to work. I wanted to know and feel the discipline—the mastery of stone carving—and I learned that in the hours of working up on the scaffolding in the heat of the summer and through the winter."[8] It was not easy, especially in the early years as a stone carver, when Hart had to subjugate his ego and his impulses to the artistic visions of others, but, unlike his experiences in formal higher education, Hart felt that he and his colleagues had a definite mission: "We felt that we were doing something important, selflessly for the ages, in a manner that

---

6. Tom Wolfe, "The Artist the World Couldn't See: Frederick Hart, b. 1943," *The New York Times Magazine*, 2 January 2000.

7. Homan Potterton, "Metamorphosis: Stone Carver to Artist," in *Frederick Hart: Sculptor*, ed. Marshall Lee (New York: Hudson Hills Press, 1994), 19.

8. Frederick Hart, as quoted in Potterton, 19.

21

was meant to last in a society that no longer valued things that last."⁹

When the cathedral, which had been under construction since 1907, announced a design competition in 1971 for the main entrance on its west façade, Hart decided to come up with a plan. All the entries, including Hart's, were rejected in the first round of competition, but eventually, in 1975, his revised design was announced as the winner. That his proposal—the entry of a young and unknown American in a profession dominated by older Europeans—was accepted is still hard to believe. But it was accepted, and Hart jumped from apprentice to visionary.

His design called for a bas-relief sculpture in each of the tympana (the arched, triangular surfaces) above the three sets of doors on the façade. On the left would be the creation of day, on the right, the creation of night, and in the center, "Ex Nihilo," a swirling portrayal of God's creation of man and woman "out of nothing." Below each of the bas-reliefs would appear a statue: the Apostle Peter on the left, Adam in the center, and the Apostle Paul on the right. For years, Hart worked on clay models, slowly honing the exact lines of this last major sculptural addition to the cathedral. Then he and the other stonecarvers spent years more bringing his vision to life.

The result was remarkable. In the central tympanum, "Ex Nihilo," the figures of four men and four women emerge from a swirling, churning mass of earth and cloud, the primordial chaos. The beauty of the finely formed human figures, in contrast to the rough, jagged, and seemingly random edges of their surroundings highlights the unique nature of the human person, formed in the image and likeness of God himself, unlike all else in creation. The facial expressions of the figures, one of which is serene, but most of which are solemn, quizzical, or concerned, emphasize the profound and challenging nature of human existence, and especially of the

---

9. Frederick Hart, quoted in Bill Ruehlmann, "Sermon in Stone: Washington National Cathedral Has Been an 83-Year Labor of Love," *Virginian-Pilot* (Norfolk VA), 23 September 1990; Frederick Hart, interview by Noah Adams, *All Things Considered*, NPR, 7 May 1998.

search for meaning. That all of them have their eyes closed emphasizes their lack of understanding but promises greater insight as they slowly come to see.

Hart's friend, the writer Tom Wolfe, describes what happened after the official unveiling of his work:

> The next day, Hart scanned the newspapers for reviews... *The Washington Post*... The *New York Times*... nothing... nothing the next day, either... nor the next week... nor the week after that. The one mention of any sort was an *obiter dictum* in *The Post's* Style (read: Women's) section indicating that the west facade of the cathedral now had some new but earnestly traditional (read: old-fashioned) decoration. So Hart started monitoring the art magazines. Months went by... nothing. It reached the point that he began yearning for a single paragraph by an art critic who would say how much he loathed "Ex Nihilo"... anything, anything at all!... to prove there was someone out there in the art world who in some way, however slightly or rudely, cared.[10]

What Wolfe called the "biggest and most prestigious commission for religious sculpture in America" of the century, and what another writer later called "without question the major architectural sculpture" of its era, had attracted no critical attention at all.[11] The style and subject matter of Hart's work simply no longer mattered to the self-styled custodians of the art world. In fact, Hart's work was by no means a stale copy of bygone approaches. As a perceptive critic later pointed out, "The style of the work does not try to recreate Gothic art; its Renaissance and romanticist predecessors are readily apparent, but its lyrical, humanistic, and ultimately spiritual effectiveness successfully transcend art-historical pigeonholing."[12] The Creation pieces transcended traditional sculpture in both style, by combining fine detail work with rough, chaotic edges, and content,

10. Wolfe.

11. Wolfe; Sarah Booth Conroy, quoted in Potterton, 38.

12. J. Carter Brown, introduction, in *Frederick Hart: Sculptor*, ed. Marshall Lee (New York: Hudson Hills Press, 1994), 10.

by a vision of creation far different from previous sculptural evocations of the subject. Nevertheless, the intentional beauty and unabashed spirituality of his work, without any attempt at irony, put it beyond the pale. Its earnestness had no place in the world of serious art.

Hart was hurt but did not give up. And his next major public work immediately attracted all sorts of attention, both elite and popular. In 1980 he submitted a proposal in a national competition for a proposed Vietnam War memorial, to be built on the National Mall in Washington, DC. Maya Lin, a Yale undergraduate, won the competition with her plans for a 400-foot-long black granite wall, but some veterans, led by Tom Carhart, objected to what they saw as the sterile and impersonal character of the wall, with Carhart going so far as to call it "a black gash of shame" that was an affront to those who had served.[13] To be fair to Lin, the competition rules had virtually mandated something like her wall, since the memorial was supposed to be nonpolitical and had to list the names of those who died in the war. After some political wrangling, a compromise resulted in Hart being asked to design a figurative sculpture to be combined somehow with Lin's wall. Although some hot heads wanted to put the sculpture right next to the wall, Hart himself did not want the wall and the figures to be in conflict. He suggested moving his sculpture far enough away, "so there was an interaction between the two elements" and "making them all work together by having the figures themselves gaze at the wall."[14] As J. Carter Brown, director of the National Gallery of Art, recognized, Hart's sculpture deferred to Lin's and actually "solved the problem of the culture wars that broke out over the monument."[15] A veteran agreed: "the Wall reminds me that I am one of three million men and women who served in the Vietnam War, who sacrificed, bled, and

13. James M. Goode, "Three Soldiers: A Solution to a National Controversy," in *Frederick Hart: Sculptor*, 44.

14. Frederick Hart, interview by Ben Wattenberg, *Think Tank with Ben Wattenberg*, PBS, 24 July 1999, www.pbs.org/thinktank/transcript730.html.

15. Irvin Molotsky, "Frederick Hart, 56, Designer of Vietnam Statue," *New York Times*, 17 August 1999.

died because that is what we were asked to do; the bronze figures of Frederick Hart's memorial remind me that I am more than that. They remind me of my humanity."[16]

After research and long conversations with veterans of the war, Hart had decided to make bronze statues of three Marines that would be situated about 300 feet from the wall, as a complement, not a rival, to Lin's project. The men seem to be gazing at the wall. Their stance signals their comradeship and mutual dependence, but also shared weariness, not so much of body but of soul. As in "Ex Nihilo," the facial expressions are the key to the meaning of the work. This time, though, the eyes betray depths of suffering, an almost palpable sense of ongoing experience of loss. But their eyes and stances also reveal a sense of shared resolve. "There is about them the physical contact and sense of unity that speaks of love and sacrifice, and this is the nature of men at war," said Hart. "And yet each one is alone. Their true heroism lies in these bonds of loyalty, in their aloneness, in their vulnerability."[17]

Hart's statues were unveiled in 1984 and this time the world took note. Maya Lin herself said, "Three men standing before the world— it's trite, it's a generalization, a simplification. Hart gives you an image—he's illustrating a book."[18] "Hackneyed realism" that clashed aesthetically with Lin's wall, said one scholar.[19] Another writer critiqued Hart's simplistic use of "physical analogy," because the statues "must in fact be quite different from the actual bodies of those who served" and therefore prevented "a more inclusive representation."[20] For another observer, the statues represented a "singular narrative and totalizing image" that supported the "official story"

---

16. Frederick Downs, Jr., "A Soldier's Reflections," in *Frederick Hart: Sculptor*, ed. Marshall Lee (New York: Hudson Hills Press, 1994), 10.

17. Frederick Hart, quoted in Goode, "Three Soldiers," 45.

18. Maya Lin, quoted in Michael Kammen, *Visual Shock: A History of Art Controversies in American Culture* (New York: Vintage, 2007), 5.

19. Michael Clark, "Remembering Vietnam," *Cultural Critique* 3 (Spring, 1986), 24.

20. Josephine Lee, ed., *Performing Asian America: Race and Ethnicity on the Contemporary Stage* (Philadelphia: Temple University Press, 1997), 213.

of the war.[21] The *Washington Post's* art critic called the soldiers "plastic toys" without a shred of grandeur, done in by Hart's lack of taste and his superficial approach.[22]

The details that Hart had so painstakingly crafted, from shoe laces to bullets, from folds in each garment to the names on the dog tags, from blood vessels visible in arms to individual strands of hair, were to these critics an impediment to true representation and generalization. Hart described his work as "a heroic sculpture disguised as a realistic statue" that was trying to reveal "the true nobility of spirit of the Vietnam veteran," but to the critics the heroism and nobility of the three men, even in the understated form in which Hart presented them, was an endorsement of the war itself.[23] Without going into an extended discussion of the critics, it should be enough to say that Hart himself had been a Vietnam War protester and that the pathos and suffering on the men's faces surely belies any ingenuous "official story."[24] Similarly, it is almost laughably literalistic to say the realism and specificity of the three figures depicted makes them *less* representative of all those who fought, for human beings only exist as individual, embodied persons. Had any of these intellectual critics heard of allegory? Did any of them understand analogy? The bigger issue, though, was that Americans, especially the members of the intelligentsia, had become uncomfortable with the virtues and spiritual qualities that infused Hart's work, including bravery, dignity, and longsuffering patience. If it was an annoyance for the intellectual class to come face to face with realism, it was a shock for the public to encounter non-ironic depictions of virtue and traditional spirituality.

---

21. Marita Sturken, "The Wall, the Screen, and the Image: The Vietnam Veterans Memorial," *Representations* 35 (Summer 1991), 126.

22. Richard Paul, "Frederick Hart's Heavenly Bodies; He Carved Out Quite a Niche, But His Reputation Isn't Set in Stone," *The Washington Post*, 20 August 2000.

23. Frederick Hart, interview by Ben Wattenberg, *Think Tank with Ben Wattenberg*, PBS, 24 July 1999, www.pbs.org/thinktank/transcript730.html.

24. Jonathan Darman and Evan Thomas, "To the finish—Bring it on: Can the Dems exploit public worry about the war and retake Capitol Hill? A case study in Virginia," *Newsweek* (18 September 2006).

Here is where Hart excelled. Unlike many of the talented (and untalented) artists of his generation, who wasted their gifts in puerile attempts to shock or transgress, his love of beauty was much stronger than his desire for critical acclaim. As "Ex Nihilo" should have made clear, he was not a kneejerk conservative or a blind traditionalist, the kind of person who likes old things simply because they are old and refuses salutary changes. That sort of reactionary traditionalism actually has more in common with the so-called *avant garde* than it does with Hart's views and practices, for the *avant garde* is just the opposite side of the coin, endorsing the new because it is new. In Hart's mind it was just common sense to know and learn from the past. "I'm not trying to go back to anything," he said. "I am trying to use what is in the past. When you do something and you don't seem to be getting it right, whether it is a new century in art or it's a building or a bridge, you go back to try and find out who's done it before, and how they were successful and how you can learn from them in order to go forward."[25] To learn from the past is wisdom; to ignore the past is a form of pride.

Hart believed that the *avant garde* was not merely wrong in its criticisms of his work, but wrong in its approach to the public. Where the *avant garde* lamented the poor taste and stinginess of the public, especially in the context of controversies over funding by the National Endowment for the Arts, Hart instead blamed "a practice of art that refuses to nourish the public." Bullied by so-called experts, people resigned themselves to tolerate all sorts of odd objects that were presented as art. "But the common man has his limits," said Hart, "and they are reached when some of these things emerge from the sanctuary of the padded cells of galleries and museums and are put in public places, when the public is forced to live with them and pay for them." The art world feigned outrage but actually welcomed the opportunity to play the martyr, hated by the rude masses. To Hart, art as practiced in the late twentieth century displayed "a belief system of deliberate contempt for the public" and was often involved in "ridiculing traditional values, and trying

25. Glenn Terry, "Presence of Light: An Interview with Frederick Hart," *Classical Realism Journal* 3, no. 1 (1996).

to destroy them."[26] Hart took the opposite approach. He believed that public art, in particular, should reflect "meaning and value" in a way that the public could appreciate. "The central metaphor for all of that in art is, and always has been, and always will be, the human figure," he said. "It's the metaphor, the language of expression, of visual art that means the most to the greater public." Abstract forms and animals could play a part, but "the figure will always remain the dominant element, especially within a public art form such as sculpture, where you're always dealing with the monument's meaning in terms of cultural history and the future."[27] The elite of the art world scoffed, but Hart's human-centered approach was built on the perennial wisdom of humanity and it appealed to the public.

The best example of the vitality of Hart's artistic vision was his innovative work with acrylic resin, known commercially as Lucite. Years of experimentation allowed him to pioneer a process of embedding a translucent acrylic resin sculpture inside another piece of acrylic resin, enabling him to employ light and shadow as constituent elements of the sculpture. This specific methodology allowed him to address "the constant challenge that specificity can descend into mere literalism" in a realist style like Hart's.[28] Starting at about the time that his cathedral and Vietnam projects were coming to fruition, Hart began a series of acrylic works that he called "Sacred Mysteries: Acts of Light." Although reminiscent of the figures in "Ex Nihilo," these male and female nudes represented "an aesthetic and attitudinal change" in Hart's work, as the figures appear to be "emerging now from light—and disappearing into light as well."[29]

The new medium enabled Hart to use light in way that was impossible in traditional sculpture. Later in the 1980s he "began to equate light with life and spirit" and by the 1990s Hart's acrylic work

26. Frederick Hart, *American Arts Quarterly* (Fall 1989).

27. Terry, "Presence of Light: An Interview with Frederick Hart."

28. J. Carter Brown, introduction, in *Frederick Hart: Sculptor*, 11.

29. Robert Chase, "Transcending Tradition: The Cast Acrylic Resin Works," in *Frederick Hart: Sculptor*, 75.

had become "increasingly allusive rather than representational," with his creations now "depicting the undeniable existence of two levels of being, the physical and the spiritual."[30] Hart achieved what seems contradictory: he crafted painstakingly detailed and finely rendered human figures that, in their ethereal beauty and their combination of translucency with embeddedness, pointed beyond the physical realm to the spiritual. As Michael Novak points out, the vision and mastery displayed in these works is extreme, for Hart "had to see them imaginatively from multiple angles, reflections, and light effects *before* they were cast in final form."[31] His focus on the human body paradoxically led him beyond the body to the spirit; his very focus on human beauty led him beyond human beauty to hints of the divine. In Hart's own words, "the figures are translucent and disappear into the light, creating a spiritual relationship between light and form, and a sense of mystery around being and non-being."[32]

The most important of Hart's acrylic resin works is probably "The Cross of the Millennium," which in 1993 was selected as Best in Show at Sacred Arts XIV, the nation's largest religious art competition, and also won the visitors' choice award. This work, in which Christ is crucified not on the cross, but inside of it, "simultaneously represents the birth, death, and resurrection of Christ."[33] The transparent cross holds the translucent Christ like a womb, imprisons him like a tomb, and raises him like a tidal wave. This is a suffering Christ who is already triumphant, a victorious Christ who yet bears his wounds; it is the play of light, doubled, tripled, quadrupled by the cross's hexagonal arms, refracted and reflected, that allows the figure to speak clearly yet not univocally. This is not ambiguity. It is clarity, multiplied and intensified, made possible by the one figure of Christ embedded in a medium that produces new perspectives.

In 1973, while working on the National Cathedral, Hart was

---

30. Chase, "Transcending Tradition," 76.

31. Michael Novak, "Beauty is Truth: The Changing Tides," in *Frederick Hart: Changing Tides*, ed. Frederick Turner and Michael Novak (New York: Hudson Hills Press, 2005), 8.

32. Ibid.

33. Chase, "Transcending Tradition," 76.

received into the Catholic Church, converted as much by beauty as by the inquiry classes he took at the Cathedral of St. Matthew the Apostle, and the beer and pizza he often shared with Father Stephen Happel.[34] His apprenticeship to Roger Morigi, his constant struggle to perfect his craft, his days spent in the midst of the otherworldly splendor of the cathedral: these experiences of beauty demanded, of beauty pursued, and of beauty imbibed led him beyond beauty to the good and the true, which, of course, are most abundantly found in God himself. As Tom Wolfe puts it, he "fell in love with God."[35] Hart's work a decade later on "The Cross of the Millennium" indicates that this love deepened and matured, at last finding expression in a vision of Christ whose suffering mirrored the bloody terrors of the modern age but whose rebirth in light was the hope of the next millennium.

One of Hart's last major pieces before his death in 1999, "Daughters of Odessa," like the "Cross of the Millennium," displays his growing spiritual depths. The sculpture portrays four girls in thin, almost transparent gowns, sisters or close friends, walking together.[36] The eyes of the figures are closed and they seem to be in prayer or some sort of reverie. Whatever they are doing, their faces reflect love for each other and a sort of serious, joyful innocence.

In fact, their innocence and beauty are so marked that this easily could have been a work of naïveté. After all, it is hard to imagine that such pure creatures could exist in the twentieth century. The girls' almost radiant purity raises the specter of kitsch and sentimentality. The sculptor has laid himself open to the charge that, although he might be talented, he must have been living in a dream world to produce something so devoid of complexity and nuance.

The title of the composition and Hart's commentary on it demonstrate that such a charge would be mistaken. Hart explained that the sculpture started as a sketch of the royal Romanov sisters who

34. "Frederick Hart: Giving Form to Spirit: A Leader's Guide," Frederick Hart Exhibit, University of Louisville, 2007.

35. Wolfe, "The Artist the World Couldn't See."

36. Hart died at the age of 55 in 1999 from lung cancer that had not been diagnosed until two days before his death.

were murdered by Vladimir Lenin's Bolsheviks in 1918. "Then," he says, "it turned into a larger allegorical work, as a tribute to the all of the innocent victims of the twentieth century." For a time he even called it "Martyrs of Modernism," as a protest against the "deliberate destruction of things that are lovely, beautiful and filled with life." The final name refers to the great suffering endured by Ukraine, which endured pogroms, intentional famines, collectivization, invasion by the Nazis, the Holocaust, and further oppression by Stalin.[37]

"Daughters of Odessa" is an affirmation of beauty and goodness that was created not only in full knowledge of the massive suffering and death of the twentieth century but also in answer to those evils.[38] It is not blind or naïve or sentimental. Its beauty is not irrelevant to Stalin and Hitler. In fact, it is a direct response to the diabolical evil that littered Europe with the corpses of the innocent. And that response is to emphasize beauty and goodness all the more. Hart's answer to death and the culture of death is life and the culture of life, not resignation or nihilism. The transcendental beauty of "Daughters of Odessa" does not downplay evil and suffering; it highlights it.

Here is Frederick Hart at his boldest. First, he is referring directly to the great evils of Marxism, a topic few artists have wanted to challenge. Many, in fact, have wanted to support revolution and to present various Marxian visions of the world. Second, he is responding to those evils with goodness and beauty, the very values that the *avant garde* rejects. "The very lyrical, elegant, flowing design and the kind of delicate attention to the female form is treated with great contempt today," Hart admitted. "So, this is done in defiance of that contempt."[39] Third, he is "doubling down" on beauty, presenting not a hidden beauty or a beauty mixed with the

---

37. Frederick Hart, interview by Ben Wattenberg, *Think Tank with Ben Wattenberg*, PBS, 24 July 1999, www.pbs.org/thinktank/transcript730.html; Frederick Hart, memorandum, in *Frederick Hart: Changing Tides*, 53.

38. Novak, "Beauty is Truth," 8.

39. Frederick Hart, interview by Noah Adams, *All Things Considered*, NPR, 7 May 1998.

mundane and the ugly, but the pure, unadulterated form of four innocent girls, unmarred by sin or suffering.

The force of "Daughters of Odessa" comes from the girls' vulnerability, for the viewer knows that these girls will die, that they will be brutally murdered. Their beauty, the beauty of innocence, shines forth and arrests the viewer because it hints at truths at once terrifying and transcendent. The innocent and good suffer and die—this is a hard word, a message almost impossible to accept. Yet, and yet, that very fact cannot help but resonate with the suffering and death of the most innocent man, Jesus Christ; and his suffering, we know, was also a victory, the greatest victory. In the Christian tradition, the deaths of the martyrs are tragic but also triumphant. They follow Christ into death, but they will rise again on the last day. Their weakness is somehow a strength. Their suffering, somehow, will be redeemed.

Hart's work thus provokes a crisis for the viewer. It forces a decision about the nature of beauty, which ultimately points to the nature of reality itself. The encounter with beauty, as long as that beauty is accepted and welcomed, is never with beauty alone. Of course, many will decide that the beauty portrayed in "Daughters of Odessa" is false, a betrayal of the difficult human condition. They will conclude that such beauty glosses over the harsh realities of life.[40] Beauty, in this view, is a fraud. Others—and I hope you are one!—come from this confrontation challenged both to accept beauty and to look beyond beauty. Then, beyond beauty they find goodness. If beauty is real, they conclude, so too is goodness.

Hart's Legacy

Beyond his sculpture, Frederick Hart left at least four important legacies. First, in the 1990s, in the last decade of his life, Hart gathered around himself a community of artists, architects, musicians, and writers who were seeking beauty and were not afraid to learn

---

40. For example, Richard Paul evaluated Hart's opus and concluded that Hart was a skilled "professional" who "caught the mercantile, woozy spirit of his age": "Frederick Hart's Heavenly Bodies," *The Washington Post*, 20 August 2000.

from tradition. At Chesley, his estate in rural Virginia, Hart welcomed these fellow artists and thinkers and gave them hope, which they needed, because many of them had felt alone and ignored. In encouraging them, he made clear that his words about the moral duty of the artist were not just talk.

In a sense, Hart was giving these men and women what he himself had rarely received. As a traditionalist resister of the zeitgeist, Hart almost never encountered established artists who could support, encourage, and guide him. Especially in his early years as a sculptor, his was a lonesome path. In fact, the most obvious weaknesses in Hart's work—the puerile Teilhardian theology of "Ex Nihilo" and his overreliance on the female nude—reflect his lack of older and wiser Catholic mentors who could have pointed him to a more insightful depiction of Creation and a more judicious and less sensuous approach to the glory of femininity.

Second, Hart renewed the centrality of beauty and the human figure in the arts.[41] In a time of crisis, this was exactly what Western culture needed. The body, as Pope John Paul II elucidated in his "theology of the body," has its own language and its own logic. In a time of confusion about marriage, family, and sexuality, the body has a message of sanity and meaning for those who will listen. Simultaneously, Hart also did American culture the inestimable favor of reminding us that beauty is essential to any art worthy of the name. After decades in which artists were embarrassed to produce paintings, sculptures, and musical compositions of beauty or were convinced that somehow the human form had been eclipsed in serious art, Hart gave them the confidence to tread the old, wise paths.

Third, Hart restored serious thought to art, in contrast to the kneejerk nihilism and deconstruction of many of his fellow artists. "Part of the silent power of Hart's work is that it is intellectually more profound than that of his contemporaries," says poet and philosopher Frederick Turner. "It has often been praised for its romance and passion, but beneath its lush beauty and generous

41. Novak, "Beauty is Truth," 8.

expressiveness is a complex theory of being, becoming, and meaning which is best articulated by the work itself but which can be partly put into words."[42] For example, "the spiraling forms that recur throughout Hart's 'Ex Nihilo' tympanum suggest the spirals that are found in nature—in sunflower heads, nautiluses, hurricanes, and galaxies," signaling the theological, philosophical, and theological depth of Hart's work.[43] As Turner points out, the burden of proof has shifted in recent years. The almost universal acceptance of the "Big Bang" means that serious thinkers have to reckon with the beginning of all things. The mystery of the mind, which continues to elude biological or physical definition, pushes honest philosophers and scientists to grapple with metaphysics. The "strange attractors" of chaos theory raise, for fair-minded observers, the possibility of meaning or design in the universe. The "new atheists" like Richard Dawkins might be attracting all the attention, but the late twentieth and early twenty-first centuries actually were difficult times to sustain an honest and scientifically rigorous atheism. As atheist philosopher Anthony Flew indicated with his conversion to deism in 2004 after years of leading the philosophical fight against the existence of God, the evidential tide has turned dramatically.[44] It is now Hart's theistic view that reflects the cutting edge of contemporary science.

Finally, Hart revitalized public art. He believed that art could not be merely a vehicle for self-aggrandizement and should not even be done for its own sake. "Art for art's sake," Hart said, "excludes the notion of public service, or that there is something more important about the artistic endeavor than art." To remind himself of this truth, he always carried with him a quotation from G.K. Chesterton: "Nothing sublimely artistic has ever arisen out of mere art, any more than anything essentially reasonable has arisen out of pure reason. There must be a rich moral soil for any great aesthetic

---

42. Frederick Turner, "Evolution Out of Chaos: The Creation Sculptures," in *Frederick Hart: Sculptor*, ed. Marshall Lee (New York: Hudson Hills Press, 1994), 59.

43. Ibid., 60.

44. Antony Flew, *There Is a God: How the World's Most Notorious Atheist Changed His Mind* (New York: Harper Collins, 2007).

growth."[45] Part of the reason why Hart was one of the great artists of his day was that personal greatness was not his highest goal; he saw himself as a servant of beauty and of the public. The artist, he believed, had a duty to be "a moral force in society" by "bringing beauty and value into the cultural mainstream."[46] The importance of Hart's view is evident in his response to a question about whether the money spent on the National Cathedral might have done more good if given to the poor. "To serve the poor," replied Hart, "you must have a value system in place that makes that important. A cathedral is a repository of that value system. You have to have a libretto to make all that music accessible."[47]

Frederick Hart was great, in other words, because he was humble. He did not see his task as reaching within himself and expressing the depths of his inner genius. Rather, he believed "there really is only one creator and artists are people who are reflecting upon creation and compose our reflections into a statement." Only God truly creates *ex nihilo*. Hart had real freedom and real vision because he knew that human artists "are really composing our reflections of the great beauty and majesty of creation itself."[48]

---

45. Ruehlmann, "Sermon in Stone." Chesterton continues, "The principle of art for art's sake is a very good principle if it means that there is a vital distinction between the earth and the tree that has its roots in the earth; but it is a very bad principle if it means that the tree could grow just as well with its roots in the air. Every great literature has always been allegorical—allegorical of some view of the whole universe. The 'Iliad' is only great because all life is a battle, the 'Odyssey' because all life is a journey, the Book of Job because all life is a riddle." G.K. Chesterton, *The Defendant* (London: R. Brimley Johnson, 1902).

46. Frederick Hart, interview by Ben Wattenberg, *Think Tank with Ben Wattenberg*, PBS, 24 July 1999, www.pbs.org/thinktank/transcript730.html.

47. Quoted in Ruehlmann, "Sermon in Stone."

48. Terry, "Presence of Light: An Interview with Frederick Hart."

2

Brilliant Innocence

The Sisters of Life

IN 2009, WRITER HEATHER KING encountered the Sisters of Life at a booth they had set up after Mass at St. Patrick's Cathedral in New York City. "I hung around the fringes for a while," she says, "and I can't describe the light these nuns threw off: anything but hokey, anything but contrived, anything but patronizing, anything but with an ulterior motive, anything but weird." Eventually King talked to one of the sisters, admitted the secret she had carried for twenty years—that she had had three abortions—and began to sob. "I didn't seek help for many more months," King says. "But it was the face of that young nun—healthy, wholesome, sane, compassionate, joyful—I really have to thank her. Love is how you treat those who have nothing to give. I had nothing to give her. And she gave me back my life."[1]

The Sisters of Life are a relatively new religious order that takes four vows, the usual vows of poverty, chastity, and obedience, and a fourth vow "to protect and enhance the sacredness of human life." The order first came to public attention in 1989 when New York's Cardinal John O'Connor put an announcement in the archdiocesan newspaper:

> I would like to establish a new religious community of women. I would like as many of its members as possible to be lawyers or paralegals, doctors or nurses. I want to call them the Sisters of

---

1. Heather King, "The Sisters of Life," *Shirt of Flame*, 1 May 2012, https://shirtof-flame.blogspot.com/2012/05/abortion-straight-up-sisters-of-life.html. Accessed 16 September 2016.

Life. My community of sisters would take the customary three vows of poverty, chastity, and obedience, and a fourth vow to defend human life against abortion and "mercy killing."[2]

The Sisters of Life were part of the new approaches to the fight against abortion that developed in the late 1980s and early 1990s as the pro-life movement grappled with the reality that the Supreme Court showed no signs of reversing itself on abortion and no pro-life amendment to the US Constitution was on the horizon.

In addition to the carnage of the approximately 30,000,000 abortions that had been performed by 1990, the Roe vs. Wade decision of the Supreme Court, which had asserted a "right" to abortion, had philosophical implications that both reflected and contributed to America's moral decline.[3] The Roe decision was logically and morally incoherent. It recognized no rights in the unborn child, yet presumed that the moment of birth somehow conferred "an essential difference, a real (not merely conventional) transition to a living entity, human in nature."[4] This distinction between a fetus with no rights and a baby who becomes fully human at the moment of birth is illogical and untenable.

Even more worrying than the rationale of the Roe decision was the evolution of pro-abortion "logic" over the ensuing decades. Many supporters of abortion now assert that even the recently born baby is not fully human, in the sense of being a rights-bearing individual. Pro-life scholar Richard Stith refers to a study in the *Journal of Philosophy* that "showed that all pro-choice theories developed by 1989 deny that there is anything wrong *prima facie* with killing infants" and notes that none of the pro-abortion scholarship he has encountered will admit that the killing of young infants is intrinsically wrong.[5] Princeton philosopher Peter Singer, for instance, has

2. Quoted in Charles Connor, *John O'Connor and the Culture of Life* (New York: Alba House, 2011), 63.

3. "Abortion Statistics: United States Data and Trends," National Right to Life Committee, nrlc.org.

4. Richard Stith, "Nominal Babies," *First Things: A Monthly Journal of Religion & Public Life* no. 90 (February 1999): 16.

5. Stith, "Nominal Babies," 18.

famously argued for the legitimacy of infanticide in various circumstances: "Newborn human babies have no sense of their own existence over time. So killing a newborn baby is never equivalent to killing a person, that is, a being who wants to go on living."[6] In other words, America under the abortion regime was becoming a place where acclimation to the great horror of abortion was opening moral doors that had been shut for centuries.

The Supreme Court's 1992 revisiting of the abortion issue in Planned Parenthood vs. Casey had some positive aspects—it gave states more freedom to regulate, and thus restrict, abortion—but it upheld the basic "right" to abortion and it did so on the basis of an ominous philosophical development. Justice Anthony Kennedy declared that the "right" to abortion was based on a new kind of freedom: "At the heart of liberty is the right to define one's own concept of existence, of meaning, of the universe, and of the mystery of human life."[7] Although there is a sense in which people do have a right to their own opinions, Kennedy was going far beyond that truism. He was asserting that one person's concept "of the mystery of human life" could justify taking the life of another innocent person. He was also asserting this right to define meaning and the universe without any reference to an obligation to do so truthfully. Kennedy's reasoning sounds like the feel-good morality of the 1970s, but in the context of abortion it functions as a statement that one person's beliefs trump another person's right to exist. The project of "defining" reality might sound like no more than a process of naming and explaining, but its use in the justification of abortion exposes it as a rejection of the traditional attitude of submission to reality in favor of a new attitude of *redefining* reality to suit one's preferences. In short, if Casey's "logic" were applied systematically, the strong would run roughshod over the weak. The tragedy of abortion in America is not just that by 2021 the strong had aborted 60,000,000

---

6. Jessica Chasmar, "Princeton bioethics professor faces calls for resignation over infanticide support," *The Washington Times*, 16 June 2015.

7. 505 U.S. 833, Planned Parenthood of Southeastern Pennsylvania v. Casey (Nos. 91–744, 91–902), 29 June 1992, 851, https://www.law.cornell.edu/supremecourt/text/505/833.

of the weak but also that this crime had perverted the moral reasoning of millions of Americans to the extent that they now can muster no argument against infanticide.[8]

Cardinal O'Connor

John O'Connor was a friendly, hardheaded, outspoken man whose self-deprecating humor and sardonic wit obscured a deep intellect and profound moral vision. Before becoming archbishop of New York in 1984, he served as chaplain for the Third Marine Division in Vietnam during the Vietnam War and as the Navy Chief of Chaplains. He also earned a Ph.D. in Political Science from Georgetown University and wrote several books. He was neither a political partisan nor the kind of culture warrior who looks at the world through ideological glasses. He devoted much of his free time to caring for those suffering from AIDS, which in the 1980s was associated strongly with homosexuality.[9] His support for labor unions was not just notional. During a 1984 strike of hospital employees, when the top administrator of New York's Catholic hospitals wanted to bring in replacement workers, O'Connor told him, "Over my dead body will you bring in scabs."[10]

One of the pivotal events in O'Connor's life occurred in 1975. On a visit to the Dachau concentration camp in Germany, he was overwhelmed by a sense of the sacredness of human life. "Good God," he wondered, "how could human beings do this to other human beings?" Although he did not understand the full meaning of what he had experienced, he recommitted himself to working for the dignity of human life. In later years he was convinced that he had received a special grace at Dachau.[11] "My life was changed radically,

---

8. J. Budziszewski, "The Future of the End of Democracy," *First Things: A Monthly Journal of Religion and Public Life* no. 91 (March 1999): 15–21.

9. George Marlin, "Cardinal O'Connor vs Governor Cuomo," *Human Life Review* (Fall 2014): 17.

10. Nat Hentoff, "Remembering Him," *Human Life Review* (Spring–Summer 2009): 67.

11. Patty Knap, "Sisters of Life Thrive at 25," *National Catholic Register* (1 June 2016), http://www.ncregister.com/site/article/sisters-of-life-thrive-at-25.

not modestly, not fractionally but radically when I put my hand into the oven at Dachau for the first time," O'Connor said. "I knew that with all my studies and all my degrees up until that moment, I knew no real theology. I learned it at Dachau. And it radically changed my life."[12]

O'Connor was not the typical American bishop. Throughout his career, but especially after his experience at Dachau, he spoke publically, boldly, and repeatedly about the evil of abortion. When he was ordained as a bishop in 1979, O'Connor later explained, "I vowed publically that from that day on there would be some reference to the dignity of the human person and, in particular, to the defense of the most vulnerable—the unborn—in every public address I made." In one instance, when asked about the red rose pin that he was wearing at a gathering of Jewish activists, he said, "This is the rose that lives in my heart for all the beautiful, unborn roses not allowed to live."[13] Unlike most clerics, he was willing to offend the powerful and to be seen as uncultivated. In 1984, he said, "I do not see how a Catholic, in good conscience, can vote for an individual expressing himself or herself as favoring abortion." At the time, Mario Cuomo was the governor of New York and an important figure in the Democratic Party who was backing away from the Catholic position on abortion. O'Connor also rebuked Geraldine Ferraro, Walter Mondale's running mate in the 1984 presidential election, for saying that the Catholic Church allowed for a variety of positions on the abortion issue. He made clear that there was no ambiguity about the issue: Catholics simply could not support abortion.[14] Ferraro, Cuomo, and many commentators criticized O'Connor for meddling in politics.

Cuomo gave an infamous speech at the University of Notre Dame on 13 September 1984, in which he articulated a position that countless Catholic politicians emulated in the following years. He said that he accepted the Catholic teaching on abortion but that,

12. "Dachau: A trip that radically changed me," *Imprint* (Fall 2014), 8.

13. Sandi Merle, "Of Life, the Law, and Roses," *Human Life Review* (Winter 2009): 91.

14. Marlin, "Cardinal O'Connor vs Governor Cuomo," 13–14.

since public morality "depends on a consensus view of right and wrong," it would be wrong to impose his own religiously informed moral views in a context of pluralism and disagreement. This philosophically inane but politically pragmatic position enabled him to assert his Catholic *bona fides* while simultaneously appealing to pro-choice voters. O'Connor responded, publically, by making the indubitable point that all laws legislate morality. He saw clearly the political costs of coming out against abortion, but he made clear that abortion was not an issue on which compromise was possible. He was not being unreasonable, or overstepping his bounds, or taking a partisan stand; he was just teaching what the Church taught. The politicians who imagined that his public words were the problem were missing the bigger issue: "As I see it, their disagreement, if they do disagree, is not simply with me but with the teaching of the Catholic Church."[15] After a similar controversy in 1986, in which Cuomo and various commentators lambasted O'Connor for endangering free speech and implied that his anti-abortion comments amounted to a sort of theocratic censorship, O'Connor characterized such complaints as "nonsense" and "hysterics." He asked, "Are we to have a Church in which everyone's judgment is equal to everyone else's? That's not a Church, it's chaos."[16]

After becoming Archbishop of New York in 1984 and while he was involved in the public defense of life in the ways mentioned above, O'Connor continued meditating on the Church's work against abortion and euthanasia. He had become one of the most vocal opponents of abortion in United States and no one could doubt his commitment or his bravery. Nevertheless, he wondered why the many efforts by Catholics, evangelical Protestants, and other people of good will in the decade since the Supreme Court's Roe vs. Wade decision had not achieved more. During the late 1980s and early 1990s the anti-abortion protesters of Operation Rescue were active in several American cities and thousands of protesters were arrested. Despite the movement's individual successes, there was no sign that abortion would end any time soon. As far as the

15. Ibid., 15–17.
16. Ibid., 19.

larger anti-abortion movement was concerned, it became clear that, if they continued with Operation Rescue's approach of blocking access to clinics, all of the most committed anti-abortion activists would soon be in jail. After meditating on his own experiences and on the larger pro-life movement, Cardinal O'Connor came to believe that the spiritual aspect of the work had been neglected and that "the demon of contempt for human life at every point of existence" was at the heart of the modern culture of death. Struck by Jesus's statement in the Gospel of Mark that certain demons can be driven out only by prayer, the Cardinal came to believe that a religious order devoted to prayer would be the best response to what was at root a spiritual crisis.[17] Activism, protest, legal efforts, and media work were all important, but they would now be undergirded by prayer. "It is not perchance that contemplation comes first," the Cardinal explained:

> Until we contemplate the Word, until we remind ourselves that all things are made in the image of this Word, until we commune with this Word, until we become identified, we cannot really begin to understand the sacredness of human life. This why every life is sacred; it is sacred in the Word. Hence contemplation comes first, and then action, the apostolic activity, including works upholding the sacredness of human life. The apostolic activity must flow from contemplation. It is an extension of contemplation. If you remove contemplation, separate yourself from union with the Word, then what you do is nothing, it's meaningless. We are not the Light. We are only witnesses to the Light. The Light must be able to shine through us, as it shone through Mary.[18]

Instead of adding prayer to the list of activities that the sisters would perform, Cardinal O'Connor decided to make prayer the foundation of their lives.

In 1989 and 1990, as women began to respond to O'Connor's invitation, he organized a series of discernment retreats where he

17. Mark 9:29; Knap, "Sisters of Life Thrive at 25."
18. Quoted in Charles Connor, *John O'Connor and the Culture of Life*, 85.

laid out his vision for the new religious order. On 1 June 1991, the Sisters of Life welcomed eight postulants, who would be trained in the religious life by the sisters of another religious order, the Parish Visitors of Mary Immaculate, at a convent in Monroe, New York. The new order would be committed to "a ministry of reverence for every human person." Some liberal Catholics scoffed at the idea of establishing a new order at a time when most women's orders were having trouble finding vocations. Sister Ann Patrick Ware of the Sisters of Loretto warned, "There are not swarms of young women entering communities, and the face of religious life is very different today; people are not about to take vows of poverty and chastity."[19] Nevertheless, the new order grew steadily throughout the 1990s under the leadership of its superior general, Mother Agnes Mary Donovan, a former psychology professor at Columbia University who had been one of the original eight postulants.

Mother Agnes's story illustrates why, *contra* Sister Ann Patrick, American women might actually find traditional religious life attractive. Agnes had what she describes as "a fabulously interesting career as a psychologist, good friends, a happy family, a lot of material comforts," but she had a sense that she had not found her true vocation.[20] She was deeply bothered by the ways in which the abortion license in the United States had wounded millions of women, not to mention the loss of millions of their children, since the Roe decision. She was active in the pro-life movement and prayed every Saturday outside of the Eastern Women's Clinic, a New York abortion facility. Other pro-lifers had noticed that Agnes "had the demeanor of a special grace" and were encouraged and strengthened by her "serene yet determined face," but she was not considering religious life.[21] When she took an eight-day Ignatian retreat in 1990, she was simply trying to grow closer to God. "I left that retreat," she

19. Nadine Brozan, "O'Connor Proposes Order of Nuns to Fight Abortion and Euthanasia," *New York Times*, 4 November 1989.
20. Quoted in Patricia Edmonds, "Group of nuns to focus on life," *USA Today*, 3 October 1991.
21. Brian Caulfield, "Twenty-five Years Consecrated to Life," *Human Life Review* XLII, no. 4 (Fall 2016): 16–17.

says, "certain that God wished to have my life."[22] On another occasion she described the experience as being "surprised by Love."[23]

The problem, though, was that Agnes was already thirty-nine years old, too old for most religious orders. The three that she contacted showed little interest in her. Then, at a Mass at St. Patrick's Cathedral Agnes heard Cardinal O'Connor explain his vision for the new Sisters of Life. She agreed with the cardinal that the fabric of culture had been torn and human life had been cheapened. She also agreed that activism and political action were not enough. The abortion crisis was a spiritual crisis and it needed a spiritual solution. When O'Connor shared, as he often did, his idea that "God raises up religious communities to address the needs of the time" she began to sense not only that he was right but the she was being invited to participate in this move of God.[24]

Theologically innovative watered-down orders of sisters were seeing few vocations because they were offering a thin faith and careers in social work and education that were not that different from what women could experience without joining a religious order. An accomplished professional woman and committed Catholic like Agnes Mary Donovan therefore had little to gain from joining a liberal order of sisters. On the other hand, the combination of a serious prayer life and ongoing work for the most vulnerable, as proposed by Cardinal O'Connor for his new order, was extremely attractive. The sisters originally wore a sort of business uniform, but soon switched to a traditional blue and white habit. This traditional religious attire actually attracted would-be sisters and encouraged Catholics in the streets. People came up to Sister Maria Kateri Frazier and said, "Sister, thank you for wearing the habit. Thank you for not taking God off the street." Other people, after seeing her traditional habit, asked her for prayer.[25]

22. George Anderson and Agnes Mary Donovan, "The Sisters of Life," *America* 182, no. 11 (April 2000): 9.

23. Sean Salai, "On Fighting for Life: 15 Questions for Mother Agnes Mary Donovan, S. V.," *America*, 21 January 2015.

24. Edmonds, "Group of Nuns."

25. Charles Lewis, "Word on the Street: The Sisters of Life are out of the convent and working with women contemplating abortion," *National Post*, 13 February 2010.

In 1993, after two years of formation, Agnes became the first, and so far only, superior of the Sisters of Life. Working closely with Cardinal O'Connor, who came to see the order as his greatest legacy, she moved the community from Monroe to the Throgs Neck neighborhood in the southeastern corner of the Bronx. By 1996, the order had twenty-seven women, including postulants, novices, and those who had taken final vows, and was working with both pregnant women who needed aid and encouragement and post-abortive women who needed healing.[26] By 2000 the sisters had forty-seven women, and about seventy in 2010.[27] In 2016 there were about one hundred members, including eleven postulants, seventeen novices, twenty-four who had made temporary vows, and forty-two who had taken their perpetual vows.[28] In 2013 the Sisters of Life received the Evangelium Vitae Medal, the nation's highest honor in the field of pro-life work, from the University of Notre Dame. Professor David Solomon called the Sisters of Life "much needed witnesses of the beauty and sanctity of life" who "bring joy and hope to the world."[29] Although O'Connor originally had expected the order to attract doctors and lawyers who, presumably, would engage in medical and legal work, the order attracted women from a variety of backgrounds, but few medical or legal professionals, and evolved in the direction of emotional and spiritual care.[30]

Formation and Ministry

As the order grew, it developed a more specialized system of training and formation. Today, a woman discerning whether she had a vocation to the Sisters of Life would spend nine months as a postulant at St. Frances de Chantal Convent in the Bronx. Then she

---

26. Connor, *John Cardinal O'Connor and the Culture of Life*, 70.

27. Anderson and Donovan, "The Sisters of Life," 11; Maggie Gordon, "Ten Nuns join Sisters of Life community in Stamford," *Stamford Advocate*, 6 August 2010.

28. Caulfield, "Twenty-five Years Consecrated to Life," 18.

29. "Mother Agnes Mary Donovan, Sisters of Life to Receive 2013 Evangelium Vitae Medal," *Targeted News Service*, 10 October 2012.

30. Edmonds, "Group of Nuns."

would go the Annunciation Motherhouse in Suffern, New York, for two years of prayer and study as a novice. Next would come temporary vows and, finally, perpetual vows.

A life of prayer and service, without television, email, cell phones, or the Internet, might seem impossibly challenging to modern women, but there has been steady interest in the order since it began accepting postulants in 1993. Not all of those who attend discernment retreats or who start as postulants stick with the order, but many do. One of the first women to join the order had had no previous knowledge of the group before she told her pastor in Colorado that she was thinking about religious life and he told her to contact the Sisters of Life. Many of the sisters, however, come from the Catholic pro-life movement and from circles of faithful Catholics who are supportive of orthodox religious orders. The sisters have included a computer engineer, a graphic artist, a doctor, a mechanical engineer, a teacher, a lawyer, an opera singer, and a nurse; by 2014 there were sisters from Canada, Europe, Australia, and New Zealand. The one group that is no longer accepted is women with living children—a few joined at first but their adult children "were not willing to let go of them."[31]

Angela Karalekas of Ludlow, Massachusetts, was serious about her faith as a teenager and felt that God was calling her to give him her life. She attended the Naval Academy and became a Naval officer. Starting in 2001, she served as the gunnery officer on a destroyer that hunted narcotics smugglers in the Pacific Ocean. Then, while serving in Italy, she was particularly impressed by the young women who were becoming religious sisters. They were not joining religious orders because they had no other options; they were "bright and talented" women who believed they would have wonderful lives as sisters.[32] "It was actually while I was in the military stationed in Europe that I really grew in my faith. I saw the

31. Mary Voboril, "'There's a Need for the Work': for these nuns, protecting human life is a sacred mission," *Newsday*, 11 September 2000.

32. Sarah Kuta, "Veterans Speak: Sister Maris Stella grateful after serving in US Navy," *Daily Camera*, 5 November 2016.

beauty and privilege of religious life there."[33] She joined the Sisters of Life in 2006 and is now Sister Maris Stella.[34]

Sister Bethany Madonna, who professed her vows in 2010, had a religious conversion at the age of seventeen that opened her to the possibility of religious life. "I grew up always thinking I would be married with a family. The desires of a feminine heart are to be a spouse, to love someone to the fullest and be a mother," she said. But after growing closer to God, she said, "I began to hear the Lord offer me an invitation to be his bride, and love his children as my own." After investigating other religious orders that did not quite fit her, she met the Sisters of Life at the March for Life in Washington, DC, in 2005, and sensed that this was the religious community for her. Her first assignment was to work with the order's vocations director in the Bronx.[35]

Mother Agnes herself says, "I have never done anything so difficult, but delightfully difficult. It takes all of myself, and requires a total integration of heart and mind to lead and to summon the energies of women who wish to dedicate their lives to God." Of course, she had the additional challenge of leading an order without having been in one herself. She was learning to be a sister even as she had to be a mother.[36]

The order now has seven convents in the New York City area, newer convents in Toronto, Denver, and Philadelphia, a retreat house in Connecticut, and a house of studies in Washingnton, DC. The Sacred Heart of Jesus Convent in the Hell's Kitchen section of Manhattan, which opened in 1998, functions both as a place a prayer and contemplation for the sisters and as a home, or "Holy Respite," for pregnant women. The seven or eight sisters who live in the convent can host up to eleven women. These women are usually referred to the convent by pro-life groups and crisis pregnancy centers in the New York area, and many of the women are immigrants.

---

33. Rosemary Fernandez, "Young Nuns: Meet Suffern's Sisters of Life," *Hudson Valley Magazine*, April 2014.
34. Kuta, "Veterans Speak."
35. Gordon, "Ten Nuns join Sisters of Life."
36. Anderson and Donovan, "The Sisters of Life," 12.

In its first few months, the convent welcomed women from Liberia, Kenya, France, Italy, and the Philippines. In later years the women living there included a nanny from Trinidad who had barely escaped an abusive boyfriend and a Polish woman who was hoping to become a doctor. The most important aspect of the ministry to the pregnant women, many of whom have been forced out of their homes or pressured to abort their unborn children, is to give them a place of security and stability where they can live during their pregnancy.[37]

The sisters connect the women to social services and counseling, but the heart of the ministry is spiritual. Mother Agnes says, "We think of the environment we create here as a 'holy respite,' a place where the women can be nurtured and where they can step aside from the busy-ness of the world and have an opportunity to reflect on the direction their lives are taking and the very big decisions they have to make." The women include Protestants, members of non-Christian religions, and the unaffiliated, in addition to Catholics, but most appreciate the prayerful environment in which they live and the personal attention that they receive. They usually work during the day and then return to the convent for dinner with the sisters. That time around the dinner table allows the women to befriend each other and form a community that shares information and resources. After a few months in the convent, most women give birth and then keep their child, but some place the child for adoption. In the eyes of the sisters, "both kinds of decisions are equally heroic," because they are forms of "self-sacrificing love."[38] As Sister Rita Marie, the superior of the convent, says, the sisters rejoice in "the beauty of a mother coming to the understanding of the dignity of her calling and how that gives life back to her."[39] The women usually stay in the convent for a few months after giving birth, as they adapt to their new lives and make plans for their next steps. Between

37. William McGowan, "Life and Faith in Hell's Kitchen," *Wall Street Journal*, 29 July 2011.
38. Anderson and Donovan, "The Sisters of Life," 11.
39. McGowan, "Life and Faith."

1998 and 2011, the convent welcomed 150 babies into the world.[40] It is important that some of the work of the Sisters of Life takes place in New York, for the city has become the nation's unofficial abortion capital, with seven abortions for every ten births in 2010.[41]

The sisters help the women with tasks such as housing applications and requesting back pay. They even go to doctor's appointments with their guests, partly to learn about the woman's specific health issues, but also simply to give support. "I was so cranky and so unhappy trudging outside," says one former guest, "but they always made it seem fun and exciting, like it was a picnic or something." The sisters also visited her in the hospital once she had given birth: "Every hour on the hour I had two or three visiting. It really helped me, because I placed my baby for adoption."[42] Once the baby is born, the sisters help with diapers and more encouragement.

Although there is no requirement that guests pray or attend Mass with the sisters, many guests do pray with their hosts. Many become closer to God during their time in the convent and want to be confirmed or to convert to Catholicism but do not have the ability to attend the Rite of Christian Initiation for Adults (RCIA), a slate of classes in preparation for admission to the Church that most Catholic parishes offer. The sisters therefore have designed their own RCIA program that fits their guests' schedules and needs. In 2016, fifteen guests at the New York convent entered the Church after going through the in-house RCIA program and being baptized and confirmed by Bishop John O'Hara.[43]

Mother Agnes and her sisters developed a schedule that allowed them to devote significant time to both prayer and active ministry:

> In prayer, we follow the Liturgy of the Hours, setting aside the first two hours of the day for prayer in common, meditation, and the holy sacrifice of the Mass. By rising early we experience a sacred space and time to pray, to be with God. We practice silence

---

40. Ibid.
41. Christine Spampinato and Erin O'Donnell, "Living faith in medicine," *Linacre Quarterly* 80, no. 1 (2013): 3.
42. Voboril, "There's a Need for the Work."
43. Knap, "Sisters of Life Thrive at 25."

in the morning so as to continue our recollection. Then at the end of the afternoon, we gather for prayer again—the rosary and silent adoration before the Blessed Sacrament. Thus prayer marks our day and creates a rhythm within which we live our lives. Here in this house, where pregnant women are our guests, our lives of prayer create the consistency and structure of each day. Prayer forms the walls of our home.[44]

This emphasis on prayer, just as Cardinal O'Connor had hoped, has distinguished the Sisters of Life from other pro-life ministries. It is not merely that the sisters pray for about four-and-a-half hours every day; it is that they consciously base their lives and ministries on prayer.

The Sisters of Life based at the Bronx and Toronto convents are usually involved in the order's preaching and teaching ministry. They travel to churches and other sites to speak about various pro-life issues. They teach Catholics to understand the psychology of women who are considering abortion, many of whom see pregnancy as "the death of their identity." As Sister Catherine Marie explains, these women know that a new life has begun inside them, but they are deeply afraid that who they are and all they have achieved will be destroyed. Desperate for a quick and easy solution, they grasp at abortion as the answer to their problems; abortion therefore often occurs in the days directly after a woman learns that she is pregnant. "The first thing I tell a woman in crisis," says Sister Catherine Marie, "is to take some time. Circumstances can appear tough, but I reassure her that things can change." The sisters help the women come to see that, although it will be difficult, it will not be impossible to survive and even to prosper as they bring the baby to term.[45]

In Manhattan and Toronto the sisters also have Visitation Missions, which are telephone, email, and walk-in ministries to women who are considering abortion. About 900 women call or visit the

44. Anderson and Donovan, "The Sisters of Life," 10.
45. "Sisters Educate on Psychology of Women Facing Abortion," *BC Catholic*, 7 March 2012.

Manhattan mission each year, and the sisters offer them encouragement and advice, both in an initial contact or meeting and in follow-up calls or texts. Some are being pressured by boyfriends, husbands, or family members to abort. Many, even the wealthy and professionally successful, believe that pregnancy is going to ruin their lives. Sister Magdalene, the coordinator of the Manhattan ministry, says that many of them, though, receive a "moment of grace," a check in the spirit, that makes them open to counsel. The Visitation Missions continue to provide advice and encouragement throughout the pregnancy or connects the women to pregnancy help centers and maternity homes in their areas. Some of the women are invited to stay at the Convent of the Sacred Heart in Manhattan or other Sisters of Life convents.[46]

In 2004 the Sisters of Life took over the Villa Maria Retreat House in Stamford, Connecticut, about one hour outside of New York City, from a shrinking group of Franciscan Sisters. The new facility gave the sisters an excellent site for its retreat ministry, especially their "Entering Canaan" healing retreats for post-abortive women. "Our experience," says Mother Agnes, "is that they are desperately waiting for an invitation to come home to the Church, to be reconciled with God, and to find forgiveness in their own hearts for themselves—which is sometimes the hardest part."[47] Theresa Bonapartis, a post-abortive woman who, after her own healing, helped the sisters develop their healing ministry, says that the "Entering Canaan" retreat is unique, "not because of what the sisters do, but because of who the sisters are." Their prayerful, loving, merciful, welcoming attitudes create a safe space for women who often see themselves as unforgivable. The retreat is not a one-time experience; the sisters see it as the beginning of a relationship that can last for years or a lifetime. Mother Agnes believes that these women will become "the ultimate evangelizers of our society" because of the depth of their experience of God's mercy and healing.[48]

---

46. McGowan, "Life and Faith."
47. Anderson and Donovan, "The Sisters of Life," 11.
48. Knap, "Sisters of Life Thrive at 25."

Charism and Message

The charism of the Sisters of Life is a commitment to the sacredness of all human life that includes reverence for every human being. Although the basic idea was there from the start and can be traced to Cardinal O'Connor's experience at Dachau in 1975, over the years the sisters have come to a deeper understanding of its meaning. Their understanding in 2014 was that their Charism of Life "proclaims that every human being bears the imprint of God" and that "every human being is a sacred, unique, unrepeatable expression of God's love in the world." They had found that "in contemplating Jesus Christ in the Eucharist, the eyes of our hearts are opened so that we may recognize His presence in each human being."[49] Mother Agnes Mary puts it this way:

> We've come to learn that this spiritual love is not about doing more but about allowing oneself to first be moved in delight by the good of the other, and then outwardly manifesting that delight. This idea can sound simple enough, but do we truly live in this way? Do we love like this? Are we open to receive another person, allowing our hearts to be moved by some goodness we see and notice in them—such as beauty, strength, vulnerability, generosity? And then do we mirror that back to them, before acting, giving advice or stepping in to help, so that they experience being confirmed in their own goodness?[50]

Sister Mary Elizabeth, the order's vicar general, says, "One of the reasons for the joy in the community is we believe each person has some beautiful, unique goodness and we have the joy of discovering that in them and reflecting it back so she has the experience of her own dignity, goodness, and strength. That person becomes a gift to us in our recognizing her for who she is. She reveals to us the splendor and beauty of God."[51] The order's charism gives the sisters a

49. "One Man with a heart for the most vulnerable," *Imprint* (Fall 2014), 4.

50. Mother Agnes Mary, "A Woman's Heart: Made for Maternal Love," *Imprint* (Spring 2014), 2.

51. Beth Griffin, "Sisters of Life hold up dignity of single moms in 25-year-old ministry," *Catholic News Service*, 9 May 2016.

message of hope for all those they meet: "God loved you into exist-ence, continuously upholds you and calls you forth to become your best self and chooses you in each moment."[52]

The sisters also came to a deep appreciation of femininity and maternity, of what Pope John Paul II called "the feminine genius." The nature of their ministry as women serving mothers who either were about to deliver children or were mourning lost children, led to a growing understanding of women's gifts and orientations. At the heart of femininity, they came to see, is maternity. "Maternal love brings the other to life and sets him or her free to join the living chain of heroic love," explains Mother Agnes Mary. This is true for women who have given birth and women, like the sisters them-selves, living lives of celibacy. "Every woman, regardless of her state in life and whether or not she has physical children, has the power to love in this revolutionary way," she believes. Cardinal O'Connor had said that the sisters' mission was "to mother the mothers of the unborn so that they could mother their children."[53]

This appreciation of femininity is by no means a rejection of mas-culinity. In fact, the sisters have also developed a love for authentic masculinity, which they see as complementing authentic femininity. Many of the women they work with, who have been hurt by irre-sponsible and callous men, need healing for their wounded femi-ninity and benefit greatly from living with strong, pure women who model a kind of feminine virtue that some of them have never seen before. But these women also benefit from contact with strong and upright men who model the affirming and strengthening sort of masculinity. Male volunteers, who fix appliances, move furniture, and perform a variety of other tasks at the convents and visitation missions, can also be part of the healing process: women see the ser-vice-oriented kind of masculinity that perfectly complements authentic femininity.[54]

For instance, a woman named Laura was considering abortion

---

52. "One Man with a heart," 4.
53. Mother Agnes Mary, "A Woman's Heart," 2.
54. "Men's Gift: To Uphold," *Imprint* (Spring 2014), 4.

but talked often with the sisters. If she gave birth, she was afraid that the baby's father would fight her for custody. The sisters arranged for her to meet with a lawyer to counsel her about her rights and options. At the end of the meeting, the lawyer, impressed by Laura's courage and not realizing that she was thinking about abortion, said, "I want you to know, I really believe in what you are doing." These simple words flooded Laura with hope. When she called the sisters to inform them that she had decided to go through with the pregnancy she sounded like a new woman. The sisters saw this episode as a demonstration of man's special calling of "upholding women in the gift of their maternity." The lawyer had thought he would help Laura with his legal expertise, but his gift to her was more fundamental. "Rather, through his supportive presence and a few heartfelt words he stepped into his God-given capacity to confirm and uphold a woman in one of her greatest gifts—that of giving life. Not only that, but he uncovered what so many fears, challenges, and discouraging voices were stifling—the incredible strength she possessed, both as a woman and a mother, to love."[55] In other words, the sexes are not at war—they are made for each other. Rediscovering and healing wounded femininity is in fact closely related to healthy expressions of masculinity.

The general approach to ministry of the Sisters of Life is positive and affirming. It focuses on the good, not on the bad. It is premised on loving what is good, not denouncing what is bad. The sisters do, of course, hate and reject abortion, violence against women, and all offenses against human life, but they lead with their love of what is good. According to Sister Mary Rose, superior of the sisters' house of studies, the Catholic response to abortion "is to proclaim the truth, beauty, goodness, and sacredness of human life." She emphasizes that "each human person is a unique and unrepeatable gift, made in the likeness of God, the Author of life." This is, of course, applicable to the unborn child that women carry within them, but it is also applicable to the women who come to them, who often feel burdened and alone. The sisters try to show the women "the goodness

55. Ibid., 4.

and beauty of their own lives." "She really needs to know that she is loved and supported," says Sister Mary Rose. "Only then can she love and nurture the child growing within her."[56] Sister Grace Dominic puts it this way: "When a woman comes to us, she can need a thousand different things, but mostly she just needs to know she's not alone. . . . Once she knows she is loved, she can make a decision of love for her child."[57]

For women who have had an abortion, the message is not condemnation, but mercy and the hope of healing. The sisters look especially to the encyclical of Pope John Paul II on life issues, *Evangelium vitae*, which has a short but powerful section for post-abortive women:

> I would now like to say a special word to women who have had an abortion. The Church is aware of the many factors which may have influenced your decision, and she does not doubt that in many cases it was a painful and even shattering decision. The wound in your heart may not yet have healed. Certainly what happened was and remains terribly wrong. But do not give in to discouragement and do not lose hope. Try rather to understand what happened and face it honestly. If you have not already done so, give yourselves over with humility and trust to repentance. The Father of mercies is ready to give you his forgiveness and his peace in the Sacrament of Reconciliation. To the same Father and his mercy you can with sure hope entrust your child. With the friendly and expert help and advice of other people, and as a result of your own painful experience, you can be among the most eloquent defenders of everyone's right to life. Through your commitment to life, whether by accepting the birth of other children or by welcoming and caring for those most in need of someone to be close to them, you will become promoters of a new way of looking at human life.[58]

---

56. Joseph Martin Hagan, "The Sisters of Life," *Dominicana*, 22 January 2014.
57. Fernandez, "Young Nuns."
58. John Paul II, *Evangelium vitae* 99.

Mother Agnes Mary puts it this way: "Many of our apostolates give women whose femininity, maternity, or sexuality has been wounded the space to heal and reclaim the brilliant innocence of a pure heart and fruitful love. These wounds can result from the effects of pornography, distortion of body image and sexuality born of media culture, the suffering after abortion, etc. Underlying all of these effects of the culture of death is a contempt for human life."[59]

There is a sense in which the sisters' life is one of suffering. This is not to deny their real joy, which is evident to anyone who meets them, but to recast that joy as joy-in-the-midst-of-pain. For the sisters willingly put themselves, daily, into the worst that the modern world has to offer. They experience, over and over again, the wrenching pain of women who have turned on their own children, of men who have used and deserted women, of parents who have pressured their daughters to abort and even turned them out into the streets if they did not. It is hard to imagine a more emotionally searing set of experiences than those that bring women to the Sisters of Life.

For most families the crisis of an unwanted or unplanned pregnancy is a rare, if not once-in-a-lifetime, event. The Sisters of Life live, day by day, in a world of crisis pregnancies. In addition to their intense prayer life they are able to do so because they understand and accept the world of pain in which they are immersed. They do not run from it but, rather, seek healing in the mercy of Christ and in the tears of the Virgin Mary. Despite all this suffering, it is difficult to avoid the "b-word" when describing the sisters. Dominican friar Joseph Martin Hagan puts it this way: "Beautiful. Merciful. Inspiring. Do these words describe the Catholic response to abortion? If you hesitate to say yes, you probably haven't met the Sisters of Life." To Hagan, the sisters embody "the tender heart of the Church." In the darkness of pain and confusion their joy shines through.[60] In a similar way, Brian Caulfield of the Knights of Columbus describes

---

59. Salai, "On Fighting for Life."
60. Hagan, "The Sisters of Life."

the Sisters of Life as "a hint of the hidden God whispering within each heart amid the dust and din of New York."[61]

Life and Hope

Jane came to the New York convent from a small town in another state to escape the "scorn" and "daily pressures" she was experiencing for being an unwed pregnant woman.[62] She felt depressed at some times and emotional at others. The sisters would put notes of encouragement, prayer cards, and rosaries in her lunch bag. They put more notes on her door, especially when she was in a bad mood. "So the next morning," she says, "I yelled at them. I'm, like, 'Stop putting notes under my door! You're going to kill me!'" They responded by smiling at her.

Jane found the pure and chaste environment both difficult and reassuring. The younger sisters, especially, seemed naïve and sheltered. They would blush, for instance, if she said a workman was cute. Jane keenly felt the absence of electronics and media and wondered how intelligent women, as she admitted many of the sisters were, could give up so much, for the rest of their lives. But she loved the environment of emotional and physical safety in the convent. The sisters were "very supportive and not judgmental." Unlike her experience in college, there was no gossip. On campus, "when you were being a snot, you just knew there was a dorm full of women in the next room talking about you," but that simply did not happen at the convent. Jane knew she had often acted "grumpy," "cranky," and "snappish," but she says that the sisters "never responded in kind, not even once."

A notable aspect of Jane's story is that, although she had a certain respect for the sisters' devotion to prayer, her stay with them does not seem to have deepened her own faith or to have made her more religious. During her last month at the convent she did not attend any prayers or religious services at all. She says she will try to repay them and will always be grateful, but gives no sign of recognizing

---

61. Caulfield, "Twenty-five Years Consecrated to Life," 13.
62. Client names are pseudonyms.

that the love she experienced is, at its source, the love of Christ. However, this is not a failure. Her baby was saved and she was loved and this is what the Sisters of Life exist to do. "I needed to feel loved and accepted, no matter what, and I was," Jane says.[63]

Another woman, Greta, found out that she was pregnant at about the time she was finishing up graduate school in the United Kingdom. Instead of supporting her, her boyfriend broke up with her. Greta says she was "in a horrible state of depression." She came back to the United States and thought seriously about abortion. Like many educated women, she looked at abortion as "the most practical thing," the best way to solve her many problems. After staying with the Sisters of Life, though, she found new hope. She gave birth, found a job, and even reunited with her boyfriend. Greta is now happily married and professionally successful.[64]

Racquel was sick, pregnant, and unemployed. She did not want to go on welfare and turned to the Sisters of Life as her only other option. Initially, she thought the sisters were naïve or foolish to welcome strange women into the convent and did not understand how they could spend so much time in prayer and service to others, but she was reassured by the sister she first met at the convent. "She made me feel good and strong in the decision I had made to have this baby," Racquel says. "I was doing the right thing." As she lived, ate, and prayed with the sisters she developed a deep appreciation for their lives of service. "By the end you see that it's a beautiful expression of what it means to be a woman on the deepest level," Racquel said. By the time she gave birth, she was comparing the ways the sisters had welcomed her to the way she wanted to welcome her son.[65]

Sometimes women find the Sisters of Life in surprising ways. Once, a young woman named Amy and two of her friends showed up at the Visitation mission in New York. The sister in charge welcomed them into the mission and asked how she could help. Amy

---

63. The story of "Jane" and all her words are from Voboril, "There's a Need for the Work."

64. McGowan, "Life and Faith."

65. Hagan, "The Sisters of Life."

shared that she was about three months pregnant and that the father of her child was insisting that she have an abortion. Feeling alone and unsupported, she had made an appointment for an abortion at Planned Parenthood but had prayed that God would give her a sign if she was doing the wrong thing. In the Planned Parenthood waiting room, she found a brochure from the Sisters of Life. Amy read the brochure, sensed it was the sign she had asked for, started to cry, and left the abortuary with her two friends. She then took a bus to the Visitation mission.[66]

As Amy poured out her heart to one of the sisters, a weight seemed to leave her shoulders. The sister asked her delicately what her heart was telling her to do. Amy replied, "My life is not over. I just have to let go and let God. I am keeping this baby." She did keep the baby. No one discovered how that brochure came to be in a Planned Parenthood facility, but Amy and the Sisters of Life see its presence in that terrible place as evidence of the providential care of their loving God.[67]

The retreats for postabortive healing that the sisters conduct are other places where God's touch is manifest. Magda, for instance, approached the portrait of Jesus, the Divine Mercy, to lay a rose in front of it, as the retreat participants have the opportunity to do at the end of each retreat, as a way of entrusting their lost children and themselves to the mercy of God. Kneeling in front of the image, she began to cry, releasing all the anger, pain, regret, and self-hatred that she had bottled up inside of her for years, and receiving the sweet mercy and forgiveness of God. "Afterward I had the chance to speak with her," says Sister Mariae Agnus Dei, "and she was hardly the same person who had walked in. Her face and eyes were filled with light. She possessed a new sense of dignity and innocence. She was truly made new. And while she knew there was still a long road ahead in healing, she had the peace, hope, and support to move forward in the journey."[68]

66. "Weaving a tapestry," *Imprint* (Fall 2014), 6.
67. Ibid.
68. Sister Mariae Agnus Dei, "When His mercy touches our wounds," *Imprint* (Fall 2014): 8.

The stories of mercy and healing could be recounted for hundreds of pages. The Sisters of Life are fulfilling a great need not because of innovative programs or professional expertise, but because of their great love, their hospitality, and their devotion to prayer, which makes their love and hospitality possible and, it seems, leads a steady stream of women to their doors. While the Roe and Casey decisions of the Supreme Court reflect and encourage a culture of death, the Sisters of Life reflect and foster a culture of life, which is a culture of truth about sin, consequences, and mercy; a culture of goodness, especially the goodness of human life; and a culture of beauty, the beauty of love, holiness, and chastity.

3

Reality, Wonder, and Delight

The Integrated Humanities Program

> *An ancient philosopher said that to look at the*
> *stars is to become a lover of wisdom—a philosopher.*
> *Since the Pearson Program aims to make all students*
> *philosophers in that sense, we say, with a modern poet,*
> *"Look at the stars! Look, look up at the skies!"*[1]

UNTIL ABOUT 1970 the University of Kansas offered a course in observational astronomy, otherwise known as star-gazing. But after the professor who had taught the course retired, it was replaced with astrophysics. The major problems with twentieth-century university education were encapsulated in that single incident, believed English professor Dennis Quinn. Freshmen who had not mastered the basics were thrown into specialized classes; young people who had barely glanced at the night sky began their study of the stars by learning abstract mathematical formulas; the mystery of the heavens faded into the task of measurement. The problem was not merely that the university was assuming too much of its students—assuming in this case a familiarity with the night sky that most students actually lacked—but that the university did not value a certain type of knowledge at all. The university assumed

---

1. "Pearson Integrated Humanities Program" brochure, in Robert Carlson, *Truth on Trial: Liberal Education Be Hanged* (n.p.: Crisis Books, 1995), 145. The poem is "The Starlight Night" by Gerard Manley Hopkins.

that valuable knowledge was the type that came from scientific measurement and calculation and that the experiential sort of knowledge typified by observational astronomy was not worthy of an "advanced" institution.[2]

Professor Quinn and two colleagues, John Senior and Franklyn Nelick, lamented the demise of observational astronomy and, more importantly, the loss of the form of knowledge that it represented. In 1970 they started the Integrated Humanities Program as an antidote to the disintegration of the modern university, which they saw as splintered, overly specialized, incoherent, and ultimately meaningless. Their four-semester program, they hoped, would provide a united, holistic introduction to Western culture by using the Great Books approach developed by Mark van Doren and Mortimer Adler, but with two twists that made it unlike anything else in American higher education at the time: the whole program would be taught through the poetic mode of knowledge, the participatory sort of learning exemplified by observational astronomy, and the Western tradition would be taught from the perspective of what the professors called "Realism" or "The Perennial Philosophy," not "objectively" or from a supposedly neutral viewpoint. At the heart of the IHP's realism was the belief that the real exists and is beautiful, good, and true; the three professors contrasted this belief with "anti-realism," or the "perennial heresy" that reality is an illusion, which they saw in Western philosophies like nominalism, relativism, and voluntarism, and in Eastern thought, such as Buddhism.[3]

---

2. Dennis Quinn, "The Muses as Pedagogues of the Liberal Arts," *Classical Homeschooling Magazine* 2 (2000): http://www.angelicum.net/classical-homeschooling-magazine/second-issue/the-muses-as-pedagogues-of-the-liberal-arts-by-dennis-quinn/. Quinn and his colleagues, of course, were not alone in noting and critiquing the dominance of the scientific method of inquiry in education. For a comparison of the modernist position, with its elevation of the scientific approach, and a traditionalist approach that accepts "many valid methods of inquiry, each appropriate to its own subject matter," see Mortimer J. Adler and Milton Mayer, *The Revolution in Education* (Chicago: University of Chicago Press, 1958), 157–73.

3. By Realism, the professors meant "the conviction that there is an absolute truth, that the exterior world can be known in itself, and that the mind depends on the senses to know it." For Senior, the "Perennial Philosophy" was best represented

The program was wildly successful. Before it was shut down by worried administrators, it saw at least 200 of its students convert to Catholicism and many of its alumni become teachers, priests, and monks.[4]

Poetic Knowledge

Although the professors were Catholics and Thomists, they taught neither Catholicism nor Thomism in the classroom, the former because they strove to teach literature and not to proselytize, and the latter because they did not think their students were ready for it. We get a sense of the approach from Senior's later plans for a boys' boarding school: "Don't intrude religion. Just let the world be there. Let God teach as he intends in the language of nature which he himself invented for the purpose. . . . Wrestling in the dirt under a clear sky in the flat light of the October sun, licked by the fiery tongues of maple leaves as they roll in them, the cool indifferent pines observing—well, you don't have to say God made all this; it's in the excitation of their blood."[5] Reality, he believed, was the greatest evangelist.

In a similar way, Senior loved Thomas and saw the *Summa Theologiae* as "the greatest theological opus in history" and the "norm and measure of all Catholic theology" but believed that Western culture had become so exhausted and "depleted" that Americans were like "stuffed, stitched dolls walking mindless among the broken statues of a devastated civilization." He had tried to teach Thomism to undergraduates earlier in his career, but he had decided that this "age of spiritual aridity, dissolution, a Dark Night of history and the Church," was a time for more modest endeavors.[6] The issue was not

by Plato, Aristotle, Thomas Aquinas, and John Henry Newman: Francis Bethel, *John Senior and the Restoration of Realism* (Merrimack, New Hampshire: Thomas More College Press, 2016), 3, 7–8, 60–61.

4. Mason Becraft, "Let them be born in wonder: Catholic legacy from the humanities program at the University of Kansas endures," *Eastern Oklahoma Catholic* (June 2013): 12–15.

5. John Senior, as quoted in Bethel, *John Senior*, 254.

6. John Senior, *The Restoration of Christian Culture* (San Francisco: Ignatius, 1983), 77–83; Bethel, *John Senior*, 135–39.

just that Thomas's *Summa* had been written for students who already had mastered philosophy, Scripture, and the seven liberal arts—the *trivium* of grammar, logic, and rhetoric, and the *quadrivium* of arithmetic, geometry, music, and astronomy—which almost no American college students had done, but that they had not even started on a more elementary program of memory, singing, dancing, nature study, and gymnastics that was the necessary preparation for the liberal arts. Senior believed that the American way of life was so artificial that young people lacked the basic sort of experiential knowledge on which all higher learning is predicated:

> Generations brought up in centrally heated and air-conditioned homes and schools, shot from place to place encapsulated in culturally sealed-off buses, who swim in heated, chlorinated pools devoid of current, swirl, or tide, where even the build-up from one's own pushing of the water is suctioned off by vacuums so as not to spoil the pure experience of sport-for-sport's sake; they play summer games like shooting balls through hoops, but reinvented as "basketball," and on winter nights, dressed in short pants; they play football under geodesic domes in heavy jerseys, and ski on artificial snow in July—poor little rich suburban children who have all these delights, and living in a constant fluorescent glare, have never seen the stars, which St. Thomas, following Aristotle and all the ancients, says are the first begetters of that primary experience of reality formulated as the first of all principles in metaphysics, that *something is.*[7]

This "primary experience of reality" is what Senior, Quinn, and Nelick meant by "poetic knowledge." It was based on "direct and vicarious experience that engages and awakens the senses" in a state of "passive receptivity." Knowledge of something through the senses is "a natural transcendental gazing into the forms of things" and a "virtually unconscious act." Often this knowledge is associated with wonder, "knowing the good and beautiful in some thing, knowing this simply in repose, love, and adoration," which in turn motivates

---

7. Senior, *Restoration*, 83.

desire. Without this poetic knowledge, higher (intellectual) knowledge cannot exist because it has no content or foundation.[8]

Poetic knowledge involves experience, participation, sympathy, and intuition, in contrast with the measurement associated with the scientific mode of knowledge and with the fragmentation associated with the critical mode of knowledge. Where the scientific and critical modes are external to the object, the poetic mode participates in the object.[9] For example, the star gazer experiences the star, while the astronomer measures light or movement. The astronomer knows facts and theories about the star, but the star gazer knows the star. In the same vein, the critical approach to a poem about a star brings knowledge of many things, but not of the star itself, while the poetic mode approaches the star itself: "The poet says to us: Here it *is*. He presents it as a gift. This is the mourner, the lover, the moon, the smile, the soldier, the ship, the horse. Part of the wonder of poetry is that it does give us things in the present, puts us in their presence, a certain inner quality we glimpse but seldom and fleetingly."[10] Without poetic knowledge, scientific and critical knowledge have no foundation. Without poetic knowledge, science and literature are abstract and vain; they presuppose knowledge of stars.

The Integrated Humanities Program

In the 1960s, the University of Kansas experimented with an initiative called "Colleges within the College" that was designed to foster community and friendship for freshmen and sophomores, who often felt alone and anonymous in what had already become a massive university. In 1970, English Professor Dennis Quinn, the director of the new Pearson College, one of the new colleges inside the College of Arts and Sciences, added an academic dimension to what had been up to then merely a living arrangement by starting the Integrated Humanities Program (IHP) with his friends John Senior

8. James S. Taylor, *Poetic Knowledge: The Recovery of Education* (Albany: State University of New York Press, 1998), 34–58.

9. Ibid., 83–84.

10. Dennis Quinn, *Iris Exiled: A Synoptic History of Wonder* (Lanham, Maryland: University Press of America, 2002), 43.

(Classics) and Franklyn Nelick (English) in the new college. The IHP featured a four-semester sequence that would count for several of the college's general education requirements: Greek works in the first semester, Roman works in the second, the Bible and Medieval European works in the third, and Modern Western works in the fourth.[11] Although the texts studied were similar to Great Books programs at other institutions, the IHP's leadership, orientation, and methods made it distinctive. First, the professors were united by a common vision of truth and by their willingness to go against the flow of contemporary higher education. Second, the professors insisted from the beginning that the texts under discussion actually had something to teach American college students. Homer, for instance, was to be studied not simply to discern his technique but to appreciate his message. Third, there were no lectures, at least in the traditional sense. Instead, the three professors had spontaneous conversations during which students were forbidden to take notes. Fourth, the students memorized ten poems each semester. Finally, although it was not required, students were strongly encouraged to study Latin.

Quinn and Nelick had met as graduate students at the University of Wisconsin and both of them had taught at the University of Kansas since the 1950s. Senior had studied with Mark van Doren at Columbia and then had taught at Hofstra, Wyoming, and Cornell before coming to Kansas in 1967.[12] The three men had different life

---

11. Carlson, *Truth on Trial*, 152–53. The full program was as follows. Semester I: Homer, *Odyssey* and *Iliad*; Plato, *Republic*; Aesop, *Fables*; Herodotus, *Persian Wars*; Thucydides, *Peloponnesian War*; Aeschylus, *Oresteia*. Semester II: Virgil, *Aeneid*; Caesar, *Conquest of Gaul*; Plutarch, *Makers of Rome*; Lucretius, *The Nature of the Universe*; Cicero, *On Duty*; *Old Testament* selections. Semester III: *New Testament*; Augustine, *Confessions*; *Two Lives of Charlemagne*; *Song of Roland*; *Memoirs of the Crusades*; *Sir Gawain and the Green Knight*; Boethius, *Consolation of Philosophy*; St. Francis, *Little Flowers*; Chaucer, *Canterbury Tales*. Semester IV: Cervantes, *Don Quixote*; Cellini, *Autobiography*; Shakespeare, *Henry IV*, part I, and *Hamlet*; Descartes, *Meditations*; Hume, *Dialogues Concerning Natural Religion*; Scott, *Ivanhoe*; Burke, *Reflections on the French Revolution*; Newman and Huxley, *Selections on Education*; Parkman, *The Oregon Trail*; Dostoyevsky, *Crime and Punishment*.

12. Carlson, *Truth on Trial*, 4.

experiences and different personalities, but they were united in their rejection of the educational status quo and in their willingness to swim against the tide. There were many professors who felt uncomfortable with the directions universities were taking in the 1970s, but few of them spoke up and even fewer joined with like-minded colleagues to create an actual alternative to the relativism, over-specialization, and vocationalism that pervaded academia.

Quinn was a convert to Catholicism and a generally happy man who was an excellent administrator and a smooth talker, but he was also a passionate advocate of the humanities who was willing to fight to restore them to their former glory.[13] He believed that the humanities were in crisis because they had sold their heritage for a "mess of methodology." Their "distinctive appeal," he argued, was "love of knowledge for its own sake." But the professionalization of the humanities—really their inappropriate aping of the laboratory sciences—meant that scholars emphasized dispassionate investigation more than love. Quinn wanted to restore love to its central place in the humanities.[14] Doing so, he believed, would not only restore the humanities to their proper mode, but also "revitalize" the whole university.[15]

He based his approach on the words of Plato in *The Laws*: "Shall we begin, then, with the acknowledgment that education is first given through Apollo and the Muses?" In this traditional scheme, the nine muses, including Clio, goddess of history, and Calliope, goddess of epic poetry, "introduce the young to reality through

13. Ibid., 5.

14. John Senior's mentor, Mark van Doren, had a philosophy of the liberal arts that differed from that of Quinn and Senior, but he too saw that his deep love for many works of literature caused a certain tension when he approached those works critically. When asked to give a series of lectures at Emory University on a work of his choice in the field of the humanities, he said, "I replied that there was one great book in that field—possibly the greatest of them all—which I almost feared to discuss formally because I loved it so much and had perhaps too many ideas about it." Mark van Doren, *Don Quixote's Profession* (New York: Columbia University Press, 1958), vii.

15. Dennis Quinn, "Education by the Muses," *Classical Homeschooling Magazine* 2 (2000): http://www.angelicum.net/classical-homeschooling-magazine/second-issue/education-by-the-muses-by-dennis-quinn/.

delight" in a holistic form of education that includes "the heart, the memory, and passions and imagination, as well as the body and intelligence." Why would this form of education be so attractive to young people and why did it have such a profound effect on them? He believed that *wonder* was the key: "Wonder is no sentimentality but, rather, a mighty passion, species of fear, and awe-full confrontation with the mystery of things. Through the Muses the fearful abyss of reality first calls out to that other abyss that is the human heart; and the wonder of the response is, as the philosophers have said, the beginning of philosophy, not merely the first step but the *arche*, the principle, as one is the principle of arithmetic and the fear of God the beginning of wisdom. Thus wonder both starts education and sustains it."[16] Although, like his colleagues, Quinn devoted himself to classroom teaching and had little time for research and writing, his *Iris Exiled: A Synoptic History of Wonder* is a tour de force of literary and cultural insight that integrates not only the wide range of Western literature from ancient Greece to modern Europe, but also the Western philosophical and theological tradition from Plato and Aristotle to John Henry Newman and Jacques Maritain. The first half of this book, in fact, is probably the closest that today's reader can come to a direct encounter with the academic side of the IHP, for it traces the role of wonder in Greek, Roman, late Antique, Medieval, and early Modern periods, in a sequence very similar to the IHP's Great Books progression. As in the IHP conversations among the three professors, Quinn does not pull apart the various works he examines, but rather traces his theme in a languid but precise manner that shows both familiarity with and appreciation for the works under discussion.[17]

Senior, who had flirted with Marxism, Buddhism, and the occult before converting to Catholicism in 1960, had none of Quinn's optimism and was prone to sadness and harsh judgments of contempo-

---

16. Quinn, "Education by the Muses"; John Senior, *The Death of Christian Culture* (New Rochelle: Arlington House, 1978), 23–24. A key influence on Quinn's thinking about wonder was Josef Pieper's *Leisure, the Basis of Culture* (1952).

17. Quinn, *Iris Exiled*. The second half of the book examines the demise of wonder, as it is "usurped" and "in exile" in the modern age, despite the valiant efforts of Charles Dickens and Gerard Manley Hopkins.

rary culture.[18] "I happen to have a small vocation for spreading gloom," he said, and admitted that his favorite hymn, with the title adapted slightly, was "Darken the corner where you are."[19] His most famous book, *The Death of Christian Culture*, features essays with titles like "The Perennial Heresy" and "The Dark Night of the Church" and statements like "decadence has always led to the hatred of children" and "industrialism brings on a paralyzing gluttony and greed in which the quality of life is quantified." Although he was inclined to see the worst in modernity and American culture, he too was indefatigable in fighting for the truth and against the various inanities passing as wisdom in the modern university.[20] He believed that Modernism was killing literature because it elevated artificiality and sensationalism, which in turn were rejections of the realism—*"the real is really real, or, in a word, is"*—that he saw as simple common sense. For a poet to assert that his poetry had no purpose and existed for its own sake, was to Senior meaningless, impossible, and dangerous, as was the pursuit of novelty for its own sake.[21]

With Aristotle, Senior thought that "a man first simply looks, hears, smells, tastes, touches, and affirms existence." Man encounters the world and knows that it exists. He does not, as Descartes proposed, start with doubt and proceed to the recognition of autonomous cogitation. Rather, "Something exists and I know it and therefore I know that I exist and think," Senior said. "Thinking follows from existence; it does not make things so." If being is good, he argued, then the modernist retreat into artifice and hallucination was more than a retreat from reality; it was also a retreat from the good. "The divorce from *reality*," he argued, "is a divorce also from *morality*." The flight from reality ultimately becomes a nightmare.[22] The solution, of course, was reality: encountering it, embracing it, seeking more of it. Like Quinn, Senior thought that reality should first be encountered in nature, in the stars, in song and dance. Even

---

18. Bethel, *John Senior*, 27–33, 47–49.
19. Senior, *Restoration of Christian Culture*, 67.
20. Carlson, *Truth on Trial*, 5.
21. Senior, *Death of Christian Culture*, 33, 39.
22. Ibid., 33, 45.

university professors should turn from the work of criticism and return to the "humbler and greater elementary work of the conversion and education—the drawing out—of their students into the light of the good, the beautiful, and the true." Like Wordsworth, Senior invited his students to "come out into the light of *things*." Their "direct, everyday experience of fields, forests, streams, lakes, oceans, grass, and ground" was the prerequisite for any sort of deeper knowledge.[23] Senior's approach to teaching, although unorthodox, was masterful and highly attractive to students: he won various teaching awards throughout his career and was named one of the fifty best professors in the United States by *Esquire* magazine.[24]

Nelick was, if anything, more combative than Quinn or Senior. A Navy pilot in World War II, he was quick to argue and even to fight in the literal sense. IHP alumni relate stories of him challenging professors to public debates and overpowering and disarming a security guard who got on his bad side.[25] He was seen by some students as "the hard man, the harsh man, the man without patience," but those who knew him also detected a "Spartan, compassionate essence." In the beginning years of the IHP he was an Anglican, but he, as his two friends had done earlier, converted to Catholicism in 1973.[26] Also like his two friends, Nelick believed that the humanities were in trouble. In his view, the problem was that scholars of literature were "disregarding its meaning and substituting a quasi-historical analysis of its antecedents." While other scholars were focusing their attention on matters of technique, style, and influence, he called for a return to "traditional reverence for the text as a vehicle of truth." Art has "an end proper to it," he believed, and that end is "instruction of the person by delight." When a prominent poet said that a poem should not have a meaning, Nelick rejected that idea as deadly to both poetry and real education. Instead, he argued, poetry must, by its very nature, aim to delight in virtue or truth; education must, by its very nature, "address itself to an assent to truth by the

23. Senior, *Restoration of Catholic Culture*, 105, 111–12.
24. Bethel, *John Senior*, 133.
25. Carlson, *Truth on Trial*, 4, 5, 139.
26. Ibid., 139–40; Bethel, *John Senior*, 289, 355.

total intellectual, physical, moral, spiritual being, not to mere memory or the mastery of techniques."[27]

Nelick believed that the modern university had lost its way. In particular, it had confused means and ends. Great attention was given to tools, instruments, techniques, and methodologies. Little attention was given to ends. The result was "timid and endless talkative comparison of opinions in which every point of view is regarded as being equally important." At the same time, "dominance by specialty and method" was having a disintegrating effect on Nelick's discipline, literature, and, in fact, on all disciplines. "The integrity of the profession is lost," he said, "for the very notion of integration as a force which lies outside the profession has evanesced in one or another of the modern disjunctions of the good and the beautiful, the body and the soul, the means and the end." In such an environment, change and novelty were valued above truth and goodness, and "things that are self-evident, simple, plain, received, orthodox, and ordinary have no place." Modern academia, in Nelick's view, saw itself as progressive and advanced but actually had no real foundation. With knowledge splintered and disconnected, there was no longer any sort of unifying force. The façade of the university remained, but little else: "the center did not hold; it is all in pieces, all coherence gone."[28]

The three professors designed each part of their program to emphasize poetic knowledge and the wonder inspired by encountering reality. The use of conversation, rather than lecture, emphasized the friendship between the three professors and their shared love of the true, the good, and the beautiful:

> A faculty, studying the truth and conversing about it, are overheard by some who, though they don't know what it is, see something good, therefore desirable and, as such, urgent.[29]

The professors' own obvious friendship "personalized the imper-

---

27. Franklyn Nelick, "The Darkling Plain of Poetry," in *The Integration of Knowledge* (Lawrence, Kansas: IHP, 1979).
28. Ibid.
29. John Senior, as quoted in Bethel, *John Senior*, 306.

sonal education" that otherwise characterized the university and naturally overflowed into further conversation outside of class, with the professors or with other students. "Unlike many professors in academia," a former student remembers, "they weren't focused on outside research, or publishing technical scholarship, or winning grants. . . . Their primary commitment was to be teachers, to impart wisdom, convey beauty, and inculcate wonder among their students." Their friendship, he believes, "set the shape and tenor of the whole program."[30] "He loved his work, and that same love flowed into me," remembers a student of Professor Senior. "It was contagious. I remember speaking to him one day after class about a certain scene in the *Iliad*, and then later in his office about Socrates. His simple explanations of the works and the profound insights into Western Civilization spurred me on to a greater desire to learn, a desire that up to that time had remained dormant."[31]

The prohibition of note-taking fostered a sort of receptivity, presence, and openness that was quite different from the "will it be on the test?" attitude in most classes. The atmosphere, says another former student, "was intended to be meditative, not disputatious."[32] The professors were modeling poetic knowledge and their own experience of wonder as they talked, without notes, about what they loved in the week's readings. Meanwhile, students were *experiencing* literature much more than they were *analyzing* it. Freed from the expectation of writing down everything they heard, they were able to adopt an attitude of receptivity and delight.[33]

---

30. James Conley, "Friendship: A Pillar of Catholic Education," *Crisis Magazine* (19 February 2016): http://www.crisismagazine.com/2016/friendship-a-pillar-of-catholic-education.

31. "Our Schoolmaster Remembered: A Tribute to Dr. John Senior," *Edocere: A Resource for Catholic Education,* http://edocere.s15338140.onlinehome-server.com/our-schoolmaster-remembered-dr-john-senior/.

32. Taylor, *Poetic Knowledge,* 148–49.

33. The IHP, therefore, had a fundamental pedagogical difference with Thomas Aquinas College, the successful Catholic Great Books college in California, which taught in the philosophical mode. Senior argued that the Thomas Aquinas College model did not take into account "the impossibility of sending a young person to college without his having been to school" and the reality that freshmen arrived at college with wonder "pretty much crushed" out of them: Bethel, *John Senior,* 295.

Memorizing ten poems each semester seemed daunting to many freshmen. While in earlier eras memorization had been an important part not only of education but of culture more generally, by the 1970s it had become rare. Professional educators viewed memorization as restrictive, impersonal, and even damaging, while students, never having done it, initially saw it as unduly onerous, and perhaps impossible. Quinn and his colleagues, on the other hand, saw memorization as a path to delight, in the sense that when a poem is memorized it can be savored in a way quite different from reading. Memorization allows direct, unmediated knowledge. In contrast to the more common academic approach of analyzing poetry through dissection, the program sought to make poetry come alive. "Poetry, like song and dance," said the IHP brochure, "is primarily for memory and primarily for simple delight." Where critical analysis "spoils the delight and implies that the analyst should be aloof from poetry rather than participating in it," the IHP approach highlighted participation and delight. Once students got over their preconceptions, many found poetry memorization to be a highlight of the program. "At first I didn't think I could enjoy memorizing poetry," said one student, "but now it is one of the things I like best about the Program."[34]

Latin, at least as usually taught, might seem like the antithesis of the poetic approach to knowledge. Since students usually have to study noun and verb forms extensively before they can read anything complex and, even at a fairly advanced level, tend to approach a text as a sort of exercise in deciphering code, reading Latin would seem to be exactly the sort of "analysis" that the program was striving to avoid. However, the roughly half of the IHP students who took the optional four-semester Latin sequence (designed to correspond to the four semesters of Great Books), experienced Latin in a unique way. In the first semester, the course did not have a textbook. Students simply listened to the teacher who spoke simple Latin words, then phrases, repeating them and eventually answering

34. "Pearson Integrated Humanities Program" brochure, in Carlson, *Truth on Trial*, 153.

questions. The next stage involved the teacher reading simple stories, which students repeated in their own words. This was the "oral-natural method" of Cambridge scholar W. H. D. Rouse, designed to mimic the way children learn language, which was in line with the poetic approach. Students, again like children learning language, then learned Latin songs and poems by heart. By the second semester they could read simple Latin texts and by the third and fourth semesters they read Livy and Virgil.[35] As the IHP brochure boasted, "students actually speak and sing Latin as the living language of Western Civilization, rather than memorizing conjugations and declensions."[36] The vibrancy and delight of this approach to Latin led many of them to become Classics majors.[37]

Another way to provide this sort of direct lived experience was through travel. In 1972 the program sponsored a two-week trip to Greece and in 1973 students went to Greece and Rome. In 1976 the entire program moved to Ireland for the spring semester. The goal was "to get away from urbanization for a while, to rediscover some true values, and to experience silence." Senior called the semester in Ireland "a pilgrimage towards the truth" because he believed that American culture was so impersonal and abstract that students had lost contact with real life. He hoped that direct contact with a less industrialized and urbanized society that was still "people-conscious" could wake students from the American dream.[38]

One IHP student appreciated "the slowed-down pace of life that is more proportioned to man and his ability to function at a proper pace." Another student relished being able to spend two or three hours a day "just walking through the beautiful scenery and talking to people." She said that writer Henry van Dyke's words epitomized what she learned in Ireland: "Be glad of life because it gives you the chance to love and work, to play and to look up at the stars."[39] In

---

35. Carlson, *Truth on Trial*, 36–37.
36. "Pearson Integrated Humanities Program" brochure, in Carlson, *Truth on Trial*, 153.
37. Carlson, *Truth on Trial*, 37.
38. Ibid., 89; Bethel, *John Senior*, 301.
39. Carlson, *Truth on Trial*, 91.

retrospect, another student believed that "this travel to Europe is a very important and very poetic thing to do for an American."[40]

The combination of these experiences and activities, none of them complicated or extraordinary in itself, was surprisingly powerful for many students. One student explained the impact of the program this way:

> To put it as simply as possible, we were awakened, we saw that we belonged to the universe and to God, we belonged to Beauty, Truth, and Goodness, that our deepest desires were not fantasies or "nostalgia trips" or the "trips" of hippies, but the hard and often lovely truth that this world and ourselves are mysteries of greatness and of evil and that first of all we are to love a Creation that is completely loveable. To say that the good and great books that we read accomplished this for us would not be true. The program was not about books but the truth they all pointed to outside the pages, in the world, in our hearts.[41]

Rise and Fall of the IHP

After a trial session with twenty students in the fall of 1970 and the spring of 1971, the IHP began officially as part of Pearson College in the fall of 1971 with 140 students and grew to 346 students by 1972.[42] In 1979 the university closed the Integrated Humanities Program, which had been the object of attacks and complaints from its earliest days. Why was an academic program that inspired the love and devotion of hundreds of students, a program whose readings were virtually identical to dozens of other Great Books programs around the country, a program that created a real intellectual community in the midst of a large public university, controversial? And why was a

---

40. James S. Taylor, "The Restoration of Christian Education: Poetic Knowledge," *Classical Homeschooling Magazine* 4 (2002), http://www.angelicum.net/classical-homeschooling-magazine/fourth-issue/the-restoration-of-christian-education-poetic-knowledge/.
41. Ibid.
42. Carlson, *Truth on Trial*, 59, 64.

controversial program shut down during an era when controversy was generally tolerated and often celebrated?

The professors' cardinal sin, as far as the modern academy was concerned, was their lack of moral relativism. The modern American university is a strange place. It allows investigation of almost any topic and the espousal of a broad array of philosophies and religions. It encourages research into the most arcane areas and offers courses in specialized areas of ever more specialized disciplines. Professors have no qualms about challenging the most sacred beliefs of their students or of the society around them and are often rewarded for doing so, not only with the respect of their peers but also with the appreciation of students who feel liberated from oppressive traditions. In this pluralistic environment, it might be expected that devotees of the Western tradition would be just one more tribe preaching one more message in the marketplace of ideas. It might be expected that the removal of all criteria for orthodoxy would mean that all views would have equal status or at least the equal right to be heard, but the modern university rarely operates according to its stated principles. From the start of the IHP, other professors began complaining about the narrow-mindedness and rigidity of the program. Frances Horowitz, professor of Human Development, led the charge against the IHP:

> By everyone's admission and Professor Quinn's analogy, it is a cohesive experience involving personal selection of students, much personal contact, counseling, commitment, and the shared discovery of truth. It involves a form of emotional commitment that families engender. When this also involves extensive contact with three good teachers who share a basic view of what the fundamental truths are and when the personal element is strong and exciting, the outcome can motivate students to adopt the ardent advocations of the teachers and the students around them under often subtle pressure with regard to a particular philosophical and religious view of truth.[43]

43. Frances Horowitz, "Remarks to the College Assembly," 20 February 1973, in Carlson, *Truth on Trial*, 73.

Other professors criticized the program for the "dogmatic nature" of its teaching and because "its faculty advocate and defend 'the truth.'"[44] Professor Robert Lind expressed particular disdain for Senior, whom he accused of teaching Latin "with singular dogmatism," using "narrow, sectarian, and antihumanistic" methods in an effort "to indoctrinate students in his own narrow and obscurantist views."[45] Such charges convinced many professors that the IHP's approach was inappropriate and in 1973 the faculty of the College of Arts and Sciences voted to make the program's courses count only as electives. Students could enter the program, but they would have to take additional courses to fulfill general education requirements. In later years the IHP was prohibited from advertising itself in various ways, from recruiting high school seniors, and from travelling abroad. By the time administrators closed the program in 1979, they had already made life so difficult for students and professors in the IHP that there were few students left.[46]

The particular irony of the charges against the IHP was that they were made in the name of pluralism. To ensure that pluralism prevailed at the University of Kansas, one unpopular viewpoint was eliminated. As Senior pointed out, the complaints against him were incoherent and illogical. "In a university where the teaching of relatively trivial and even bizarre matters is tolerated under an inflated idea of academic freedom," he said, "it is stupid and indecent to suggest that the teaching of a magnificent, venerable, intellectually brilliant and spiritually splendid body of thought should be suppressed by an anxious and inquisitorial pluralism."[47] Quinn believed that pluralism had reached "an inquisitorial stage" in which, even as its proponents espoused moral relativism and academic freedom, they pounced on those who disagreed with them: "One simply cannot teach, for example, that anything is inferior or superior to anything else. Pluralism dictates the utter uniformity of

---

44. Carlson, *Truth on Trial*, 74.
45. Ibid., 94.
46. Ibid., 98–99.
47. John Senior, 25 April 1972, in Carlson, *Truth on Trial*, 192.

equality."[48] It should also be pointed out that, although the professors genuinely loved and found truth in most of the texts in the program, they also assigned authors with whom they strenuously disagreed—Lucretius, Descartes, and Hume—so that students could encounter the strongest examples of those who opposed the "Perennial Philosophy."

The *students'* cardinal sin was believing what they were taught. Again, one might expect, if the principles of pluralism were taken seriously, that there would be no problem with students becoming interested and engaged with the subject matter of any of their classes. One might expect, too, that students pursuing majors and careers related to the academic subjects that they had studied in the IHP would be seen as the evidence of a healthy and attractive program. In fact, however, the enthusiastic response of IHP students was so different from the usual response of American university students to academics that it frightened parents, administrators, and other professors. Particularly worrying to them were conversions to Catholicism, such as the nine students who were received into the Church during the semester in Ireland in 1976, and the handful of IHP students who went on to become monks.[49]

When it emerged that, during spring break of the 1976 semester spent in Ireland, forty students and Quinn had traveled to a French monastery, some parents became quite upset. They became even more upset when several of those students returned to the monastery that summer, seeking to become novices. Administrators defended Quinn publically, for, of course, students and faculty were free to do as they wished during breaks and the monastery visit was not part of the IHP program, but privately they questioned the trip and soon took the measures mentioned above to restrict IHP recruiting efforts and to prevent any returns to Ireland. In August 1976, Herman Goldstein, father of a student in the program, led a group of six parents in publically criticizing the IHP and asking the Jewish Community Relations Bureau and the American Civil Liberties Union to investigate. The main concerns were that "a dispro-

48. Dennis Quinn, in Carlson, *Truth on Trial*, 69.
49. Carlson, *Truth on Trial*, 91.

portionate number of former IHP students have chosen to enter a monastery in France" and "a disproportionate number of IHP students have chosen to convert to Catholicism." To Goldstein, such results suggested "a flagrant violation of the principle of separation of church and state."[50]

Kansas administrators repeatedly investigated Senior, Quinn, Nelick, and the whole program but never made any charges of misconduct against the professors. There was simply no evidence that they used their classrooms for proselytism. They really did teach Homer, Shakespeare, the Bible, and the rest of their curriculum, a set of texts similar to those taught in many other institutions, and they always welcomed parents to attend classes. Their poetic approach and their evident sincerity about the texts was what distinguished their program, but how could they be censured for an approach or for sincerity? Academic freedom obviously protected them. Parents and administrators then complained about informal settings and personal advice. Apparently students would go to the professors with questions, not only about academic matters but also about philosophical and religious issues. The dean of the College of Arts and Sciences wanted the professors not to answer such questions because, he believed, they could exercise undue influence over their students. Quinn had no patience for such a request. He insisted on his right to give private religious advice to anyone who asked for it and particularly resented the idea that IHP professors had a special duty to refrain from giving such advice. If such a restriction was put on him, he asked, why would it not be applied to all professors at the university?[51]

Quinn's complaint highlighted again the ironies of the pluralist university. Professors of various ideological persuasions were accustomed to giving advice on all sorts of topics. Many of them, of course, devoted no inconsiderable attention in class and outside of class to disabusing their students of what were seen as irrational prejudices, that is, traditional views of morality and religion. While there was no effort being made to prevent faculty from sharing their

50. Ibid., 98–101.
51. Ibid., 101–6.

views on the Vietnam War, abortion, electoral politics, or any other of a wide range of moral and political issues, the traditional beliefs of the IHP professors were somehow problematic.

The combination of the three professors' attitude toward their subject matter and the response of their students amplified the crisis: if either element of that combination had been lacking, the program probably would have survived. If the teachers had taught their ideas as true, but nobody had believed them, a few professors and administrators might have been concerned about this offense against relativism, but few people outside of the university would have cared. If the professors had taught literature in the usual way—examining forms and motivations and contexts but expressing no view about the actual meaning of the texts—but students had for some reason seized on Homer and Augustine as guides to their lives, professors and administrators would have defended "academic freedom," while parents and journalists might have been concerned but would have had only Homer and Augustine to blame. But the combination of teachers teaching truth and students loving what they were taught proved explosive.

The Fullness of the IHP

The students' serious commitment to the program raises the question of why the IHP program seemed so attractive to students. Part of the attraction surely came from its stark contrast to the mainstream culture in the 1970s. At a time when expressive individualism and moral relativism had finally vanquished most of the remnants of the Protestant cultural-moral code, anyone who asserted timeless truths was sure to stand out. At a time when the old elite seemed to have lost their nerve or had been exposed as corrupt but when the stridency and incoherence of proposed alternatives was more and more evident, the emergence of a voice for simple and enduring truths exercised a profound attraction. With all the noise, the thoughtless braying of television and popular music, it was almost prophetic for Senior and Quinn to direct their students to look at the stars or to memorize an ancient poem. Existence, being, the possibility of knowing truth: these simple ideas had a revolutionary impact because students' lives had otherwise been impoverished and denuded. Stars shine brightest in the darkest night, and the 1970s in America were indeed a dark night.

Also, there is a deep resonance between Thomism, or in this case, a sort of experiential pre-Thomism, and everyday life and wisdom. The truth exists and can be known. People know this at a deep level and rejoice in it. From the Catholic perspective, we can say that they actually were made to know the truth and they can in fact know the truth. The modern university is doubly disappointing in this vein. First, it is thoroughly Cartesian—ready to doubt anything and to criticize everything, holding nothing sacred, at once overwhelmed by endless administrative requirements and anxious never to be fooled or misled. Second, it is thoroughly devoted to means rather than ends, and these means are relentlessly administrative and bureaucratic. Students in the Cartesian administrative university find themselves in a complex impersonal system that produces a commodity called "education," characterized not by love for truth or the human person, but, rather, by procedural rigor with an undertone of angst about meaning. The IHP, on the other hand, affirmed from the first class that truth was its object and that truth was knowable. The professors were full of love for each other, for their students, and for their subjects. They were accessible after class and ready to engage the truth in all its wonderful aspects. In short, they represented a living alternative to the rest of the University of Kansas.

In a sense, the rest of the vast university was "empty." Since professors had few fixed beliefs and taught very little as true in the realm of morality and philosophy, the growing size of the university, both in number of students and number of disciplines, was only evidence of an expanding vacuum. The IHP, although tiny in comparison to the rest of the university, was "full." Inside its small confines the IHP had stars, wonder, beauty, poetry, Don Quixote, Aeneas, and an endless parade of characters and ideas. Its students knew poems by heart, learned to dance the waltz, talked to each other in Latin, and thought about the meaning of life, not as the anxious Descartes and his anxious disciples did, but with hope. They had come in contact with the greatest minds of the Western tradition and they had before them the living examples of Quinn, Senior, and Nelick, who were visibly enlivened by their ongoing encounter with the true, the good, and the beautiful. The fullness, the immensity, the expansiveness of the Great Books, encountered directly and appreciated properly, spoke to them, called to them, filled them with hope. Truth, they knew, existed and could be discovered.

Although the professors did not proselytize, they understood that truth leads to truth and that they did not have to spell out the doctrines of Catholicism in the classroom. All they had to do was to lay a foundation. Once students understood some of the basic truths of the universe, of human nature, and of the moral law, they would be hungry for more. The many conversions to Catholicism of students in the program can best be understood as logical progressions from truths to truth.

The case of James Conley is exceptional, in that he went on to become a bishop, but it is exemplary in that it illustrates the ways in which the IHP approach to education could be transformative. First, Conley was struck by the rare form of teaching practiced by the IHP professors. They emphasized their roles as friends much more than their roles as experts or functionaries. "Their friendship set the shape and tenor of the entire program," he believes. In fact, Senior taught that a school was fundamentally "a faculty of friends." This friendship-based approach to learning stood out in the modern university, where objectivity and dispassionate research often led to isolation and competition. Unlike in other classes, in the IHP Conley experienced friendship, both with other students like his roommate Paul Coakley (now Archbishop of Oklahoma City) and with the professors, especially John Senior, who became his godfather.[52]

Second, Conley was particularly influenced by his encounter with beauty in the IHP. What struck Conley first about Senior was that he "saw the beauty of this world in the light of eternity, and he helped others to acquire the same transcendent vision." Conley and his fellow students were so mesmerized by popular culture and so ill-served by the education that they had previously received that they were only dimly aware of what they were lacking:

52. Conley, "Friendship: A Pillar of Catholic Education."

At the University of Kansas, my fellow students and I had very little sense of our own cultural inheritance. We were ignorant of Western civilization's founding truths, and we had only a passing acquaintance with the beauty they had inspired. Our lives had largely been shaped by the crass appeals of the mass media and the passing fads of popular culture. There was a lack of truth in our lives, certainly; but there was also a profound lack of beauty. Our souls were starving for both, and we did not even know it.[53]

Senior, Quinn, and Nelick understood that leading with truth, especially philosophical truth, would overwhelm the students of the day, so they began instead with beauty, which served as a doorway to truth. Conley says that he was captivated. Through "the beauty of music, visual art and architecture, nature, poetry, dance, calligraphy and many other things" he gained a "sense of wonder," which then opened him to philosophical and theological truths. He and "literally hundreds" of his fellow students converted to Catholicism, but Conley emphasizes "this was not the result of proselytism in the classroom nor was it engaging in apologetics." Rather, the IHP cultivated in Conley a love of beauty which grew into a love of truth: "beauty gave us 'eyes to see' and 'ears to hear' when we encountered the Gospel and the Christian tradition."[54]

Conley, formerly a Presbyterian, was received into the Catholic Church in 1975 and was ordained a priest in 1985 and a bishop in 2008.[55] He was just one of many IHP students whose life was changed dramatically by the program. Alumni of the program know of at least 200 definite Catholic conversions of IHP students, as well as an abbot, a prior, a prioress, two religious superiors, a seminary rector, three novice masters, a judge, several lawyers, and many teachers, but the impact of the program extended also to the

---

53. James Conley, "Ever Ancient, Ever New: The Role of Beauty in the Restoration of Catholic Culture," *Crisis Magazine* (10 October 2013), http://www.crisismagazine.com/2013/ever-ancient-ever-new-the-role-of-beauty-in-the-restoration-of-catholic-culture.

54. Ibid.

55. "Bishop James Douglas Conley," *Catholic Hierarchy*, http://www.catholichierarchy.org/bishop/bconley.html.

lives that those converts touched.[56] Many IHP students led family members and friends into the Church. Bishop Conley, for example, saw both of his parents convert to Catholicism.[57] Father James Jackson says, "If one were to count the conversions that came out of the IHP, all the waves and ripples, they might number in the thousands."[58] Graduates of the program, now with children and grandchildren, continue to meet for discussions and reunions.[59] Senior's writing has been translated and published in France, where it received plaudits from other Catholic writers and inspired journalist Natalia Sanmartin Fenollera to write the novel, *The Awakening of Miss Prim*, about the beauty of small things and human community.[60] Several IHP alumni also went on to found schools and colleges, such as The Learning Alternative in Wichita, St. Joseph's Academy in Lawrence, Cair Paravel in Topeka, St. Jude's School in Minnesota, and St. Gregory's Academy (now Gregory the Great Academy) in Pennsylvania.[61] Wyoming Catholic College in Lander, Wyoming, founded in 2005 by three men among whom was IHP graduate Robert Carlson, is worthy of special note, for it is attempting to institute the IHP's Great Books program and poetic knowledge approach in a particularly auspicious environment: a committedly Catholic college in the midst of the natural beauty of America's least populated state.[62]

Some observers might be inclined to think that Senior, Quinn, and Nelick were naïve. How could they imagine that the IHP could prosper in the midst of a secular university at a time of cultural

---

56. Bethel, *John Senior*, 2.

57. "Bishop Conley appointed to lead Diocese of Lincoln," *Catholic News Agency* (14 September 2013), http://www.catholicnewsagency.com/news/bishop-conley-appointed-to-lead-diocese-of-lincoln/.

58. Becraft, "Let them be born in wonder," 12.

59. Bethel, *John Senior*, 366.

60. Ibid., 6, 361. Natalia Sanmartin Fenollera, *The Awakening of Miss Prim: A Novel* (New York: Atria, 2014).

61. Carlson, *Truth on Trial*, 128.

62. Wyoming Catholic College, https://wyomingcatholic.edu/. Carlson is also the author of the only book-length study of the IHP: *Truth on Trial*.

upheaval? How could they imagine that a poetic approach to education could succeed in the 1970s? First, none of the professors was
naïve about the culture in general or about academia in particular.
As their writings and actions make clear, they could probably more
justly be charged with pessimism, even despair, rather than naiveté.
Senior, the most prolific writer of the three, had nothing positive to
say about contemporary culture, which he saw as decadent and
unprincipled, or about the modern university, which he believed
was in the midst of an inevitable decline occasioned by its own cor-
ruption. A better adjective to apply to the IHP is "quixotic." There
was always something of the tragicomic seriousness of Cervantes's
hero in the IHP, and this was evident in the minds of the professors
as well as the students. Students not only read *Don Quixote* but also
adopted the title character as a sort of mascot of the program. As the
program's brochure said, "The spirit of the Pearson program may be
called Quixotic. Don Quixote has been both ridiculed and admired
because he lived a chivalrous life when it was out of fashion."[63]
Almost everyone in the IHP knew that the program was not just
"out of fashion" but so counter-cultural that the odds were against
its surviving long in the midst of a secular university. They nevertheless adopted the quixotic ideal that it was better to carry on as
long as they could, despite the attacks, despite the growing difficulty
of celebrating the true, the good, and the beautiful in a world of relativism and artificiality. They knew the goodness of what they were
doing, whether it lasted for one semester or one hundred semesters.
The IHP's embrace of Quixote is a reminder to those who venture
nothing because the climate is unfavorable: the students and faculty
of the IHP knew that the spirit of the age was against them, but they
persevered for as long as they could and accomplished marvelous
things, whose echoes continue to this day, because they did so.

Before he came to the University of Kansas, Senior had already
embraced this quixotic vision. He had ended an essay on the importance of Virgil and the other classical writers with an episode from
Evelyn Waugh's novel *Scott-King's Modern Europe* in which the

---

63. "Pearson Integrated Humanities Program" brochure, in Carlson, *Truth on Trial*, 22.

headmaster of an English public school confronts his classics teacher with the declining demand for his subject as students choose more "relevant courses." After the classics teacher turns down the opportunity to teach "economic history," the headmaster indicates that the teacher will probably lose his job and asks him what his intentions are:

"If you approve, headmaster, I will stay as I am here as long as any boy wants to read the classics. I think it would be very wicked indeed to do anything to fit a boy for the modern world."

"It's a short-sighted view, Scott-King," says the headmaster.

"There, headmaster, with all respect, I differ from you profoundly. I think it the most long-sighted view it is possible to take."[64]

Culture and Humility

Before concluding this chapter with a look at the most surprising element of the IHP—its orientation toward Benedictine monasticism—it is necessary to take up some of the problematic elements of the program. As is true of many successful movements, the IHP's strengths—its building of a warm and active community, its focus on truth and reality, and its ability to withstand the pressures of what would today be called political correctness—could veer in unhealthy directions.

The tight-knit IHP community rubbed many faculty and students who were not part of the program the wrong way and frightened many parents of students in the program. It seemed to some outside observers that Quinn, Nelick, and Senior were building a cult-like group that was hypnotized by its charismatic leaders.[65] Some parents, especially non-religious parents of students who converted to Catholicism or found religious vocations, felt that they had lost their children to religious confidence men. Most irksome to other professors was what they perceived as hubris: IHP's insistence on truth and reality, with its strong implication that other beliefs

---

64. Evelyn Waugh, as quoted in John Senior, *The Remnants: The Final Essays of John Senior* (Forest Lake, MN: Remnant Press, 2013), 38.

65. Bethel, *John Senior*, 125.

were untrue and out of touch with reality. In general, these charges were not completely fair, but there were elements of truth in them.

There *was* a bit of a sectarian feel to the IHP and it is difficult to avoid the conclusion that it came more from Senior than from the other two professors. Senior's biographer admits that he "tended to carry things to extremes," had "impulsive judgment" and "a tendency to overstate," and was "sometimes careless in practical historical accuracy." More seriously, "his vigorous rejection of Relativism pushed him, by reaction, to take this or that contingent conclusion as an absolute."[66] One area where these tendencies manifested themselves was in Senior's religious life, which, although not officially part of the IHP, had an influence on the general tenor of the program and on the many converts who turned to Catholicism in large part because of Senior's influence.

Senior was a strong proponent of the traditional Latin Mass and of a highly traditional approach to Catholic life, to the extent that he "never accepted the New Mass" instituted after the Second Vatican Council.[67] He participated in the Society of Saint Pius X (SSPX) —even after the leader of that society incurred an automatic excommunication for ordaining bishops without papal permission—and was buried in an SSPX cemetery.[68] In fact, when the Priestly Fraternity of Saint Peter, a traditionalist Catholic group in communion with Rome, started offering the traditional Latin Mass in his area, Senior attended briefly but quickly reverted to the SSPX because he found its liturgy and the architecture of its church more congenial.[69] Although Senior was an avid student of John Henry Newman, who wrote the classic work on the Catholic understanding of the development of doctrine (see Newman's *An Essay on the Development of Christian Doctrine*) and whose thought played a pivotal role at the Second Vatican Council, Senior tended to absolutize the value of the Tridentine Latin Mass and the European contri-

---

66. Ibid., 128, 378, 387.
67. Andrew Senior, Foreword, in *The Remnants: The Final Essays of John Senior*, 2.
68. Ibid., 3; Senior, *The Remnants*, 79–97.
69. Bethel, *John Senior*, 370–79.

bution to Christian culture, and to neglect the larger history of Christianity outside of Europe.[70]

As beautiful, reverent, and awe-inspiring as the traditional Mass is—I, for one, agree with Senior's judgment of its superiority to the liturgical banalities that have been foisted on Catholics in the post-conciliar decades—there is, and always has been, a strong Christian argument for translation into the vernacular, as Vatican II recognized. Latin, of course, was the vernacular of many citizens of the Roman Empire and was at first a replacement of Greek; the various Eastern Catholic churches have long celebrated the liturgy in languages such as Greek, Syriac, and Arabic. Christ's Incarnation is the ultimate "vernacularization" and will always serve as a corrective to any absolutization of one language or culture. Thus, the post-Vatican II liturgical reform, although painfully botched in practice, was *in principle* consonant with traditional Catholic doctrine. Senior's longstanding resistance to the council and, even more, his seeming inability to tolerate even a form of traditionalism that was in communion with Rome because it did not meet his aesthetic standards, signals a dangerous reliance on experience and private judgment that no serious Catholic should countenance. The events with the Society of Saint Pius X occurred after the demise of the IHP, but they indicate the force of Senior's convictions about liturgy and tradition, which, in general, served as a helpful corrective to the relativism of the modern academy but could make him "more Catholic than the pope."

In a similar way, Senior's view of European culture went beyond an appropriate appreciation and reverence to an inaccurate *identification* of Europe and Christianity. "The only way to bring Christianity to the Bantu or the British, however, is to bring them clothes, chairs, bread, wine, and Latin," he argued. "Belloc was exactly right in his famous epigram: 'Europe is the Faith; the Faith is Europe.'"[71] To put it simply, Belloc and Senior were wrong. To cite just one thorough refutation of the idea that "the faith is Europe" one need only

---

70. Ibid., 133; Ian Ker, *Newman on Vatican II* (London: Oxford University Press, 2014).

71. Senior, *The Death of Christian Culture*, 19. See also similar views in Senior, *The Remnants*, 22–23, 60–62, 137.

consult Robert Louis Wilken's *The First Thousand Years: A Global History of Christianity* to see that Christianity, far from being exclusively or even predominantly identified with Europe and European culture, from its earliest centuries put down roots in various cultural milieus, including Egypt, Carthage, Nubia, Ethiopia, Syria, Armenia, Georgia, India, and Central Asia. To suggest that Christian communities and traditions in these regions were part of the same process of cultural development that took place in western Europe would be profoundly mistaken, as would be any denial of the deeply Christian nature of those cultures and traditions.[72] One can agree with Senior about the value of the "Great Books" of "Western Civilization" without having to agree that "the Faith is Europe." One can agree with Senior about the wonderful synthesis of Athens, Jerusalem, and Rome in the West, without having to agree that other syntheses were not possible or did not occur. In short, to the extent that Senior's extreme views on European culture permeated the program—and it should be said that it is not clear how much they did—it is likely that they encouraged an unwarranted cultural exclusivism in the IHP students. A more humble approach to the traditional Latin Mass and to European culture in general would have softened some of the IHP's edges; what is more important, it would have reflected a more biblical and catholic view of culture, which, as significant as it is, is never an absolute. Senior was right to insist on *moral* absolutes in an age of relativism, but he was on dangerous ground when he made a specific culture the bearer of those absolutes.[73]

72. Robert Louis Wilken, *The First Thousand Years: A Global History of Christianity* (New Haven: Yale University Press, 2012).

73. Also extreme was Senior's occasional rhetorical elevation of the rural and devaluation of the urban—he once called modern cities "irrational monstrosities"—but these outbursts did not reflect the breadth of his own thought. He appreciated "the classic human city," such as Siena or Assisi, and taught a class on the appropriate human scale of the "The Village," but he probably did not reflect sufficiently on the urban nature of early Christianity or the biblical elevation of the city, the new Jerusalem, in the book of Revelation. In retrospect, there is a definite resonance between his thought and the contemporary movement known as the New Urbanism, which supports walkable, mixed-use, human-centered neighborhoods: Bethel, *John Senior*, 196, 219, 225; Michael Leccese and Kathleen McCormick, eds., *Charter of the New Urbanism* (New York: McGraw-Hill, 2000).

The Benedictine Connection

If Senior needed a dose of humility in his treatment of culture, it is not to say that he generally acted with hubris or an inflated sense of his own dignity. In fact, in other areas of life, it might be fair to call him a prophet of humility. Remarking on the way in which the world "human" comes from the Latin word for "earth" or "soil," Senior once said, "*Humus* is the root of 'human,' 'humility,' and 'humor,' because, knowing our humble origins, we can never take ourselves too seriously."[74] This emphasis on humanity's humble origins fit well with his advocacy of farming and ranching, which he saw as the normal sort of human work because they put man in direct contact with the real, with the *humus* from which he had come. It is necessary to understand this aspect of Senior's thought to understand the Benedictine connection that perplexed and angered many outside observers of the program.

Even for outsiders, James Conley's journey from uncommitted Presbyterian to Catholic convert to priest to bishop has a certain logic to it. The move from wonder to truth to the truth of God to a life of service through ordination is well known in Catholic circles and has its parallels in Protestant life and in most religions, but the choice of *monasticism* by several of the IHP students might seem less consistent. What explained the move from the big and broad truth of God to the small world of the cloister? Did that jump betray the grandeur of the IHP vision?

One explanation is simply that Senior had an abiding interest in monasticism that he shared with his students.[75] The deeper answer is that there is a deep resonance between the poetic knowledge emphasized by the IHP and the way of life of Benedictine monasticism. To outsiders, the monastery often represents a strange sort of self-denial and isolation. Monks take vows of poverty, chastity, and obedience and live in one place, not traveling, not interacting with the larger world. Many are not even aware of many of the events going on outside. Such a life might seem shallow, circumscribed,

---

74. Senior, *The Restoration of Christian Culture*, 126.
75. Ibid., 95.

and incomplete, but to focus only on what they give up is to see less than half of the picture. Monks give up so much because they want to gain more: closeness to God, the greatest prize of all. In the Benedictine tradition, the path to such closeness is summarized in the Latin phrase, "ora et labora," "pray and work." The Benedictine rule sets times of prayer and times of work for the day. The way of life created by the rule is therefore full of poetry and reality, just like the IHP. The poetry comes in the form of the liturgy, including the liturgy of the hours and the Mass, both often sung in Gregorian chant. The reality comes in the form of mud and grass and pigs and cows and all the other gritty elements of agricultural work.

In fact, Senior believed that it was time for a new Benedictine age:

> Today, we are, I think, in times like those of St. Jerome, moving rapidly toward those of St. Benedict. Barbarians have destroyed our cultural institutions, this time mostly from within; and now as then, it is true that there is nothing for the world to offer anyone. If I were a young man or woman seeking God today, I should enter, if I could, a Benedictine monastery. And if I were a Benedictine seeking God, I should work to reform my monastery so it conformed to the Rule of St. Benedict in its strict integrity, praying seven times a day the great Latin Office as recovered by the painstaking, sanctifying scholarship of Solesmes; and in the spaces between the hours, work with my hands at the immediate tasks of food and shelter. Or if I were called to other vocations, the secular priesthood or marriage, I should become an oblate of such a monastery or at least keep as close to it as I could consistent with my obligations.[76]

Senior loved the "profound simplicity" of the Rule, which had nevertheless "transformed the history of Western Civilization." He loved the Rule for its "intimate, affectionate" manner and for its silence, the silence not of emptiness but of patience, humility, recep-

---

76. Ibid., 87. Writer Rod Dreher has proposed a more generalized "Benedict Option," a call for Christians to focus on community, discipleship, and training as a response to the decadence of Western society: *The Benedict Option: A Strategy for Christians in a Post-Christian Nation* (New York: Sentinel, 2017).

tivity, and wonder.[77] The Rule, in its fundamental humility, was the antithesis of the modern university, characterized by the "aggressive, brute bureaucracy" of the "shrewd administrative caste," the "pop carnality" of the students, and the indolence and "essential pusillanimity" of the faculty.[78] It is no surprise that several IHP students went on to become monks. Benedictine monasticism proved to be the best way to continue the journey they had started in Kansas, to continue living lives based on poetic appreciation of the true, the good, and the beautiful.

77. Senior, *Restoration*, 92–93.
78. Ibid., 95.

4

The Splendor of Truth

The Dominicans of the Province of St. Joseph

DOMINIC LEGGE left his position as a lawyer in the Justice Department in Washington, DC, to become poor, chaste, and obedient. He first thought that he might be hearing God's call on a weekend retreat at a Benedictine monastery. There the Yale Law School graduate for the first time asked God for specific guidance about the path of his life. A monk at the monastery had encouraged him to meditate on a passage of Scripture throughout the weekend and Legge had chosen Jesus's words, "Ask and it will be given to you; seek and you will find; knock and the door will be opened to you. For everyone who asks, receives; and the one who seeks, finds; and to the one who knocks, the door will be opened" (Mt 7:7–8).

Frustrated at first because he did not see how the words applied to him, Legge soon recognized that Jesus was asking him to open himself to God's plans for his life. On his knees in the chapel, he grappled with God, afraid even to ask what God wanted, for fear that God would ask him to become a priest, and thus ruin his career and plans for marriage and family. He realized, though, that if he avoided the question and went on with his life, he would be saying, in effect, that he knew better than God. "On some level," he knew, "that would be turning my back on the Lord and refusing him." Once he did open himself to God, he felt joy and peace rather than fear. Although he had wanted to be a lawyer since childhood and had a beautiful girlfriend whom he was hoping to marry, he left the

95

chapel open to the possibility that God was asking him to leave both the law and his girlfriend to become a Catholic priest. Over the next year, despite some frustrations and confusions, he came to believe that God was in fact calling him to the priesthood, not to test him or torment him, but out of deep love for him.[1]

The next question was whether he should become a diocesan priest, serving like most priests under a bishop in a specific locale, or whether he should join a religious order, such as the Franciscans or the Jesuits. He immediately thought of the Dominican friars he had met at St. Mary Church, which was located in the middle of Yale's campus. They had helped Legge get back on track with his Catholic faith during his years at Yale Law School. The Dominican House of Studies, a combination seminary and center of formation for young friars, in Washington, DC, offered him the opportunity to investigate the Dominicans in some depth. Many visits to Mass and two "discernment weekends" with the friars gave Legge a basic understanding of the Dominican way of life, which is devoted to prayer, study, and preaching. The more he experienced Dominican life, the more he felt at home. One day at Mass, viewing the dozens of young friars in the choir stalls of their chapel, he realized, "I could entrust my soul to these men." He saw, in a deeper way than he had before, that Dominicans did not just live alongside of each other, but were brothers who shared a profound spiritual fraternity, who cared for each other sincerely and intensely.

Legge left the Justice Department in 2001 and spent a year at the Cincinnati novitiate of the St. Joseph province of Dominicans, where new friars for the eastern branch of the order (there are three other provinces in the United States) learn how to live as Dominicans. After a year of philosophy and four years of theology at the House of Studies in Washington, he was ordained a priest in 2007. He taught undergraduate theology at Providence College and then studied for his doctorate in theology in Switzerland, before return-

---

1. "Vocation Story of Fr. Dominic Legge," St. Joseph Province, 2010, Vimeo, https://vimeo.com/15071001; Tim Bradley, "Campus Vocations: A Dominican Visits Notre Dame," *Irish Rover*, 31 January 2016, https://irishrover.net/2016/01/campus-vocations-a-dominican-visits-notre-dame/.

ing to the House of Studies, this time to teach theology and to help lead the Thomistic Institute, a Dominican initiative to bring orthodox theology to secular universities. His first book, *The Trinitarian Christology of St. Thomas Aquinas*, came out from Oxford University Press in 2018. The former trial attorney and graduate of the most prestigious law school in the country was now penniless, his earthly possessions limited to a few robes and books, and even these were not technically his own personal possessions.

Legge's story is intriguing, but it is not really out of the ordinary for the Dominicans of the Province of St. Joseph. The province's recent years are full of new novitiate classes featuring a dozen or so aspiring friars. Some of them hail from Catholic colleges, but others attended Ivy League universities and other schools not known for fostering Catholic faith and devotion, and many had begun various professional careers. For instance, the men who began their novitiate in 2016 included graduates not only of Catholic institutions like Franciscan University of Steubenville, Providence, Duquesne, and Notre Dame, but also of large state schools like Minnesota, Cincinnati, Kansas State, Indiana, Texas, North Dakota State, and the University of Alberta, and of top private institutions like Brown, Vanderbilt, and Yale.[2] The province today is full of men with graduate degrees in theology and philosophy, as one might expect, but also of men with doctorates in physics, biology, and other secular fields of knowledge. The ongoing decisions by North America's "best and brightest" to join a literally medieval religious order—it was founded in 1216—in which they wear robes, renounce sex and marriage, own no possessions of any kind, and devote their lives to prayer and study raises some obvious questions. What is this Order of Preachers and why is it so attractive to educated young men? What explains its counter-cultural appeal?

At the heart of the St. Joseph province's vitality and appeal are its reverent liturgy, vibrant orthodoxy, and life of intellectual achieve-

---

2. Benedict Croell, "Jubilee Grace: Men accepted for the 2016 Novitiate," 17 May 2016, Dominican Vocations, Province of St. Joseph, http://vocations.opeast.org/2016/05/17/jubilee-grace-men-accepted-for-the-2016-novitiate/.

ment, all of which are attractive at a time when most parishes and even most other orders are struggling to stay orthodox and are hardly thinking about reverent liturgy or genuine intellectual endeavors. For serious Catholic young men in submission to the Magisterium of the Church, men who love learning and value traditional Catholic liturgy, there are simply few other options. There are orthodox dioceses and religious orders, but few are committed to the liturgy as envisioned by the Second Vatican Council's *Sacrosanctum concilium* and the *General Instruction of the Roman Missal*. Even fewer of these orthodox dioceses and orders are committed to high-level intellectual engagement with the issues of the age. In some ways, then, the answer to the questions at the end of the previous paragraph is a simple one: there are not many other options for intellectual, orthodox, liturgically serious young men. The Dominican order in general and the Province of St. Joseph in particular offer talented men of a particular bent an attractive combination available in few other places. The three qualities that distinguish the Dominicans have proved difficult to sustain in recent American Catholicism, and especially difficult to sustain in combination with each other.

As anyone who has encountered professors, doctors, lawyers, and other highly educated people is surely aware, intellectual achievement is no guarantee of holiness or even of basic decency. In fact, those who achieve the most academically are often full of pride and self-importance. This is as true in theology as in any other academic discipline. All one has to do is to look at the awards given by the Catholic Theological Society of America to see how easy it is for the intelligent to act foolishly. Almost as if to thumb its nose in the faces of the bishops and anyone so retrograde as to imagine that orthodoxy and morality are requirements of good theology, that society often gives its highest awards to dissenters and the notoriously immoral.

It is not even necessary to turn away from Church teachings to run into trouble as an intellectual. As Franciscan University president Michael Scanlan once told his school's most famous professor, theologian Scott Hahn, God opposes the proud, *even when they are right,* especially when they are right. It is tempting for intellectuals to see their work as something they have created rather than something they have unveiled with God's help. They can easily become proud and then to go off track spiritually, even when the content of their scholarship is true.[3] God loves them too much to let them glory in their own accomplishments.

Finding orthodoxy would seem to pose less of a challenge. The 904-page *Catechism of the Catholic Church* explains exactly what Catholics are to believe. Denzinger's compendium of Catholic doctrine has been available since 1854.[4] The teachings of Vatican II, the most recent church council, can be purchased in book form or accessed at the Vatican website. So many copies of the Bible are floating around that the average second-hand bookstore has Catholic versions available at nominal prices. Nevertheless, the post-Vatican II era has often been one of confusion and dissent.

Catholics in most nations in Europe and the Americas experienced the years after the Second Vatican Council, which ended in 1965, as a time of rapid but poorly explained liturgical change. The new order of the Mass, shortened and simplified, now celebrated in the vernacular and with the priest facing the people, rather than in Latin with the priest facing the altar, looked radically different from the older form. If the Mass could change so much, many Catholics thought, might not Church teaching change as well? The resulting confusion about what could and could not change in the Church was amplified by two unfortunate circumstances. First, the 1960s and 1970s were globally an era of cultural ferment and rebellion. In the United States, for example, the African American civil rights movement, the women's movement, the anti-war movement, and several similar movements coincided with rapid cultural change in areas such as sexual morality, music, and drugs. In 1968 alone there were large protests and student movements in France, the United

---

3. "There is no road which leads so directly and so quickly to Modernism as pride": Pius X, *Pascendi dominici gregis* 40, 8 September 1907, Vatican, http://w2.vatican.va/content/pius-x/en/encyclicals/documents/hf_p-x_enc_19070908_pascendi-dominici-gregis.html.

4. Heinrich Denzinger and Peter Hünermann, eds., *Enchiridion Symbolorum: A Compendium of Creeds, Definitions, and Declarations of the Catholic Church*, 43rd edition (San Francisco: Ignatius, 2012).

States, Mexico, Brazil, and Czechoslovakia. Second, bishops and priests generally failed to explain Vatican II to their people in a helpful or detailed way. In fact, catechesis fell by the wayside after the council in most dioceses.

The years after any Church council are always difficult because the new ideas and emphases need to be accepted and implemented by Catholics who may have no desire to do so. After Vatican II, Catholics were in the midst of political crises *and* deep cultural change *and* the changes called for or catalyzed by the council, with little effective leadership and teaching about how to proceed. It is no wonder that the post-council era has been one of discordant voices. Despite the attempts of good popes, bishops, priests, and lay leaders, a dominant theme of the half-century since the council has been confusion. It is just not clear to many Catholics what they are to believe and do. In such an environment, those who question and even reject clear doctrines of the Church have multiplied and the trajectory and momentum of the age is toward dissent and misunderstanding. Religious orders have not been immune. This book is trying not to focus on the bad, the false, and the ugly, so I will say only that many religious orders of both men and women have been weakened by dissent and confusion, and some have made shipwreck of their faith. All of which is to say that, no, it is actually not as easy as one might think to find an unabashedly orthodox religious community.

The Dominican Province of St. Joseph's third distinctive trait, its liturgical sanity, is even rarer than its intellectual achievement and orthodoxy. The liturgy in the United States, defying and rejecting the actual words of the Second Vatican Council, has become casual, trite, and human-centered. The songs in many cases are so banal that, with minimal changes, they could function as soft drink jingles or theme songs for game shows. The preaching is often moralistic, therapeutic, and superficial. Church architecture is not only ugly but, even worse, often intentionally designed to focus more on the human community than on God and the transcendent. An order that values and seeks beautiful and reverent liturgy is like an oasis for those who love the tradition and wisdom of the Church. To be able, daily, to live the liturgy of the Church as the Church has prescribed it, is an incredible grace, and one rarely found in American parishes or even religious orders.

The Dominican triptych of liturgy, orthodoxy, and intellect is therefore a beacon on a hill. It casts a bright light far and wide; few other such lights are visible because combining these three elements is much more challenging than maintaining one or two of them. Intellectuals, on one hand, are notoriously willing to challenge orthodoxy and decorum. On the other hand, liturgical traditionalists, like the Priestly Fraternity of Saint Peter (a community of priests who celebrate the traditional Latin Mass), are also guardians of orthodoxy, but they are not known for daring intellects.

For many centuries the Jesuits were the trend-setting order in the Church. Today the Jesuits, at their best, are great thinkers, but no one goes to a Jesuit for beautiful liturgy, and Jesuits, especially since Vatican II, certainly seem prone to pushing the boundaries of orthodoxy. Mother Teresa's Missionaries of Charity are paragons of loving service and orthodox belief, but their charism of sacrificial love for poorest of the poor leaves little time for scholarship.

So how do the Dominicans of the Province of St. Joseph do it? How do they thrive intellectually *and* stay orthodox *and* worship in spirit and truth? There are many answers to those questions, some of which cannot be investigated in much depth because they are supernatural. It seems clear to many Dominicans and to this writer that the Dominican vocation boom of recent years is a grace from God, an unmerited work of the Holy Spirit. It is also likely that the prayers of Dominican nuns—there are several monasteries of contemplative Dominican sisters in the United States and around the world, who pray daily for their brother Dominicans—have great spiritual consequences, in both initial vocations and the ongoing ministries of the order. The suffering and prayers of the early Dominican friars in the United States surely play a role. The province also has an ongoing devotion to Mary and a sense of being "under her mantle," which would explain much of how the Dominicans emerged from the chaos of the 1960s and 1970s, not exactly unscathed, but still in better shape than most religious orders. Other sources of Dominican success are more open to historical investigation and the rest of this chapter examines three reasons for the current Dominican prosperity: the Dominican charism and way of life, the thought of Thomas Aquinas, and the uncharacteristic, for Dominicans, commitment to parish ministry.

The Dominican Charism

The first source of the Dominicans' tripartite vitality is the Dominican charism and way of life. Domingo Félix de Guzmán (1170–1221), the founder of the order, was a Spanish priest and canon of the cathedral chapter of Osma, meaning that he followed the rule of Saint Augustine in his position as one of the members of a community of priests at the diocesan cathedral. After encountering the Cathars, also known as the Albigensians, a heretical group with gnostic and Manichean views, Domingo, or Dominic as he is known in English, attempted to turn the Cathars back to the Catholic faith through preaching and debate. Eventually he founded a new religious order that kept the monastic rule of Saint Augustine as far as prayer and liturgy were concerned, while making some significant changes in the area of work and orientation toward the secular world.

The traditional monastic orders such as the Benedictines lived lives of prayer and work in monasteries. If they did teach or conduct other ministries, they did so in monastery schools or other facilities attached to the monastery. Monks and nuns, by definition, were not supposed to wander from place to place but to practice "stability," the attachment and commitment to a specific community in a specific place. Dominic's idea, shared by his contemporary Saint Francis, founder of the Franciscans, was to take vows, like monks, but to give up stability for the greater good of preaching. His brothers, or friars, would be poor, chaste, and obedient, like monks, but they would travel wherever they were needed to preach against heresies and to defend the faith.

It was not just mobility that differentiated the Dominicans. Like monks, they would dedicate themselves to prayer, but their work would be of a special type: they would *study* intensely so that they could learn the truth so that they could preach with excellence. A Dominican motto that comes from the writing of Thomas Aquinas,

contemplata aliis tradere, to share with others the fruits of one's contemplation, gets to the heart of the matter. The idea is that contemplation and study, although good and worthy in themselves, are
even better when their results are shared. This would be an order
oriented toward preaching, but Dominic knew that his preachers
needed to be holy, or their preaching would be less credible and
ultimately corrupted, and that they needed to be wise and learned,
or their preaching would not be as clear and deep as it could be.
Thus was formed a religious order committed to holiness, scholarship, and serious preaching.

Through 800 years of Dominican history, the order has expanded
from Europe to North America, South America, Africa, and Asia.
Like most orders, it has seen its ups and downs, including persecu-
tions in revolutionary France and communist China and rises and
declines in apostolic fervor, but unlike many other orders it has
maintained its unity. All Dominican friars around the world are
part of one body that is under the guidance of the Master of the
Order, who is elected to a nine-year term by a General Chapter,
which is a meeting of representatives from all the constituent provinces of the order, of which the St. Joseph province is one. The St.
Joseph province is therefore part of a religious order formed in the
heart of the Middle Ages.

It would not be pejorative to call the Order of Preachers a medieval institution. In fact, the medieval roots and traditions of the
order help to explain its ability to navigate the rough seas of modernity. Compared to thirteenth-century Cathars determined to
destroy Catholicism and the traditional family, or to French revolu-
tionaries who guillotined Catholics and tried to eliminate all hints
of Christianity from society, the moral and cultural difficulties of
the 1960s and 1970s were challenging but not overwhelming. The
Dominican order is "underreactive" in the sense that it does not
respond quickly or overwhelmingly to changes around it.[5] Its caution and deliberation protect it from the sort of ill-considered over-
reactions that many orders and parishes made in the post-conciliar
period. While the enthusiastic but poorly informed were adopting

5. Thomas Joseph White, OP, interview, 1 June 2016, New York City.

all sorts of liturgical "reforms" that the council had not recommended and which were, in many cases, actually against the explicit words of the council, the Dominicans resisted the spirit of the age. They read the documents of the Second Vatican Council carefully and reflectively. They were convinced, for instance, that the words "The Church acknowledges Gregorian chant as specially suited to the Roman liturgy: therefore, other things being equal, it should be given pride of place in liturgical services" were not a coded demand for the adoption of folk songs but were, just as they seem, a statement that gave priority to Gregorian chant.[6]

The Dominican emphasis on contemplation and study ordered toward truth and preaching also bore great fruit at exactly the time when it was most needed in the United States. The history of the Province of St. Joseph is not, in fact, an altogether edifying one. The early days in America, starting in Kentucky in 1806, were rough, physically and spiritually. Many early American Dominicans did not have a clear idea of the Dominican form of life or of the distinctive Dominican charism. The annals of American Dominicana are full of complaints and controversies, mostly about friars who did not follow or did not even understand the tripartite model of prayer, study, and preaching established by their founder. The historical accounts are also full of provincials (leaders of the province) who abused their authority, favored cronies, fixed elections, misspent funds, ignored the Master of the Order, and generally conducted the business of the province as if it was their own personal fiefdom.[7]

What all these recalcitrant friars and conniving provincials did not do, however, was to give up on the attempt to be Dominicans, particularly to be preachers. The history of the province in its first 150 years is not one of obvious triumphs, but it is one of slow

6. *Sacrosanctum concilium* 116, http://www.vatican.va/archive/hist_councils/ii_vatican_council/documents/vat-ii_const_19631204_sacrosanctum-concilium_en.html; Darren Pierre, OP, interviewed 1 June 2016, New York City.

7. Reginald Coffey, *The American Dominicans: A History of Saint Joseph's Province* (New York: Saint Martin de Porres Guild, 1970); John Vidmar, *Father Fenwick's "Little American Province": 200 Years of the Dominican Friars in the United States*, (Dominican Province of St. Joseph, 2005).

growth and development. Although few friars distinguished themselves as scholars, many displayed great zeal for preaching and for souls, as even the most critical visitors from Europe had to admit. Continual calls for reform, repeated regrets that the province had few scholars of the first rank, and ongoing tensions with European masters of the order could mask some promising trends. The reality was that a young province, starting from scratch on the Kentucky frontier of a nation mainly hostile to Catholicism, gradually built up a network of parishes and educational institutions, gave birth to new Dominican provinces in the central (1939) and southern (1977) regions of the United States, and generally laid the foundations for a sort of American Dominican renaissance during the pontificate of John Paul II (1978–2005).

Around 1950 the province came into its own. It was far from perfect, but it had the resources and the infrastructure, in terms both of physical plant and of personnel, to go to a new level. The American Dominicans had always been preachers, in the sense that they took their sermons and their lectures at parish "missions" quite seriously. But the kind of contemplative study that produced Dominican Doctors of the Church like Albertus Magnus and Thomas Aquinas, the two great medieval thinkers, had rarely taken place, and so it probably crossed the minds of few friars that the American province could or should nurture scholars who could change the world as Albert and Thomas did. In a sense, the Dominicans were simply mirroring the American culture around them, which focused more on action—expansion, settlement, industrialization, and commerce—than on the life of the mind.

The establishment of the Dominican House of Studies in Washington, DC, in 1905, across the street from the Catholic University of America, was pivotal for the province's spiritual, fraternal, and intellectual development. The House of Studies is not a seminary. Or perhaps it would be more precise to say that it is not *just* a seminary. It combines the spiritual life proper to Dominicans, prayer and the Mass shared with a community of brothers according to the hours and days set by the Church, with intellectual formation in philosophy and theology. Although the House of Studies and Catholic University have a close relationship—the order provides professors, chaplains, and administrators to the University and some friars take classes at the university—the friars who spend five or six years at the House of Studies do not emerge as intellectuals in the contemporary American or European style. They are not specialists in narrow bodies of knowledge who hope to secure positions in the academy so that they can produce academic work of even greater degrees of specialization. Instead, friars leave the House of Studies as part of a community of brothers with shared experiences and shared moral and theological commitments.

Ivan Illich, a critic of modern education, once said, "Learned and leisurely hospitality is the only antidote to the stance of deadly cleverness that is acquired in the professional pursuit of objectively secured knowledge. I remain certain that the quest for truth cannot thrive outside the nourishment of mutual trust flowering into a commitment to friendship."[8] Today's universities, dedicated to specialized research, disdain what Illich sees as fundamental: the community of friends searching for the truth together, in partnership with each other. Instead, they consist mostly of isolated individuals whose research, as brilliant as it might be, stands alone and does not even attempt to engage the big picture. It is no surprise that academia is often characterized by rivalry, acrimony, and, in private, loneliness and despair. Even worse, for the former are at least *human* sentiments, are the vast administrative systems designed to deliver "education" as if it were a commodity, as if the classroom and the laboratory were in some way analogous to the assembly line. Cold, empty, and inhuman, these educational production systems attempt something almost blasphemous, teaching without human relationship, knowledge without truth, progress without a goal.

The great advantage of the Dominican House of Studies was that it formed men spiritually, philosophically, and theologically *in community*. Taught by their older brothers, praying with the whole Church, sharing with each other the challenges of poverty, chastity, and obedience, they learned philosophy and theology, not as paths

---

8. Ivan Illich, "The Cultivation of Conspiracy," in *The Challenges of Ivan Illich: A Collective Reflection*, eds. Lee Hoinacki and Carl Mitcham (Albany: State University of New York Press, 2002), 235.

to personal attainment or hoops to be jumped through, but as goods worthy in themselves and as truths that illumined the way of life.

In other words, young Dominicans did not so much study theology, as one might study law or medicine in contemporary professional schools, as much as they were welcomed into a family, with its own distinctive form of life. To be a Dominican, after all, is not to practice a trade or a profession. Rather, the Dominican life is still very much based on the medieval Augustinian monastic life of prayer and work from which it sprang, and includes study as the specific form of work. Less obviously to outside observers, key features of Dominican life are communal liturgy, silence, and recollection ("inner awareness not only of the presence of God but of the importance of divine things"). Even unscheduled time should be characterized by "an air of tranquility that disposes the powers of the soul to pursue the noble actions that embracing the Dominican form requires of them." In the Dominican understanding, prayer is not primarily a kind of self-fulfillment for the person praying or a "spirituality" in the modern sense, but rather "something owed to God."[9]

In 1916 Cardinal Gibbons of Baltimore, the leading prelate in America, said that the Dominicans had saved Catholic University by providing friars to serve in academic and administrative roles, and that therefore they were "the center, the corona, the diadem, the saviors of the Catholic University of America."[10] Some thought he was exaggerating, but he was surely correct that by the early twentieth century the Dominicans had started to produce a stream of theologians and philosophers who greatly aided the intellectual growth of the Church in America, through their service at Catholic University and more generally. For instance, Ignatius Smith, OP, (1884–1957), after founding *Torch* magazine and editing the *Holy Name Journal*, taught at Catholic University for thirty-seven years and chaired the university's philosophy department for twenty years, in addition to various assignments within the order, includ-

---

9. Romanus Cessario, "The Grace St. Dominic Brings to the World: A Fresh Look at Dominican Spirituality," *Logos* 15, no. 2 (Spring 2012), 7–12.

10. Vidmar, *Father Fenwick's "Little American Province,"* 125.

ing serving as prior of the House of Studies. He also founded a preaching institute "for the relief of laymen who had to sit through bad sermons" and led it for twenty-three years. He edited *The New Scholasticism* for a decade, and served as the president of the Catholic Philosophical Society.[11] Walter Farrell, OP (1902–1951) lectured widely on Thomas Aquinas, wrote a four-volume companion to Aquinas's *Summa Theologiae*, started a "Theology for Laity" program, and served as a chaplain in World War II.[12]

One of many prominent priests of the Dominican Province of St. Joseph is theologian Romanus Cessario, who earned his doctorate from the University of Fribourg in 1982 and has taught at Providence College, the Dominican House of Studies, and Saint John's Seminary in Massachusetts. His more than one hundred articles and eighteen books, including academic works like *Introduction to Moral Theology* and *A Short History of Thomism*, and devotional ones such as *The Seven Joys of Mary* and *Perpetual Angelus: As the Saints Pray the Rosary*, demonstrate not only his integration of intellect and traditional Catholic spirituality, but also the continuing utility of Thomism in illuminating matters from the Rosary to the nature of being. Similarly, he has served not only on the editorial boards of academic journals but also as the senior editor of *Magnificat*, a liturgical and devotional periodical that has become the most popular religious magazine in the United States. His book *Theology and Sanctity* exemplifies the Dominican emphasis on the centrality of truth, as he shows that sanctity can never be divorced from truth, because "only the truth has grace."[13]

---

11. Obituary of Henry Ignatius Smith, OP, *Dominicana* 42, no. 2 (1957): 143–46.

12. Vidmar, *Father Fenwick's "Little American Province,"* 126. Farrell joined the new central province of Dominicans in 1939 but continued to work closely with the St. Joseph province.

13. Romanus Cessario, *Introduction to Moral Theology*, revised ed. (Washington DC: Catholic University of America Press, 2013); Romanus Cessario, *A Short History of Thomism* (Washington, DC: Catholic University of America Press, 2005); Romanus Cessario, *The Seven Joys of Mary* (San Francisco: Ignatius, 2011); Romanus Cessario, *Perpetual Angelus: As the Saints Pray the Rosary* (New York: Alba House, 1995); Romanus Cessario, *Theology and Sanctity* (Ave Maria, Florida: Sapientia Press, 2014).

The province's intellectual coming of age was recognized by the Vatican and Catholics around the world by the 1960s. The province worked closely with the English Dominicans on the sixty-volume *McGraw-Hill Summa* during the 1960s and 1970s and was asked by the Vatican to play a leading role in producing new critical editions of the *Summa* and other important works by Aquinas, in the years between 1966 and 2000.[14] Today the province has many excellent scholars, not just in philosophy and theology, but also in literature, history, medicine, and the sciences, as will be seen below.

Thomism

The second major source of the Dominican ability to be orthodox, intellectual, and liturgically sane is Thomism, the thought of Saint Thomas Aquinas (1225–1274), often known as "the Angelic Doctor." His thought is the leading example of "scholasticism," the theology of the medieval schools. A Dominican himself, Thomas was a theologian and philosopher who digested, evaluated, and in large part restored to Christian thought the philosophy of Aristotle, which had been lost to Europe for centuries. His most famous work, the *Summa Theologiae*, opens with these words: "Because the master of Catholic Truth ought not only to teach the proficient but also to instruct beginners . . . we purpose in this book to treat of whatever belongs to the Christian Religion, in such a way as may tend to the instruction of beginners."[15] These words explain much that is valuable in Thomism and point to its great utility for an order like the Dominicans. First, Thomas wants to teach everyone, from "beginners" to the "proficient." Second, his topic is broad: "whatever belongs to the Christian religion." Third, his method is one that focuses on beginners.

Starting with the existence of God, Thomas methodically treats creation, the human person, ethics, politics, and law. He thus develops a highly detailed account of reality that is at the same time a lesson in thought and argumentation. His usual method is to raise a

14. Vidmar, *Father Fenwick's "Little American Province,"* 127.
15. Thomas Aquinas, "Prologue," *Summa Theologiae*.

question and to present the three (or more) most important objections to his view before presenting his own answer and his response to each of the three objections. In doing so he is scrupulous in presenting the strong version of the objections, rather than any sort of "straw man." In fact, it is common for his readers to find themselves nodding in agreement with an idea, only to realize that they are accepting one of the objections. His students therefore learn intellectual fairness as well as a rigorous approach to thinking and learning, in addition to the actual philosophical and theological content of his arguments.

The Catholic Church does not have one official philosophy, but it has long given Thomism a prominent place and called for its study. For example, in 1879 Pope Leo XIII reminded his readers of the many popes before him who had called for the study of Thomism and asked for bishops "to restore the golden wisdom of St. Thomas, and to spread it far and wide for the defense and beauty of the Catholic faith, for the good of society, and for the advantage of all the sciences."[16] Pius X, in his battle against theological modernism, saw Thomism as his most valuable philosophical ally. He reaffirmed Leo's words and ordered that the thought of Thomas "be made the basis of the sacred sciences" in the seminaries and warned that professors "cannot set St. Thomas aside, especially in metaphysical questions, without grave detriment."[17]

Pope John Paul II, an advocate of the modern philosophy known as personalism and the originator of the "theology of the body," was also a convinced Thomist. In fact, it was his Thomism that allowed him to range so widely and to drill so deeply, just as Thomas himself had done. Like his papal predecessors, John Paul affirmed that "the Church has been justified in consistently proposing Saint Thomas as a master of thought and a model of the right way to do theology." And just like Leo XIII and Pius X, he called the Church back to Thomas, and expressed his concern that previous such directives had been ignored:

16. Leo XIII, *Aeterni patris* 31, 4 August 1879, Vatican, http://w2.vatican.va/content/leo-xiii/en/encyclicals/documents/hf_l-xiii_enc_04081879_aeterni-patris.html.
17. Pius X, *Pascendi* 45.

If it has been necessary from time to time to intervene on this question, to reiterate the value of the Angelic Doctor's insights and insist on the study of his thought, this has been because the Magisterium's directives have not always been followed with the readiness one would wish. In the years after the Second Vatican Council, many Catholic faculties were in some ways impoverished by a diminished sense of the importance of the study not just of Scholastic philosophy but more generally of the study of philosophy itself.[18]

In short, the study of the thought of Thomas Aquinas has a special place in Catholicism and has been advocated by popes since the Middle Ages.

The Dominicans, as Thomas Aquinas's order, not surprisingly have played an important role in studying and disseminating his thought. Where other orders have minimized or even jettisoned once-important thinkers, Dominicans remain committed to Aquinas and influenced by him. The Dominicans' Thomism is one of the three major sources of their success because it has given Dominicans an organized and systematic method of seeking and assimilating truth, reinforcing their orthodoxy even as it enables research and analysis of the most pressing contemporary issues.

A medieval philosophy based on a still older Aristotelianism might seem ill-fitted for an age characterized by mechanized industry, nuclear science, and the Internet, but it works surprisingly well. As the St. Joseph province's Thomas Joseph White, following in the tradition of the French Dominican Yves Congar, has pointed out, "you don't win over the culture of your age unless you can solve its internal intellectual problems." Thomism, he argues, is able to do this, while once-influential theologies, like that of Karl Rahner, are too entangled with the spirit of the age to do so. For example, the culture of today's university is a mix of post-modernism and scientific positivism, two reductionist and incompatible views of reality.

18. John Paul II, *Fides et ratio* 43 and 61, 14 September 1998, Vatican, http://w2.vatican.va/content/john-paul-ii/en/encyclicals/documents/hf_jp-ii_enc_140919 98_fides-et-ratio.html.

"Thomism," White believes, "has become one of the only plausible contenders left that offers an authentic vision of the sapiential unity of human knowledge amidst the diversity of university disciplines." Even more, Thomism has begun and will continue an intellectually rigorous engagement with cosmology, evolutionary theory, and sexuality, disciplines and issues of fundamental importance to today's intellectual culture.[19]

The key, argues White, is a Thomistic approach known as "degrees of knowledge." In a nutshell, this approach looks at reality on progressively deeper levels, with the first level being quantity, the second natures and essences, the third metaphysics (the study of the existence of things), and the fourth ultimate causes. "One of the strengths of St. Thomas's view," White says, "is that he shows you how different scientific forms of understanding (broadly speaking) help you penetrate reality at different levels." This approach at once recognizes the validity of different methods yet still enables the different disciplines to interact with each other. In the Thomistic perspective, "all learning is united by a common goal—the pursuit of truth about reality, considered under various aspects." At a time when the university is "trapped in a factional, fragmented view of education," Thomism offers both "intellectual nuance" and the promise of synthesis.[20] Does any other philosophy, worldview, or ideology provide this possibility?

Part of the genius of Thomism is its ability to make clear distinctions about causality. Thomism encourages its practitioners to distinguish between different levels of causality, with God, of course, as the first cause, but all sorts of other beings as secondary causes and instrumental causes. "Part of the dignity of creatures," White explains, "is that they are created in such a way as to be themselves true causes." Many believers are concerned that some scientific discovery or theoretical breakthrough will undermine their faith in

---

19. Thomas Joseph White, OP, "Thomism after Vatican II," 1 July 2013, paper given at the "Dominicans and the Renewal of Thomism" conference, Washington, DC.

20. Thomas Joseph White, OP, *Thomism for the New Evangelization* (Washington, DC: Thomistic Institute, 2016), 5–7.

God. For Thomism, such an event is simply impossible: "There's no conflict because everything that you discover in the world—in the web of physical, chemical, and biological causes—is what God has given being and so has given to be causes of other things in the created order."[21] In today's culture this insight is particularly helpful in the area of creation and evolution, but it applies to all disciplines.

Finally, many Christians accept that Thomism might be true but worry that it is dry and impersonal. They see it as dull intellectualism with little room for love, wonder, and joy. Much of the rejection of Thomism that occurred in American and European seminaries after Vatican II probably came not from considered investigations and comparisons with other philosophical systems but from the sense that Thomism was an arid and inert system that would stifle its adherents. The well-known charismatic persona of the twentieth century's most famous Thomist, John Paul II, should be enough to dispense with this idea. So too should the life and work of Peter Kreeft, "America's C.S. Lewis," the Thomistic philosopher, surfer, and novelist. For both men, Thomism was energizing and empowering, not shackling or enervating. It enabled them to see clearly, to argue cogently, and to range widely. John Paul's intimate and insightful treatment of sexuality and Kreeft's sympathetic and illuminating analysis of Tolkien's *Lord of the Rings* demonstrate the vitality of real Thomism.[22]

In a sense, Thomism is like jazz. Great jazz players are able to improvise because of their deep and extensive knowledge of music, their mastery of mechanics, and their refinement, all won through years of practice and listening. "Because they mastered that basic level, when they get to the hard cases of innovation, they can move with the flow of the music, and that's what the moral thinking of Aquinas is about," says White. Aquinas teaches his disciples to develop prudence and the other virtues, enabling them to negotiate difficult and confusing environments. The Thomistic approach is

---

21. Ibid., 7–8.
22. John Paul II, *Man and Woman He Created Them: A Theology of the Body* (Boston: Pauline Books and Media, 2006); Peter Kreeft, *The Philosophy of Tolkien: The Worldview Behind "The Lord of the Rings"* (San Francisco: Ignatius, 2005).

"getting into the stream of knowledge and love and staying there" and "staying in the rhythm of the Holy Spirit," and is not at all the "hollow moralism" that critics imagine.[23] Studying Thomas is hard work that takes years to bear fruit, but it enables Dominicans to be the jazz musicians of contemporary theologians and philosophers, loving tradition and rooted in it, yet navigating confidently in the winds of modernity, able to respond nimbly in the midst of the chaos.

A young Dominican, for example, was giving a lecture on angels for Theology on Tap, a program that brings Catholic thinking into bars and restaurants. After the talk, a local news reporter asked a series of queries about the Church's moral teaching, its supposed connection to violence, and its apparent scientific backwardness. The friar quickly realized that the questions were coming from anger and distrust of the Church that would not be dispelled even by the best answers he could give. He decided to turn the tables and asked her, "Do you believe that Love created the universe?" She turned away, at last confronted by the most central issue of all.[24] The friar's knowledge of angels, morality, science, and the Bible was helpful, but his ability, in the midst of an intense conversation, to recognize the reporter's fundamental issue was the kind of discernment that indicates a deeper level of human understanding. Answering a hundred more questions would have been less valuable than identifying the one question that mattered to that specific person. The point, of course, was not that he confounded her or won an argument, but that he pointed her to the one question at the bottom of all her questions, and, it is to be hoped, one that she eventually faced and answered.

Thomism, however, is not useful only in theology and apologetics. It also helps in the laboratory, as the work of St. Joseph province priest Nicanor Austriaco illustrates. In 1996, shortly before receiving his doctorate in biology at MIT, Austriaco had a powerful experi-

23. White, *Thomism for the New Evangelization*, 13–14.

24. Gregory Maria Pine, "Grounded on Love: St. Thomas and the Logic of Subsidiarity," 11 November 2014, *Dominicana*, http://www.dominicanajournal.org/grounded-on-love-st-thomas-and-the-logic-of-subsidiarity/.

ence in Mass that convinced him that Jesus loved him and that he should devote his life to God.[25] A year later, he left a position at the Ludwig Institute for Cancer Research at University College London to join the Dominicans.[26] He earned his theological licentiate from the House of Studies in May 2005, started teaching biology at Providence College that fall, and earned a second doctorate in theology from the University of Fribourg in 2015. The titles of his two dissertations and his licentiate thesis tell his story: "UTH1 and the Genetic Control of Aging in the Yeast, Saccharomyces" (MIT); "Life and Death from the Systems Perspective: A Thomistic Bioethics for a Post-Genomic Age" (Dominican House of Studies); "The Hylomorphic Structure of Thomistic Moral Theology from the Perspective of a Systems Biology" (Fribourg). This is a biologist with the most advanced training from one of the leading research universities in the world who is also a Thomistic theologian. It is important to note that his theology is not something apart from or parallel to his biological studies. The two are utterly integrated and intertwined. He can apply Thomism to bioethics and he can apply "systems biology" to Thomism. Thomism for Austriaco is not a prison cell but a key that unlocks door after door, even at the highest levels of human knowledge.

Father Austriaco has taught general biology and Western Civilization courses, has served as a college chaplain, and has worked with prisoners at a medium-security prison. In all of these venues, he reaches and relates to the people around him. "General Biology with Father Nic is akin to taking your brain, putting it in an oven, and melting it into gold. You get rid of all the junk. He teaches you how to think," said one student. Another said, "as an English major who doesn't have a great love for most priests, I can honestly say Father Austriaco is one of my favorite professors." She said that he "makes everything completely clear" and is a "really interesting guy,

25. Vicki-Ann Downing, "There's a Priest in the Biology Lab," *Providence College Magazine*, 28 October 2015, https://news.providence.edu/theres-a-priest-in-the-biology-lab.

26. John Farrell, "From the Laboratory to the Lord, and Back Again," *Catholic World Report*, 3 May 2011, http://www.catholicworldreport.com/Item/519/from_the_laboratory_to_the_lord_and_back_again.aspx.

very open-minded, and genuinely incredibly nice too." Another enjoyed Austriaco's willingness to engage the moral and philosophical issues raised by scientific investigation: "One of the wonderful things about being taught by such a brilliant man is that while he's training you as a scientist, he's also reminding you that science isn't everything. The most profound memory I have is of all of us doing an experiment in the lab, but talking about whether miracles are reasonable, whether it is reasonable to believe in God, whether there is a scientific and empirical way to approach the big questions."[27] Austriaco also tries to teach humility to those who make scientific discoveries: "The fact is that you just happened to be the person to uncover this treasure. But that treasure was never yours. It belongs to all of us. It's a gift. And you just happened to be the privileged one, the messenger to deliver the message. But it was never yours."[28]

His lab, which works on the genetics of "programmed cell death" in yeast and is supported by grants from the National Science Foundation and the National Institutes of Health, combines scientific rigor with the kind of mentorship for its fourteen student assistants that is rare even in the best colleges. Austriaco introduces freshmen to research with small projects and gives each one an upper-class mentor. They gradually take on more responsibility and spend more time in the lab. "When the senior student graduates, the younger can take over that project," he says.[29] He also takes his students to the conferences of the American Society for Cell Biology and the International Meeting for Yeast Apoptosis, partially to catalyze their interest in the subject by showing them how much there is to learn and partially to encourage them about how much they have already learned.[30]

The alumni of Austriaco's laboratory are the best evidence of the impact that he has had on his students. Emily Roblee, now a medi-

27. Downing, "There's a Priest in the Biology Lab"; "Nicanor Austriaco," Rate My Professors, 3 April 2007, http://www.ratemyprofessors.com/ShowRatings.jsp?tid=700430.

28. Farrell, "From the Laboratory to the Lord."

29. Ibid.

30. Downing, "There's a Priest in the Biology Lab."

cal student, says, "While I was working in Father Nic's lab, I was often challenged by confusing results and became frustrated when I couldn't obtain perfect data. Father Nic taught me how to 'think like a scientist' by realizing that there often isn't a 'right answer' to scientific inquiries, and researchers can only design and perform experiments, determine their results, and interpret the results according to the trends observed." Daniel Gittings, now a physician, says, "He has always encouraged me to think independently, be able to translate and communicate the complex language of science to those who may not understand, and also to be compassionate." For Katherine Helming, who earned a doctorate from Harvard in 2015, his academic influence was not what made the biggest difference. When she learned that she had leukemia, she immediately called Austriaco: "He came to the hospital in Boston that same day and provided an indescribable amount of support and comfort to my family and me during a very scary time."[31]

Austriaco is also involved in "Thomistic Evolution," a Dominican initiative to respond to the creation-evolution debate from a Thomistic perspective. At heart it is an attempt to argue that many aspects of evolutionary theory are compatible with Scripture and Catholic doctrine. Austriaco and his brother Dominicans argue that Thomistic premises and approaches are especially useful because they "transcend and reconcile the dichotomies—for instance, the oft-cited dichotomy between chance and design—that shape the contemporary science and religion debate." Thomism allows them to accept both chance and design: "God designs with chance." In the book *Thomistic Evolution: A Catholic Approach to Understanding Evolution in the Light of Faith* and its companion website, Austriaco and his colleagues examine issues such as how faith and reason work together, the evidence for evolution, the meaning of the biblical creation narratives, the fittingness of evolution, how God might have created human beings through evolution, and the historicity of Adam and Eve.[32] In the piece on the

31. Ibid.
32. Thomistic Evolution: A Catholic Approach to Understanding Evolution in the Light of Faith, http://www.thomisticevolution.org/.

fittingness of evolution, for example, Austriaco uses an argument from the *Summa Theologiae*:

> It was fitting for God to have worked via evolution rather than to have created all species at the beginning because in doing so, He was able to give His creation—the material universe and the individual creatures within it—a share in His causality. In this way, He more fully communicates His perfection to His creation, more clearly manifesting His glory. As St. Thomas points out: "If God governed alone, things would be deprived of the perfection of causality."[33]

Since the presumed incompatibility between evolutionary science and Christianity is one of the major barriers to faith for educated people today, the Thomistic Evolution initiative speaks directly to a real intellectual need in today's culture. Many Americans accept evolutionary theory and assume that in doing so they have made a choice against any sort of supernatural explanation of life. At the same time, many Christians who accept evolution cannot account for the creation narratives in Genesis or the idea of a creator God; the danger for them is starting to see science as the realm of facts and religion as the realm of feelings and preferences. Such a bifurcation can produce a sort of "faith" that avoids or even opposes truth. The great value of the Dominicans' work on this project is its refusal to make such a compromise. Underlying the whole project is the proposition that all truth is God's truth and that, therefore, Christians do not have to flee from controversial topics. Pursuing truth, the Thomistic Evolution project makes clear, is always the best policy.

Parish Ministry

Dominicans have also done good work in areas like history, literature, and medicine, but I would like to close this chapter with a look at a kind of service that American Dominicans take for granted but

33. Nicanor Austriaco, "The Fittingness of Evolutionary Creation," Thomistic Evolution: A Catholic Approach to Understanding Evolution in the Light of Faith, https://www.thomisticevolution.org/disputed-questions/.

that is rare among friars in other countries: parish ministry. Traditionally Dominicans have worked as scholars and itinerant preachers, but the circumstances of the Dominican founding in the United States led to a different approach. In the eighteenth and early nineteenth centuries the new republic had thousands of Catholic citizens but very few priests, so when the Dominicans arrived they were almost immediately asked to take charge of parishes. That model continues to this day, so that, although the St. Joseph province runs Providence College and the House of Studies, its main form of institutional presence is the parish. Even when it focuses on university ministry, as Dominic instructed the order to do 800 years ago, it does so in the form of the "university parish," which is a Catholic diocesan parish that ministers to nearby students. Saint Thomas Aquinas University Parish, in Charlottesville, Virginia, for instance, directs significant attention to students and faculty of the University of Virginia, but it includes adults, children, and families that have no ties to the university.

There might be some friars of the Province of St. Joseph who have no interest in parish ministry—and there are posts for them at Providence College, the House of Studies, or in non-Dominican academic institutions—but the majority seems to embrace what is clearly a fruitful relationship. The parishes keep the friars honest and the friars provide the sort of liturgy, preaching, and teaching seldom found in the American Church.

Intellectuals of all types are challenged to communicate their knowledge and wisdom to the less educated. Dominicans in parishes must speak to the Catholics in the pews every day, not only in homilies, but also in parish offices, meetings of budget committees, and classes for fifth graders. They must bring their formidable learning down from the lofty heights of abstraction to everyday problems, like how to appeal to high school students or what to do with a difficult employee, and their message must be clear and understandable to lay Catholics of all sorts. The commitment to the parish also serves as a sort of doctrinal protection for the order, since, through the *sensus fidei*, "the faithful have an instinct for the truth of the Gospel, which enables them to recognise and endorse authentic Christian doctrine and practice, and to reject what is

119

false."[34] Theological error that has escaped proper scrutiny in the halls of academia is often exposed in the pews. It is one thing to say something scandalous in a seminar, quite another to have to preach it, as truth, from the pulpit.

From the other side, many Catholics who do not have the opportunity for higher education do have the opportunity to attend a Dominican parish. There they encounter something rare in today's Church: a reverent liturgy, doctrinal preaching, and beauty. It is not necessary to enter into polemics against the likes of Marty Haugen or Dan Schutte—this book consciously focuses on what is right rather than what is wrong—to make clear the substandard state of the liturgy in most parishes.[35] It is possible to do this because even fans of the folk-style music that fills most hymn books would have to admit that the music is not reverent or traditional. They would say that it is not *trying* to be reverent or traditional, but rather accessible and inoffensive. In the same way, those who enjoy homilies full of personal anecdotes and moral truisms would not defend them on the ground of profundity but rather for being amusing and entertaining. In short, the defenders of folk songs and light sermons argue according to categories that either are not part of the Church's understanding of the liturgy at all, or are subordinate to higher aims that have been laid out in great detail by the Church. According not to this book or to "traditional Catholics," but to the Second Vatican Council, the Mass is "an exercise of the priestly office of Jesus Christ," the "summit toward which the activity of the Church is directed," and "the font from which all her power flows," and the Eucharist is a "divine sacrifice." These words should be enough to ensure the reverence and solemnity of the liturgy and to rule out the diverting, the banal, and the merely inoffensive.

However, in response to liturgists determined to make Mass relevant to the contemporary culture with snappy songs, impromptu

---

34. International Theological Commission, "*Sensus Fidei* in the Life of the Church," 2014, Vatican, http://www.vatican.va/roman_curia/congregations/cfaith/cti_documents/rc_cti_20140610_sensus-fidei_en.html.

35. Haugen and Schutte are the writers of peppy songs that are widely sung in American parishes.

innovations, and a casual tone, it is helpful to review the liturgical directives of the most recent Church council. There is absolutely nothing in *Sacrosanctum concilium,* the Second Vatican Council's document on the liturgy, about singing songs in a secular style or telling personal anecdotes from the pulpit. There *is* a great deal about tradition, reverence, solemnity, and order. For example, nobody, "even if he be a priest, may add, remove, or change anything in the liturgy on his own authority." The document refers to "sound tradition" and "venerable tradition" approvingly. It calls for participants in the liturgy "to discharge their office with the sincere piety and decorum demanded by so exalted a ministry" and says that they must be trained "to perform their functions in a correct and orderly manner." It refers to "the solemn liturgy" and asks for rites to be "celebrated solemnly." It calls for "reverent silence" at the proper times and makes clear that "the use of the Latin language is to be preserved." In fact, special efforts should be made "so that the faithful may also be able to say or to sing together in Latin those parts of the Ordinary of the Mass which pertain to them."

There is an entire chapter on "sacred music," which is not the same thing as religious music or Christian music, but rather music set apart for the liturgy itself. "The musical tradition of the universal Church," this section explains, "is a treasure of inestimable value, greater even than that of any other art" that "is to be preserved and fostered with great care." In case those words did not sink in, *traditional* music should be saved and encouraged in the liturgy. If there is any doubt about what this might mean, the document makes it explicit: "The Church acknowledges Gregorian chant as specially suited to the Roman liturgy: therefore, other things being equal, it should be given pride of place in liturgical services." As far as instruments, "the pipe organ is to be held in high esteem." Other instruments are permitted "with the knowledge and consent of the competent territorial authority," but "only on condition that the instruments are suitable, or can be made suitable, for sacred use, accord with the dignity of the temple, and truly contribute to the edification of the faithful."

Preaching should not be informal and simplistic, but characterized by "exactitude and fidelity." The sermon "should draw its content mainly from scriptural and liturgical sources" and should proclaim "God's wonderful works in the history of salvation" or expound "the mysteries of the faith and the guiding principles of the Christian life." Of course, the homily should be "highly esteemed as part of the liturgy itself." The church building should feature "sacred art" the single aim of which is "turning men's minds devoutly toward God." The church should be built specifically for the liturgy (not for multiple uses) and its "sacred furnishings should worthily and beautifully serve the dignity of worship." In short, the "noble simplicity" and "active participation" of the laity also called for by the council cannot be isolated from—or pitted against—order, solemnity, decorum, tradition, and beauty, but must be integrated with them.

The Dominicans are some of the few priests and religious in the United States who take these directives seriously. First, Aquinas's virtue theory plays an important role.[36] The Dominicans value the virtue of religion, in the sense of worship as something owed to God, as opposed to something primarily political, psychological, or therapeutic.[37] Thomism also provides them with a deep appreciation of law, which forms its followers in virtue, meaning that Dominicans not only accept the laws of the Church, including the rubrics that regulate the liturgy, but see them as pathways of grace.[38] These Thomistic understandings remove many of the temptations to improvise or to alter the liturgy to make it more "relevant."

Many Dominicans like to use truly Catholic music and to sing the propers of the Mass (the sections specific to that day in the liturgical calendar, ignored in most American parishes) in English. Many try to use Latin at solemn Masses. Their goal is to have Scripture as the basis of liturgical music, using the chants composed by the Church for every occasion, but most Dominicans recognize that music and liturgy are in a fallen state today, like a man beaten and robbed and lying in a ditch. They also want to avoid the chaos that

---

36. Thomas Aquinas, *Summa Theologiae,* Second Part of the Second Part, Question 81.
37. Thomas Joseph White, OP, interview.
38. Darren Pierre, OP, interview.

came after Vatican II, when radical changes were made without catechesis. Therefore, when they assume leadership in a parish, they move slowly so as not to scandalize the faithful. They try to build consensus with clear teaching that explains the liturgy and prepares people for any changes that they might make.[39]

From the pulpit, Dominicans have emphasized doctrinal preaching, rather than the social justice moralism of the left, the sentimentalism of the mainstream, or the legalism of the right.[40] They believe that preaching must not be limited to telling people to love the poor, or be nice, or avoid fornication. It must teach the great truths of the faith in a way that, once understood, enables and impels action. For instance, it is not enough to say that contraception is wrong. That knowledge alone is seldom enough to motivate virtuous action. People will avoid contraception, though, when they understand the nature of marriage, the end of the conjugal act, and the ways in which contraception subverts those ends, because then they can see both the benefits of obedience and the real relational and spiritual costs of disobedience. The temptation of many American priests, faced with extremely large parishes, is to avoid offending anyone, but this is neither effective nor honest. Some truths will offend, but if explained, expounded, and presented with love and respect, they will set people free.

The effective preaching of today's Dominicans is not primarily the result of training or technique. Neither is it primarily a matter of rhetoric or intellect. All these factors matter, but the heart of Dominican preaching is the love of truth. More than most Catholics, more even than most priests, Dominicans are captivated by the truth, committed to the truth, and in love with the beauty of truth. Since the motto of the order is "Veritas," truth, their religious vows are in a sense a commitment of themselves to Truth in all its depths. In other words, they are effective preachers more because of their vows and their embrace of the truth than because of special techniques.

39. Innocent Smith, OP, interview.
40. Thomas Joseph White, OP, interview.

Conclusion

The Dominicans are not perfect. Most tragically, they seem to be losing control of the academic and spiritual environment of Providence College by failing to hire and to form professors who embrace Catholicism and the mission of Catholic higher education and by uncritically adopting the contemporary administrative model of the university. Instead of emphasizing the spiritual fraternity and commitment to truth that are at the heart of their order and that would be so refreshing to today's students, they have allowed their college to become an impersonal "educational system" that, despite an excellent campus ministry and some brilliant Dominican professors, is in too many areas indistinguishable from non-Catholic institutions. Sadly, many of the faculty at the college have little love or respect for Catholicism and are therefore not only unwilling but also literally unable to share the mind of Christ with their students.[41] The immediate prospects for the college are poor and likely include administrative bloat, ideological conflict, and the counterproductivity that often afflicts large institutions. In the short term, this Catholic college might make its students less and less Catholic. Since, however, the rising generation of Dominicans is talented and holy, perhaps the inevitable crisis at Providence College will call forth the Dominican equivalent of the Franciscan University of Steubenville's Michael Scanlan (see Chapter 5), who emerged at the eleventh hour with a vision for renewal that saved and revitalized his institution.

The Dominicans also at times stay silent on controversial issues where their expertise, wisdom, and gentleness make them uniquely qualified to speak out. In fairness, when to speak is a prudential decision and the Dominicans speak publicly and prophetically more than most priests and religious. Nevertheless, there is a certain reluctance to address difficult moral and sexual issues in a clear and forthright manner, less justifiably for fear of giving offence, and

---

41. A Catholic college denies its nature and rejects its proper end when it puts professors who reject its beliefs and oppose its mission in front of unformed undergraduates. The Dominican consecration to truth exacerbates this contradiction.

more justifiably for fear of providing truncated and simplistic answers to complex issues. From a purely Dominican standpoint, this guardedness is hard to understand, as Dominic and the other early Dominicans boldly and publically addressed similarly controversial and complex issues. Fear of controversy and misunderstanding does not justify silence in situations where the great mass of Catholics is ignorant and the culture is in freefall.

Still, this order is one of the gems in the Church today. Its orthodoxy, intellectual vitality, and liturgical sanity make it an attractive home for some of the most gifted and most committed Catholic men of our day. Those same qualities make it a treasure to the parishioners in its churches, the students in its classrooms, and the readers of its many works of scholarship and research. The bottom line is that the Dominicans of the Province of St. Joseph bring a confused generation the message it most needs to hear, that only the truth has grace.

5

New Ardor

Franciscan University of Steubenville

"IT IS THE HONOUR and responsibility of a Catholic University to consecrate itself without reserve to the cause of truth. This is its way of serving at one and the same time both the dignity of man and the good of the Church, which has 'an intimate conviction that truth is its real ally . . . and that knowledge and reason are sure ministers to faith'": so did Saint Pope John Paul II, quoting Saint John Henry Newman, define the mission of a Catholic university.[1] The university has played a pivotal, central, and formative role in the development of men as thinkers and as men of God. In fact, it is difficult to imagine the Polish philosopher pope and the British convert cardinal apart from their years as students, teachers, and scholars in the universities of Europe. Newman's *The Idea of the University* and John Paul's *Ex corde ecclesiae* are marked not simply by erudition, but by great love. Both men loved the institution of the university because they both loved truth and knew that the university, at its best, nurtured, protected, and amplified the search for truth and the dissemination of truth. Since man is oriented toward truth at the deepest level of his being, the truth-seeking and truth-propagating institution of the university is of great importance for human flourishing and for the development of human culture.

Already, in Newman's nineteenth century, the university was coming to be seen most importantly as an engine of economic growth and national greatness, a trend which only increased in the twentieth century. Those who accepted this conception tended to

1. John Paul II, *Ex corde ecclesiae*, 15 August 1990, Vatican.va.

minimize the role of theology and philosophy, disciplines that produced no wealth but stirred up disagreements that endangered the tranquility of society. They also tended to use the bureaucratic approach to institution building, assuming that, as with the other great institutions of modernity, such as the state or the business firm, a sort of "system" of education could be planned and administrated, independent of wisdom, humility, honesty, and other virtues of teachers and students. Without denying the economic, technological, and medical benefits of universities, Newman and John Paul II did deny that Catholic universities should be oriented primarily toward pragmatic concerns and affirmed that they should be directed primarily toward truth itself. The Catholic university necessarily includes theology and philosophy, the disciplines most directly concerned with the deepest and most important truths. Also, because of the nature of God (personal and relational in essence) and the nature of man (personal and relational in essence), the faith, love, and virtue of teachers and students cannot be ignored or taken for granted, but have to receive serious attention.

Newman, sadly, never saw his vision for the university realized. Various factors beyond his control, including meager finances and the clericalism of certain Irish bishops, foiled his valiant attempts, starting in 1854, to establish the Catholic University of Ireland according to his philosophy of education. In many ways, his beloved Oxford University came closer to the ideal, but it, of course, was an Anglican institution that by definition did not pursue theology and philosophy in a Catholic manner. John Paul II had excellent experiences at the Jagiellonian University of Krakow and the Catholic University of Lublin as student, professor, and chaplain, but he realized, by the time he became pope in 1978, that many Catholic universities in Europe and the rest of the world were struggling. In many universities faith and reason were utterly divorced, two worlds of inquiry that seemed to have nothing in common; many other universities were Catholic in name only, having opened themselves up to the world to such an extent that there was little left to distinguish them from state universities.

John Paul's *Ex corde ecclesiae* therefore affirmed the value of the Catholic university, both as a university and as part of the Church, and then set out to reform it and renew it. A Catholic university, he said, had the following four essential characteristics: Christian identity on an institutional level; faith-based reflection and research on all aspects of human knowledge; faithfulness to the Christian message as taught by the Catholic Church; and an institutional commitment to the service of the Church and the world.[2] In other words, a university with a veneer of Catholicism that operated in the same manner as its secular peers was failing both in its Catholicism (because it lacked a Catholic vision and because its activities were not inspired by Catholic motivations) and in its role as a university (because it was not seeking, and therefore not finding, the most important truths of all). Only an institution infused with Catholicism at every level, from roots to branches, could truly fulfill the mission of a Catholic university. This Catholicity was especially important in theology departments, where it was "intrinsic to the principles and methods of their research and teaching in their academic discipline that theologians respect the authority of the Bishops, and assent to Catholic doctrine according to the degree of authority with which it is taught." This requirement was a *logical* necessity, not an arbitrary limitation. Those teaching the faith had to stay within the boundaries of the faith, or they would be teaching something other than the faith.

To safeguard what was already good and to reform what was not, John Paul II ended the document with norms that would apply to "all Catholic Universities and other Catholic Institutes of Higher Studies throughout the world" and would be "applied concretely at the local and regional levels by Episcopal Conferences and other Assemblies of Catholic Hierarchy." These norms included requirements that all Catholic teachers "be faithful to" and non-Catholic teachers "respect" Catholic doctrine and morals in their research and teaching, and that theologians, in particular, be "faithful to the Magisterium of the Church as the authentic interpreter of Sacred Scripture and Sacred Tradition." To maintain Catholic identity, "the number of non-Catholic teachers should not be allowed to

2. John Paul II, *Ex corde.*

constitute a majority within the Institution."[3] When the American bishops produced their application of these norms they softened them in some unfortunate respects, for instance, encouraging rather than requiring a majority of Catholic faculty, but they did require that Catholics who teach theology have a "mandatum," or permit from the local bishop.[4]

As most observers are fully aware, neither *Ex corde ecclesiae* nor its American implementation had the kind of impact on Catholic higher education for which John Paul II had hoped. Thirty years after *Ex corde*, most of the 230 Catholic colleges and universities in the United States are barely distinguishable from their state university rivals. A few took the call to reform seriously, others made small changes, and still others largely ignored the document. The extent of the problem is illustrated by *The Newman Guide to Choosing a Catholic College*, which "recommends Catholic colleges and universities because of their commitment to a faithful Catholic education." The guide listed only nineteen institutions that met criteria based on *Ex corde ecclesiae* in 2021.[5] It is not the purpose of this chapter to outline the woes of Catholic higher education, but rather to point to an institution that appears in *The Newman Guide*, meets the requirements of *Ex corde*, and, more important, displays the fruitfulness of a university that does "consecrate itself to the truth." As Franciscan University of Steubenville makes clear, the requirements of *Ex corde ecclesiae* are not onerous or arbitrary; orthodoxy (truth in doctrine) and Catholic identity (truth in public and private life) are paths to vitality, characterized in Franciscan's case by spiritual fatherhood, evangelistic zeal, and Eucharistic devotion.

---

3. John Paul II, *Ex corde.*

4. National Conference of Catholic Bishops, "The Application of *Ex corde Ecclesiae* for the United States," 17 November 1999, http://www.usccb.org/beliefs-and-teachings/how-we-teach/catholic-education/higher-education/the-application-for-ex-corde-ecclesiae-for-the-united-states.cfm. The mandatum was not invented by John Paul or first required by *Ex corde ecclesiae*, but rather was required by Canon 812 of the Code of Canon Law: http://www.vatican.va/archive/cod-iuris-canonici/eng/documents/cic_lib3-cann793-821_en.html#CHAPTER_II.

5. Cardinal Newman Society, "Recommended Colleges for Catholic Families," https://newmansociety.org/college/.

Surprising Steubenville

Once a thriving steel town, Steubenville, Ohio, like many other cities in the "Rust Belt," was hit hard by plant closures in the 1970s and has not recovered. Today the remnants of the steel industry line the banks of Ohio River, giving the city a gritty, industrial atmosphere, even though most of the industrial jobs are long gone. Downtown Steubenville has a strangely deserted feel, as if a bomb went off thirty years ago and no one has been able to rebuild. Some blocks, once home to dozens of houses and other buildings, now stand virtually empty, with only two or three houses remaining. Other blocks, in what should be the heart of the city, have run-down, dingy buildings. Steubenville does not look like the kind of place where Catholic higher education would thrive. In fact, it does not look like a place where much of anything would thrive.

Nevertheless, Steubenville has become a center of Catholic renewal because of the Franciscan University of Steubenville. Founded for a few dozen local students as the College of Steubenville in 1946, it reached university status in 1980 and was renamed Franciscan University of Steubenville in 1986. It had about 2500 undergraduates and 800 graduate students in 2020.[6] Unlike the vast majority of Catholic schools in the United States, the campus is intentionally Catholic, at every level. Seventy percent of students attend Mass at least twice a week and almost 60 percent attend daily Mass.[7] Its faculty is full of committed Catholics. Its administration accepts and embraces *Ex corde ecclesiae*. Its students not only keep their faith but grow and mature during their years on campus. Although modest in numbers and endowment and virtually unknown outside of Catholic circles, the university plays an outsized role in American Catholic life. Cardinal Francis Stafford, former archbishop of Denver, has said of Franciscan, "I am absolutely convinced, both in my experiences as archbishop of Denver and my experience as the president of the Pontifical Council of the Laity,

---

6. Office of Institutional Research, Franciscan University of Steubenville Fact Book, 2020–2021, https://en.calameo.com/read/000056854fbfbac1a8056?page=53.

7. Scott Hahn, "The New Evangelization and Franciscan University," 16 October 2013, https://www.youtube.com/watch?v=wUv1p46P3rs.

that this university has been central to the reform and the renewal of the Catholic Church after the Second Vatican Council."[8]

The university's impact is most evident in its graduates. For instance, Hanael Bianchi, who attended Franciscan in the late 1990s, always impressed his wife, who did not attend Franciscan, with all the fellow Franciscan alumni he knew whenever he attended a Catholic conference or lecture, including the more famous ones listed below and many others. He was friends with Michael Gaitley, who is now a member of the Congregation of Marian Fathers of the Immaculate Conception, the author of *33 Days to Morning Glory* and several other books, and a popular speaker on Marian themes. At Franciscan, Bianchi also met Steve Skojec, whose writing has appeared in *Crisis* magazine and in secular venues such as the *Washington Post* and who runs a traditionalist website called *OnePeter-Five*. Another friend in Steubenville was Jason Evert, author of ten books—including *How to Find Your Soulmate without Losing Your Soul* and *Theology of the Body for Teens*—and a popular speaker on chastity and relationships. During his years in college Bianchi also got to know Jeff Kirby, now a priest, conference speaker on bioethics, and author of eight books, Bob Lesnefsky, now a hip hop artist and the president of Dirty Vagabond urban ministry, Bryan Mercier, now a retreat leader, Will Bloomfield, founder of Bloomfield Books and publisher of the Sacred Art Series of devotional materials, Matthew Leonard, now an author and commentator, and Matthew Miller, director of the award-winning documentary film, *Poverty, Inc.*[9]

Bianchi's experience was not a fluke. Since the 1970s, Steubenville has been producing a vigorous flow of graduates who have played an outsized role in the Catholic Church and in the cultural world more generally. In addition to those mentioned above, alumni involved in culture and politics include the following: Patrick Cof-

---

8. "Why Franciscan?", Franciscan University of Steubenville, http://www.franciscan.edu/Admissions/WhyFranciscan/#sthash.y5VDRQnI.dpuf.

9. Hanael Bianchi, "Franciscan University: Fertile Soil for the Faith," *Catholic Review,* February 2016, https://www.archbalt.org/franciscan-university-fertile-soil-for-the-faith/.

fin, author and former host of the Catholic Answers radio show; writer Zoe Romanowsky; Fox News commentator Jonathan Morris; novelist Regina Doman; U.S. Representative Jeff Fortenberry of Nebraska; Eurovision performer Aivaras Stepukonis; John Carlos de los Reyes, president of a political party in the Philippines; novelist, playwright, and director Emily C. A. Snyder; and Princess Alexandra and Prince Sébastien of Luxembourg.

What is most important, over 400 graduates now serve as Catholic priests, including Cardinal Cornelius Sim, Vicar Apostolic of Brunei.[10] Many lay alumni have founded Catholic ministries and apostolates. For instance, in 1995 Steve Sanborn founded Crossroads, to sponsor three pro-life pilgrimages across the country each year. Since 1996 Jeff Cavins's Great Adventure Bible Studies have brought evangelical fervor to Catholic study of Scripture. Curtis Martin launched the Fellowship of Catholic University Students, a Catholic counterpoint to Protestant-oriented campus ministries such as Campus Crusade for Christ and InterVarsity Christian Fellowship, with a conference at a local Ramada Inn in 1997.[11] Today almost 800 FOCUS missionaries minister to students on 187 college campuses and 959 FOCUS students have discerned a vocation to the priesthood or religious life.[12] Franciscan alumnus Chris Stefanick speaks to over 50,000 people every year through his Real Life Catholic ministries.

Franciscan graduates have been heavily involved in Catholic higher education, including many current and former scholars and administrators: Peter Brown, academic dean of the Catholic Distance University; Roger Nutt, associate professor of theology and Vice President for Academic Affairs at Ave Maria University; David Warner (d. 2010), former academic dean of Ave Maria College of the Americas in Nicaragua; Marie J. DiSciullo-Naples, director of the Abbot David School for Spiritual Direction; Anthony Lilles, chief academic officer of the Avila Institute; Christopher T. Baglow, direc-

---

10. Priestly Discernment Program, Franciscan University of Steubenville, http://www.franciscan.edu/pdp/.

11. Hahn, "The New Evangelization and Franciscan University."

12. Fellowship of Catholic University Students, Annual Report, 2020, 4–9.

tor of the Science and Religion Initiative at the University of Notre Dame's McGrath Institute for Church Life; Peter Murphy, former executive director of the Secretariat of Evangelization and Catechesis of the U.S. Conference of Catholic Bishops; Michael Barber, former chair of the graduate school of theology at John Paul the Great Catholic University in San Diego; Vincent DeMeo, associate professor of the New Testament at the International Theological Institute in Austria; Mary Healy, professor of Scripture at Sacred Heart Major Seminary; Tim Gray, president of the Augustine Institute in Colorado; Jim Beckman, executive director of Evangelization and Catechesis for the Archdiocese of Oklahoma City; Edward Sri, professor of theology at the Augustine Institute; Nathanael E. Schmiedicke, professor at Our Lady of Guadalupe Seminary; Mark J. Zia, professor of theology and director of Academic Enrichment Programs at Benedictine College. Franciscan graduates who have come back to teach at their alma mater, almost always after earning a doctorate, include the following: Donald Asci, professor of theology; Ron Bolster, assistant professor of theology and director of the catechetics program; Andrew Minto, professor of theology; Daniel Pattee, TOR, associate professor of theology and director of mission and Franciscan charism; James Pauley, professor of theology; Bob Rice, professor of theology; Amy Roberts, instructor of theology; Michael Sirilla, director of the graduate theology program and professor of systematic theology; Scott Sollom, assistant professor of theology.

Franciscan's influence also spreads through its conferences, which hosted approximately 54,000 teens at twenty-three events in 2016, including five conferences on campus and eighteen regional conferences across North America, in cities such as Halifax, Nova Scotia; Houma, Louisiana; Lowell, Massachusetts; San Diego; and Tucson. Its four-day catechetical conference attracted about 450 catechists and other religious educators from the United States, Canada, Ireland, Nigeria, Nicaragua, and Lebanon. The university also sponsors young adult conferences on campus and in Houston, Milwaukee, and Atlanta, a charismatic conference for 700 participants from thirty-three states, a conference for 192 priests, deacons, and seminarians, an applied biblical studies conference, and an apologetics conference.[13] The impact of these conferences is illustrated by the fact that 11 percent of priests ordained in the United States in 2013 and 11 percent of women entering religious orders in 2012 had attended a Steubenville conference before entering seminary or religious life.[14]

Founding and Renewal

When the Diocese of Steubenville was formed out of thirteen Appalachian counties on the eastern edge of the Diocese of Columbus in 1945, it had only one Catholic institution other than its churches and schools, a small hospital. One year later, the new bishop, John King Mussio, invited the Third Order Regular Franciscans (TOR), a religious order that already ran Saint Francis College in Pennsylvania, to start a college. After a decade and a half in makeshift buildings in downtown Steubenville, the College of Steubenville, as it was then called, moved to a new forty-acre campus on top of the cliffs on the north side of town. The 1960s were a decade of growth for the college, as it opened new buildings and grew to a size of over 1100 students. However, new and less expensive state colleges in the area, the precipitous decline of the local steel industry, and the cultural ferment of the era led to a sharp drop in both numbers of students and the Catholic character of the institution during the early 1970s.[15]

The trend toward secularization evident in many Catholic colleges after the Second Vatican Council hit Steubenville particularly hard. The opening Mass in fall 1973, with only six students and eight professors in attendance, exemplified the spiritual and demographic trajectory of the college. Fewer students were attending the college and those who were attending demonstrated little interest in the Catholic faith. Two of the college's dormitories were empty and one was for sale. Because the college was mentioned in the national press as likely to shut its doors in the next year, professors were

13. Steubenville Conferences, http://steubenvilleconferences.com/.
14. Scott Hahn, "The New Evangelization and Franciscan University," 16 October 2013, https://www.youtube.com/watch?v=wUv1p46P3rs.
15. "Our History," Franciscan University of Steubenville, www.franciscan.edu.

starting to leave for greener pastures.[16] When the college president, Kevin Keelan, TOR, had to resign due to ill health, it was clear that the college was at a crossroads. The sense was that something drastic had to be done or the college would have to close. The new president would certainly have his work cut out for him.

Eight TOR friars were interviewed for a job that few of them wanted. When Michael Scanlan, TOR, was invited to become the new president, he was, in fact, noticeably depressed and unconvinced that he should take the position. Soon afterward, however, at a conference at Notre Dame during the summer of 1974, he felt that God had put Steubenville in his heart and he told his provincial that he was ready to commit himself to the job.[17]

Scanlan's academic pedigree was one of the strongest in his order—he was a graduate of elite Williams College and Harvard Law School and a former Air Force judge advocate—but it was one of his other associations that shaped his early years at Steubenville. Scanlan, who had served as the academic dean at Steubenville in the late 1960s and then the rector of the TOR seminary, was one of the leaders of the Catholic Charismatic renewal, a movement that emphasized the gifts of the Holy Spirit, especially "baptism in the Holy Spirit," speaking in tongues, healing, and prophecy. After the birth of the modern Protestant Pentecostal movement at Azusa Street in Los Angeles in 1906, Pentecostal phenomena had spread across the globe, spawning new denominations such as the Assemblies of God in the United States and Brasil Para Cristo in Brazil because existing Protestant denominations were reluctant to accept the legitimacy of the new phenomena. In the 1950s and 1960s, some mainline Protestants, such as Episcopalians and Methodists, began to experience the same phenomena, but managed to stay inside their denominations in so-called "charismatic" renewal movements. Charismatic Episcopalians, for example, had their own networks of prayer meetings, conferences, and healing services, but remained

---

16. Tim Drake, "The Man Who Rebuilt Steubenville," *National Catholic Register*, 31 May 2011, www.ncregister.com.

17. David Tickerhoof, "Fr. David Tickerhoof, TOR: Household Life Mass," 16 September 2015, *Youtube*, https://www.youtube.com/watch?v=xDo1EtgWssk.

part of the Episcopal Church. To the surprise of many, in 1967 a group of Catholic students from Duquesne University in Pennsylvania began speaking in tongues at a retreat. The charismatic experience soon reached other Catholics and by 1974 the University of Notre Dame was a hosting a Catholic Charismatic conference for 30,000 people. The movement spread around the world rapidly, with significant support from priests and religious in the United States and from Belgian Cardinal Léon-Joseph Suenens, one of the leading figures at the Second Vatican Council. Although controversial and scorned by many bishops, the movement offered some real benefits for Scanlan and Steubenville. First, it was a movement with little institutional support that was looking for an institutional home, while Steubenville desperately needed a new constituency.

Second, the Charismatic movement was vibrant and full of young people fully committed to their faith, while the college's spiritual life was at low ebb. Charismatics could fill not only the chairs in the classrooms but the pews in the chapel. They could add a sense of vitality and excitement to everyday life. As Scanlan explained, "The difference the Spirit makes is the difference between will-power Christianity and Christianity lived in the Spirit. The Holy Spirit empowers. . . . He equips us with gifts and abilities that are not our own."[18] If any Catholic college needed divine intervention, it was Steubenville in the mid-1970s.

Third, Charismatic Catholics were not highly traditional and Steubenville did not have much in the way of beauty and tradition that could attract other groups of committed Catholics from outside of the immediate area. The emotional worship style of charismatics, featuring contemporary music, electronic amplification, and popular instruments like the guitar, had no special resonance with Gothic architecture or hallowed academic halls. In fact, it was almost *more* at home in a gymnasium or a stadium. The movement and the college were in many ways a perfect match. Scanlan began a series of summer Charismatic Catholic conferences at Steubenville, thus introducing young committed Charismatics to the college and,

18. Michael Scanlan with James Manney, *Let the Fire Fall* (Ann Arbor: Servant, 1986), 85.

even for those who were unable to attend, associating Steubenville with the Charismatic renewal.

Scanlan realized that the college needed a spiritual transformation, not just a few cosmetic improvements. The way he went about seeking that transformation did include marketing the college to Charismatics and other faithful Catholics, but spiritual fatherhood was more important than any marketing plan. At the most fundamental level, Scanlan acted as a spiritual father to the students and staff of the college. The transformation that he fostered was primarily familial, not structural. Working with the Holy Spirit, he invited the students and staff of the college to renew their filial relationship with God the Father and their fraternal relationships with each other as brothers and sisters in Christ. On his part, Father Scanlan reshaped the college presidency in the image of fatherhood and deemphasized its administrative and institutional nature. This is not to say that he failed to perform the administrative duties proper to his position—by all accounts he was an effective administrator—but that his approach to the presidency was not *primarily* administrative. Just as any father who thought his primary role was to pay bills or make budgets would be missing the heart of fatherhood, Scanlan realized that his role had to be personal and relational first, and that his administrative tasks, although important, were secondary to and in service of his fatherly role.

One way that Scanlan emphasized the personal and relational was by spending three or four hours each morning in prayer before going to his office.[19] This prayer led Scanlan into a relationship of great intimacy with the Trinity:

> We see the Father as Jesus saw him, as his loving, caring, 'Abba'—an Aramaic word Jesus used when he prayed that means something like 'Dear Father.' We come to know Jesus as our brother. We come to know the Spirit as the strengthening, consoling, guiding, dynamic force that we can trust to direct everything in our lives.[20]

19. Drake, "The Man Who Rebuilt Steubenville."
20. Scanlan, *Let the Fire Fall*, 87.

Scanlan also spent much of his prayer time interceding for the college and its students. We cannot know the *results* of prayer with any surety, but we do know that a father prays for his children. He cannot help himself. He loves his children and he prays for them. Devotion to prayer led Scanlan into divine intimacy and modeled the sort of loving fatherhood that the college's students so desperately needed.

Another way that Scanlan emphasized the personal and relational was by embracing his own role as a Franciscan friar and a devoted son of Pope John Paul II. Providentially, before the ferment of the 1960s and 1970s, Scanlan had chosen one of the religious orders that avoided the worst pitfalls of the "spirit of Vatican II."[21] Unlike many orders, the Third Order Franciscans maintained their orthodoxy and continued to take seriously their vows of poverty, chastity, and obedience. Scanlan, therefore, was not simply a leader who told other people what to do, but also a friar living in obedience to his superiors and in community with his brothers. His very position as president was, as related above, a result of his obedience to his superiors and to God. He also realized, once John Paul II became pope in 1978, that the pope's vision for the Church applied directly to Steubenville. Catholics call the pope the "holy father" and Scanlan indeed found in John Paul II a paternal figure who was encouraging toward the Charismatic movement and whose program for the universal Church, known as the "New Evangelization," Scanlan tried to implement.[22]

Another way that Scanlan emphasized the personal and relational was by going out of his way to get to know the students, seeking them out wherever they could be found. "My first year as president I attended every group function on campus, every dance, sport event, every club, and I immersed myself in the classroom environment. I even ate in the cafeteria with the students. I kept an open door and

---

21. By "spirit of Vatican II" I mean the false interpretations of the council that ignore the actual words of conciliar documents, especially tendentious interpretations that assert that the council abolished authority and hierarchy.

22. Drake, "The Man Who Rebuilt Steubenville."

saw students whenever they dropped by," said Scanlan.[23] This approach to the presidency might sound unremarkable but it is quite rare, possibly unique. Almost all American college presidents feel the pressure to be productive, which is usually defined as doing something in an office, alone or with a small group of administrators, behind closed doors. Even the best of them, those who walk the campus and stroll the halls and make clear that they sincerely care about students, do not feel that they have the time to go to every performance and every game or to "immerse" themselves in classes. But Scanlan knew that a father lives with his children and watches over them.

From these extensive interactions Father Scanlan diagnosed a pervasive issue among his students: "I observed the students and how sad and lonely they were and how they were looking in all the wrong places for companionship." They were like sheep without a shepherd, like orphans who did not have to be orphans. After coming to believe that "the loneliest person on earth is a college freshman away from home for the first time," he began programs "to combat this loneliness and the destructive patterns it caused."[24] In this way, Scanlan was like a father who knows his children and grieves when they are suffering.

One of Scanlan's solutions to the pervasive loneliness was the creation of Faith Households. On 16 December 1974, he sent out a memo saying, "The college has adopted a policy of household as the basic principle of residential living."[25] The new system would start in the next semester and would be fully implemented by December 1975. He abolished fraternities and sororities, which were exacerbating loneliness by encouraging drunkenness and immorality, and substituted these households, in which members signed a covenant, dedicated themselves to the faith and to each other, prayed together,

23. "The Complete Q&A with Father Michael Scanlan," *Advance Magazine*, Fall 2011, http://www.cccu.org/news/advance/fall-2011/complete-qa-with-father-michael-scanlan.

24. Ibid.

25. Gregory Plow, "Fr. Gregory Plow, TOR: Homily at 40th Anniversary of Households Mass," 17 December 2014, Youtube, https://www.youtube.com/watch?v=6MGY_glfS00.

and did various forms of service. His goal was that students could experience "the good and the blessings of fraternity life," but in a way that was rooted in "faith and moral living, so students could avoid the pitfalls."[26] These new groups were not simply organizations or clubs but "households" that would become veritable families and homes away from home for their members. The new, positive peer pressure of the households helped students seek Christ and stay committed to each other.

Although the households were required for all students for three years, they were soon made optional. In the early days, Scanlan felt that he had to take drastic measures, both to break negative habits and to inculcate positive habits in the students. Today, the now voluntary communities are thriving, with about two thirds of students participating in fifty different men's and women's households, such as "Daughters of Divine Mercy" and "Living Stones," each with a different emphasis or orientation.[27] For instance, a female household called "Crown of Creation" attempts to live out the teaching of Pope John Paul II on sexuality and morality: "We aim to live out the Theology of the Body by recognizing that we are created in the image and likeness of God for interpersonal communion and are called to use our God-given dignity to be spiritual mothers."[28] The men of Koinonia, composed of students who might have a vocation to the priesthood or the religious life, "live together in brotherhood and engage in a program of spiritual formation to better discern their vocation."[29] In this way, the different households meet the different spiritual needs of different groups of students.

The households all do some form of community service. The "Fishers of Men," for instance, pray for the employees and visitors at a strip club in nearby Weirton, West Virginia. Other households vol-

26. Drake, "The Man Who Rebuilt Steubenville."
27. Emily Stimpson, "A Remedy for the Lonely and Lost: Franciscan University's Households Celebrate 40 Years," *National Catholic Register*, 30 January 2016, https://www.ncregister.com/features/a-remedy-for-the-lonely-and-lost.
28. "Women's Households," Franciscan University of Steubenville, https://households.franciscan.edu/household-list/.
29. "Men's Households," Franciscan University of Steubenville, https://households.franciscan.edu/household-list/.

unteer at nursing homes and schools. This sort of activity builds relationships and strengthens the faith of many students, Father Gregory Plow, current director of the household program, explains: "When freshmen meet upperclassmen who are excited about their faith, it has a totally different effect. They own it more. The same holds true for the upperclassmen doing the evangelizing: 'He who teaches learns twice.'"[30] In other words, the younger students are encouraged by the example of the older ones, and the older ones deepen their faith and their commitment by teaching the younger ones.

As Father David Tickerhoof, TOR, says, the households foster the "Three Cs": conversation, communication, and communion, with God, with themselves, and with their brothers and sisters. The experience of fellowship and communion with each other and God matures the household and helps them grow into missionary disciples who, by the time they graduate, are ready to share the gospel wherever they end up.[31] In one case, "The Brothers of the Eternal Song" built a house and raised money for the family of one of their alumni members who had died at thirty-four, leaving his wife and children in a difficult situation. Father Plow believes that such incidents demonstrate that the household has surpassed Scanlan's vision for them: "It gives lifelong friends, bridesmaids or groomsmen, godfathers and godmothers to your children, a whole safety net, so if something unforeseen happens, we know our family will be taken care of. It allows you to experience a brotherhood and sisterhood on this side of our last breath that foretells of what's to come."[32]

Focusing on the Mission

Scanlan knew that there was a strong trend in American Catholic higher education toward administrative expansion and doctrinal dilution, but he was convinced that God had given Franciscan a specific mission: "loyalty to Jesus as the Way, the Truth, and the Life."

---

30. Stimpson, "A Remedy for the Lonely and Lost."
31. Tickerhoof, "Household Life Mass."
32. Stimpson, "A Remedy for the Lonely and Lost."

Rather than following the conventional wisdom, he shared his vision of Franciscan's distinctive mission with students, faculty, and staff at every opportunity throughout his twenty-four years as president and eleven as chancellor. "At the bleakest times it was the mission of the school that sustained me," Scanlan said. "If our mission is founded in the Lord, then He will give us insights on what to do and He will give us insights on what's distinctive about our mission."[33]

Institutions of higher learning have the blessing and the curse of being full of professors, who are at once good at argument, independent, and traditional, in the sense of resisting change. These qualities have their advantages—it is no accident that the university, unlike most other medieval institutions, has survived for more than eight centuries—but they can pose a real obstacle to charismatic and prophetic leaders seeking to make needed changes. Modern universities also have the blessing and curse of being full of administrators. At their best, administrators facilitate conditions under which teaching and learning can thrive, but at their worst they perpetuate the lie that a properly engineered system can make education occur. The administrative university inevitably tends to avoid the unplanned, the spontaneous, and the personal; a leaner, more personal institution allows space for the serendipity of friendship, love, and invention.

Where most Catholic colleges were succumbing to the pressure to become more like secular institutions and to hide or soften their doctrinal and spiritual distinctiveness to attract students, Scanlan took the opposite approach: "You don't need to always join the pack. Don't panic and simply become like everybody else. I would rather emphasize that you take a fresh approach and fresh proclamation of the mission."[34] College administrators, who played the numbers game, trying to appeal to the broadest possible spectrum of students, actually ran the risk of hobbling or even destroying the Catholic nature of a college. It was simply wishful thinking to believe that a college full of students with no special interest in

---

33. "The Complete Q&A with Father Michael Scanlan."
34. Ibid.

Catholicism being taught by faculty with no special commitment to Catholicism would somehow come to appreciate the Catholic intellectual tradition, just as it was wishful thinking to believe that they would emerge as paragons of virtue and Catholic devotion after spending four years in fraternities and sororities indistinguishable from those at secular schools.

Instead of diluting the college's Catholicism, Scanlan chose to emphasize it. "Find ways to stir up the mission. It constantly needs to be renewed, through student life activities, through academic convocations, through special studies in the classroom, through chapel. In each aspect of university life, find a way to breathe new life into the mission of the school. Make the mission fresh each and every year," he said.[35] The households, mentioned above, were one way to do this. Another was to make academics distinctively Catholic. Again, this might sound obvious or routine, but it is not. After Vatican II many Catholic colleges and universities slowly reduced the number of required theology and philosophy courses and almost all of them hired more and more non-Catholic faculty members. Scanlan took the opposite course by requiring *more* theology courses, putting theology at the heart of the curriculum, and emphasizing Catholic commitment in hiring decisions.

The households are an official program of the university, but the emphasis on the family of faith was not merely programmatic. For example, Scott Hahn found in Father Scanlan a spiritual father, even as he and his wife Kimberley filled a similar role for many Franciscan students. Hahn, having experienced the close personal fellowship and discipleship that often characterizes evangelical Protestant communities, had been frustrated during his early years as a Catholic by priests who showed little interest in going beyond a formal relationship. He would set up appointments with them, but they had no desire to do more than answer his questions. The idea of spiritual fatherhood, encompassing not just the formal educational role of teacher and student but also the affectionate mentoring of father and son, as the Apostle Paul did for the Corinthians

35. Ibid.

(1 Cor. 4:14–15), was not even on their radar screens.[36] This is highly ironic, of course, given the Catholic custom of calling priests "father."

It was a great joy for Hahn, therefore, when he found that Father Scanlan understood and embraced the role of spiritual father. Franciscan became for Hahn not just an educational institution where he worked, but even more a spiritual home where he grew in the love of his Heavenly Father, with the help and support of an earthly father. Hahn and his wife Kimberley turned around and did something similar for Franciscan's students: they have welcomed one or two graduate students every year to live with them. These men, including Curtis Martin, Tim Gray, Edward Sri, and Cajetan Cuddy, have often gone on to distinguished careers as theologians, priests, and other leaders in the Church, and it is hard to believe that Hahn's spiritual, intellectual, and moral mentorship did not have a large role in their flourishing as men of God.[37]

What Scanlan and Hahn both understood was that education is not the same as schooling. Many well-intentioned people, including many Catholics who should know better, see education as a sort of conveyor belt: students jump on at the beginning and jump off at the end, now "educated" through a system of lectures, tests, projects, and papers. Of course, everyone realizes that many college graduates actually know very little, and are in fact less knowledgeable when they leave than when they arrive. Honest observers, when they look at their own lives, probably realize that knowledge and learning are deeply *personal*, not in the sense of subjective or relativistic, but in the sense that only persons can learn, and in the sense that persons learn best from other persons. Any approach that elevates the system over the person misses education's essence. Steubenville, probably more than any other Catholic school in America, understands and embraces the paternal, maternal, and familial aspects of education, and therefore raises up men and women who are not only more knowledgeable than the average Catholic college gradu-

---

36. Scott Hahn, interview, 11 July 2016, Steubenville, Ohio.
37. Ibid.

ate (because persons learn best when treated personally), but are also more well-rounded and spiritually mature (because their education takes place in the context of human relationships). Franciscan is also probably the only college in the United States that defines its president in its bylaws not primarily as an administrator but as the university's "spiritual leader."[38] As Hahn emphasizes in his own writing, the Kingdom of God is characterized by kinship and covenant, not by contract.[39] At Steubenville, students experience spiritual kinship and therefore thrive academically. Meanwhile, many other Catholic institutions attempt to sell education as if it were a commodity and are dismayed to find their "customers" uncommitted to the faith.

Another way that Scanlan "stirred up the mission" was by emphasizing and reforming the discipline of theology. When he assumed the presidency, the theology curriculum was in bad shape. Not only did the school lack a theology major, but it also had a theology professor who was not Catholic. To rectify this situation, Scanlan developed a theology major and a theology master's program. Then he recruited professors of unquestionable orthodoxy to be the core of the new department.[40] Alan Schreck, for example, arrived in 1978 and later served as director of the graduate program and chair of the department. Regis Martin arrived in 1988 and prominent convert Scott Hahn in 1990. Enrollment in the Theology program grew from about twenty students in 1978 to about 450 undergraduate students (more than the University of Notre Dame) in 2009, with about one hundred graduate students. In 2015 the university had twenty-three theology professors in its faculty of 120 full time professors. The university also now has a discernment program for men who might be called to the priesthood and a Franciscan house where young men can begin to practice the prayer and

---

38. "The Mission of Franciscan University of Steubenville," http://www.franciscan.edu/about/mission-statement/#sthash.SoEDbuYO.dpuf.

39. Scott Hahn, *Covenant and Communion: The Biblical Theology of Pope Benedict XVI* (Grand Rapids, Michigan: Brazos, 2009).

40. Drake, "The Man Who Rebuilt Steubenville."

spirituality of the Third Order Regulars.[41] In other words, an institution that once offered only the rudiments of theology and little in the way of vocational advisement now boasts a vibrant theology program and serious discernment opportunities. More than that, theology has become the academic heart of the university.

It was not enough, however, to have a strong theology department. All the disciplines needed to be infused with the mind of Christ. Just as Scanlan devoted himself to meeting and getting to know his students, he committed himself to personal participation in selecting professors and administrators. "You also absolutely have to hire good leaders; they've got to share in the mission and the excitement of it; they can't just look good on paper," he believed. "I made it part of my job, no matter how busy I was, to personally interview every new faculty member and many administrative and support staff positions. This was to insure we were hiring people committed to the mission."[42] He needed to be sure that the teachers in his students' classrooms were serious about the faith and the college's mission.

The issue of recruiting and hiring cannot be emphasized enough because many Catholic institutions are in denial about the impact of hiring non-Catholics and nominal Catholics, as if a school full of professors and administrators who ignore or reject the institutional mission can still be faithful to that mission. If there ever was any doubt about that proposition, there is no doubt now. The schools that hired predominantly secular liberals after the Second Vatican Council have become more and more secularized. Their students are often *less* Catholic when they graduate than when they enter.

Scanlan did not stop at hiring. He reminded the college's professors and other leaders of their mission and purpose every year because he knew that vision can fade and that it needs to be revived and refocused continually. Not all the professors appreciated the new emphasis on mission. In the early days, a group of young pro-

---

41. Cardinal Newman Society, "Franciscan University of Steubenville," *The Newman Guide to Choosing a Catholic College,* 2016/2017, https://cardinalnewman-society.org/college/franciscan-university-of-steubenville/.
42. "The Complete Q&A with Father Michael Scanlan."

fessors opposed Scanlan's changes, as did some younger Franciscans. But in the end, what could they say? Even those who had their doubts had to admit that *something* needed to change. If the college had followed a policy of "business as usual" it would soon have closed its doors.[43] In this way, Steubenville's impending doom actually gave Scanlan the kind of latitude for innovation and renewal that most college presidents only dream about. Throughout the 1980s and 1990s, he and a growing number of partners built the Franciscan University of Steubenville into a vibrant and orthodox university.

New Evangelization

In the years since Scanlan's 2000 retirement the concept of "the New Evangelization" has guided the university. Scanlan himself had seen John Paul's call to the New Evangelization as a sort of roadmap, and his successors, Terence Henry, TOR, Sean Sheriden, TOR, and Dave Pivonka, TOR, continued along the same path. In 1983 John Paul, speaking to the Latin American bishops, after noting the many Catholics who were losing their faith, succumbing to ignorance, superstition, and syncretism, and joining other religious groups, called for "a new evangelization, new in its ardor, in its methods, and in its expression." The keys to this new evangelization, he said, were "numerous and well-prepared priests," a growing number of trained lay Catholics, and a recovery of "the integrity of the message of Puebla, without warped interpretations, without distorting simplifications or faulty applications of some parts and the disregard of others."[44]

That last point about the message of Puebla needs some explanation. In 1979 Latin American bishops met in Puebla, Mexico, in what was seen by many observers as a showdown between the supporters of liberation theology and more conservative and traditionalist forces. A previous meeting of the Latin American bishops in

---

43. Drake, "The Man Who Rebuilt Steubenville."

44. John Paul II, "Discurso del Santo Padre Juan Pablo II a la asamblea del CELAM," 9 March 1983, www.vatican.va.

Medellín, Colombia, in 1968 had emphasized justice and the Church's deep commitment to the poor. In the 1970s, theologians such as Gustavo Gutiérrez and Leonardo Boff went beyond the strong but measured words of Medellín in their development of the new "liberation theology," which, at least in its early years, adopted the perspective of class conflict and asserted that the Church had to choose sides between the rich oppressors and the exploited poor. With the support of many bishops, including Helder Camara of Brazil and Samuel Ruíz of Mexico, liberation theology for a time seemed destined to become the dominant theology of Latin America. However, a conservative response led by Colombian bishop Alfonso López Trujillo, who was elected secretary general of the regional bishops organization in 1972, coupled with the election of the anti-communist John Paul II as pope in 1978, put the brakes on the liberationist project. With López Trujillo in control of the Puebla meeting and John Paul in attendance, the "message of Puebla" reaffirmed the fight for justice and "the preferential option for the poor" but placed them firmly in the context of evangelization, which also involved proclamation, catechesis, and conversion.[45]

What this means is that the New Evangelization was an initiative designed specifically for cultures in turmoil where traditional Catholicism was being buffeted from all sides, by other religious groups, by secularization and popular culture, and by distorted interpretations of Catholicism itself. Unprepared for the riot of options for many reasons, including a priest shortage, poor or non-existent catechesis, and the decay of Catholic culture, Catholics were vulnerable to all sorts of bad ideas. Soon John Paul II extended the New Evangelization beyond Latin America and made it one of the centerpieces of his papacy. As in Latin America, Catholics in Europe and North America desperately needed to be revived, reawakened, and restored through a new proclamation of the gospel.

In one of John Paul's most important writings, *Novo millennio ineunte*, he expressed his vision of the New Evangelization this way:

---

45. Todd Hartch, *The Rebirth of Latin American Christianity* (New York: Oxford University Press, 2014), 67–70.

To nourish ourselves with the word in order to be "servants of the word" in the work of evangelization: this is surely a priority for the Church at the dawn of the new millennium. Even in countries evangelized many centuries ago, the reality of a "Christian society" which, amid all the frailties which have always marked human life, measured itself explicitly on Gospel values, is now gone. Today we must courageously face a situation which is becoming increasingly diversified and demanding, in the context of "globalization" and of the consequent new and uncertain mingling of peoples and cultures. Over the years, I have often repeated the summons to the new evangelization. I do so again now, especially in order to insist that we must rekindle in ourselves the impetus of the beginnings and allow ourselves to be filled with the ardour of the apostolic preaching which followed Pentecost. We must revive in ourselves the burning conviction of Paul, who cried out: "Woe to me if I do not preach the Gospel" (1 Cor 9:16).

This mission applied to all Catholics, and could not be "left to a group of specialists." The task of presenting Christ to "all people," including "adults, families, young people, children" of every nation and culture was simply too large for anyone to remain idle. Still, John Paul thought that young people had a special role to play. Special attention to them would yield a "generous availability" and "a rich return" of passion and commitment.[46]

For John Paul II the New Evangelization of necessity involved the intellectual content of the faith. Unlike some liberationists and others who seemed to believe that "praxis" (action) should somehow replace or overshadow doctrine in the modern age, the pope emphasized the importance of teaching the great truths of the faith, which he saw as inextricably tied to action. Citing Christ's command to make disciples and to teach them all that he had commanded, his predecessor Paul VI's emphasis on catechesis as an

---

46. John Paul II, *Novo millennio ineunte*, 6 January 2001, https://w2.vatican.va/content/john-paul-ii/en/apost_letters/2001/documents/hf_jp-ii_apl_20010106_novo-millennio-ineunte.html.

integral part of evangelization, and the continuous practice of the Church through the ages, John Paul closely connected evangelization and the teaching of the faith. He therefore called for a renewal of catechesis that aimed "to reveal in the Person of Christ the whole of God's eternal design reaching fulfillment in that Person" and helped Catholics "to understand the meaning of Christ's actions and words and of the signs worked by Him." The ultimate goal was "to put people not only in touch but in communion, in intimacy, with Jesus Christ."[47] The 1992 publication of the *Catechism of the Catholic Church*, the most important catechism (collection of teachings of the Church) since the Catechism of the Council of Trent (the "Roman Catechism"), which was part of the Church's response to the Protestant Reformation in the sixteenth century, showed again the importance John Paul attached to doctrine.[48] In his address on the occasion of the promulgation of the *Catechism*, John Paul made the connection between evangelization and catechesis clear, calling the *Catechism* a great help to bishops "in fulfilling the mission they have received from Christ to proclaim and witness the Good News to all people."[49]

This short introduction to the New Evangelization should make clear that it has real congruence with the mission of a Catholic University. If the New Evangelization involves new ardor, new methods, and new expression, it is hard to imagine a group more capable of embracing and adopting its very newness than college-age Catholics. If the New Evangelization must embrace the message of Puebla and the social teaching of the Church while avoiding distortions, it is hard to imagine an institution more suited to discerning the heart of the message and exposing distortions than one composed of serious Catholic scholars. Finally, if evangelization and catechesis are inextricably intertwined, it is hard to imagine an institution more

---

47. John Paul II, *Catechesi tradendae*, 1979, www.vatican.va.

48. *Catechism of the Catholic Church*, 1992, http://www.vatican.va/archive/EN G0015/_INDEX.HTM.

49. John Paul II, "New Catechism: Gift to the Church," 7 December 1992, https://www.ewtn.com/catholicism/library/new-catechism-gift-to-the-church-8336.

suited to participating in the New Evangelization than one that emphasizes catechesis, in the sense of both teaching doctrine and teaching the future teachers of doctrine. In short, although there are many ways of participating in the initiative, a Catholic university has great potential to embrace the New Evangelization because of its population of young Catholics, its gifts of theological and philosophical discernment, and its catechetical orientation. In fact, it is difficult to imagine an institution more suited to the New Evangelization than a Catholic university: it evangelizes its students and then they evangelize the world; it contemplates the Word and then teaches the world; it ponders all things inside its walls and then magnifies the Lord outside of them.

Unfortunately, even fewer universities have embraced the New Evangelization than have submitted themselves to *Ex corde ecclesiae*. This is partially because, while *Ex corde* clearly focused on the Catholic University, John Paul's call for a New Evangelization was a wider and more diffuse initiative. Since the New Evangelization theoretically applied to all Catholics everywhere and was not a special program for higher education, it was easier to affirm on a superficial level but, in some ways, harder to see as especially suited to Catholic universities. Schools like Christendom College in Virginia and Thomas Aquinas College in California, for instance, have committed themselves fully to *Ex corde ecclesiae*, but they are not in an obvious or vocal way colleges of the New Evangelization. In fairness to them, canon law *requires* submission to specific regulations in *Ex corde ecclesiae*, while the New Evangelization is more of a call and a challenge.

Still, Franciscan University of Steubenville has benefitted itself and the world through its hearty embrace of the New Evangelization. First under President Scanlan and then under his successors, the university has been one of the few to see the deep congruence between the mission of a Catholic university and the call of the New Evangelization. The presidents, administrators, and faculty of Franciscan, as good students of *Ex corde ecclesiae*, see that that document does call for evangelization and is, in fact, an integral part of the New Evangelization, as its section 49 explains:

By its very nature, each Catholic University makes an important contribution to the Church's work of evangelization. It is a living institutional witness to Christ and his message, so vitally important in cultures marked by secularism, or where Christ and his message are still virtually unknown. Moreover, all the basic academic activities of a Catholic University are connected with and in harmony with the evangelizing mission of the Church: research carried out in the light of the Christian message which puts new human discoveries at the service of individuals and society; education offered in a faith-context that forms men and women capable of rational and critical judgment and conscious of the transcendent dignity of the human person; professional training that incorporates ethical values and a sense of service to individuals and to society; the dialogue with culture that makes the faith better understood, and the theological research that translates the faith into contemporary language.[50]

Already this chapter has explained the role of households and professors characterized by orthodoxy and passion. Both the households, where personal formation takes place, and the classroom, where committed Catholic teachers explain the faith and apply it to the world, clearly harmonize with the New Evangelization. So do the many graduates, listed at the beginning of the chapter, who have gone out from Franciscan to serve as priests and religious, to teach in schools and colleges, to found new ministries, and to serve the Church and the world in a myriad of ways. Well taught and well formed, they go out to bring Christ's light to others.

But Franciscan's living out of the New Evangelization is not just a fortuitous result of its other values. It is intentional. Father Scanlan saw in the New Evangelization a helpful path for his university. Professor Scott Hahn has made the New Evangelization an emphasis in his thinking and writing, most notably in his book *Evangelizing Catholics: A Mission Manual for the New Evangelization* and in his television series "The New Evangelization" on EWTN, but also on radio, in the classroom, and in lectures that he has given at Steuben-

---

50. John Paul II, *Ex corde ecclesiae* 49.

ville and around the country.[51] The university has hosted conferences such as the 2012 "Apologetics & New Evangelization" conference and the "Symposium on Catholic Higher Education and the
New Evangelization" in 2013. A 2015 "Fidelity and Freedom" conference featured Scott Hahn delivering a talk on "The Gospel Truth:
How the New Evangelization Fits with Catholic Higher Education."[52] The university is probably the only one in the world that has
an endowed academic chair in "Biblical Theology and the New
Evangelization." Franciscan's television show on the EWTN network, "Franciscan University Presents," often features topics related
to the New Evangelization, including a show on the role of catechetics in the New Evangelization with Professor Bob Rice and a show
on the role of Hispanic Catholics in the New Evangelization with
José H. Gomez, Archbishop of Los Angeles.[53] Special lectures on
campus have included philosopher J. Budziszewski on "Natural Law,
Conscience, and the New Evangelization." Finally, The Veritas Center for Ethics in Public Life tries to a bring a Catholic perspective
into the public square, encouraging Franciscan professors to write
for mainstream publications and sponsoring conferences, such as
"Challenging the Secular Culture: A Call to Christians" in 2015.[54]

The Humble Heart of the University

After listing so many of Franciscan's excellent qualities, it is necessary for this book on the true, the good, and the beautiful to con-

51. Scott Hahn, *Evangelizing Catholics: A Mission Manual for the New Evangelization* (Huntington, Indiana: Our Sunday Visitor, 2014). The syllabus for his 2016
class on the New Evangelization is available at http://www.scotthahn.com/newe-
vangelization/.
52. Scott Hahn, "The Gospel Truth: How the New Evangelization Fits with
Catholic Higher Education," 18 September 2015, https://www.youtube.com/wat
ch?v=-fAiuKGfYic.
53. "Bob Rice—A New Pentecost for Catechesis," Franciscan University Presents, EWTN, 5 July 2012, http://www.faithandreason.com/2012/07/a-new-pentecos
t-for-catechesis/.
54. "Challenging the Secular Culture: A Call to Christians," 11 April 2015, Franciscan University of Steubenville, https://institutes.franciscan.edu/challenging-the-
secular-culture-a-call-to-christians-2015-conference/.

clude with two important caveats. First, the university is not beautiful. Its chapel is surprisingly charmless and the campus features a great deal of pedestrian architecture. Only the Portiuncula, a replica of the small Italian church rebuilt by Saint Francis of Assisi, and a few newer buildings offer anything like the peaceful transcendence that should mark a seriously Catholic campus. Still, the university is young and there is hope that generous patrons and visionary leaders will remedy the school's most obvious deficiency in the coming decades. Second, like all successful institutions, Franciscan faces the temptation to emphasize the bureaucratic and the administrative at the expense of the truly educational. As this chapter has demonstrated, the heart of Franciscan University is personal and familial. Current plans for physical and numerical expansion and online degree programs may tempt faculty, staff, and students to see education as a system that can be regulated and administered by experts, rather than as a familial relation between persons. As Pope Benedict XVI has pointed out, "If there were structures which could irrevocably guarantee a determined and good state of the world, man's freedom would be denied, and hence they would not be good structures at all."[55] Even if the university maintains its theological orthodoxy, an impersonal "educational system" would gravely lessen the distinctiveness and value of a Franciscan education.

Finally, though, there is great cause for hope. The university has a built-in Franciscan humility that accounts for much of its success, particularly its ability to prosper while staying orthodox and vibrant. Many Catholic schools have expanded by downplaying doctrine, while many of the orthodox institutions in the *Newman Guide* have remained quite small. Franciscan humility allows the university to do what few intellectuals of any stripe are willing to do today, to give "full submission to the teaching authority of the Catholic Church." The university does this because it "understands that it proceeds only by God's mercy." It dedicates itself to prayer "so that it may be humble before the face of God and receptive to those

---

55. Benedict XVI, *Spe salvi* 24, 30 November 2007, Vatican.va.

graces and blessings it needs to serve [its] mission."[56] True humility, especially in today's world, where the temptation is to soften doctrine to appeal to a wider audience, is to submit to the Magisterium. But Franciscan knows that minimizing doctrine is actually a form of pride, thinking one knows better than God. Similarly, Franciscan knows that its greatest accomplishments are gifts from God and that no human being can take credit for them.

This humility and devotion is best seen in the university chapel, where a high percentage of students, faculty, and staff attend daily Mass, which is not required or monitored by the administration. This devotion to the Mass, supplemented by round-the-clock Eucharistic adoration, keeps students and faculty focused on Christ himself and is one of the secret sources of the thriving academic life at the university. For example, once Scott Hahn was driving Norris Clarke, S.J., a celebrated Thomist philosopher who was teaching a course at Steubenville during a sabbatical, back to the Jesuit residence in Wheeling, West Virginia. Hahn asked Clarke about his experience, and Clarke responded that, although his students at Fordham might have higher SAT scores, he found his experience teaching Franciscan students "amazing." When Hahn asked what he meant, Clarke explained that his classroom was full of philosophy students hungry to learn and that he had been wondering about the source of their academic passion. It was only after attending a noon Mass at the university chapel and seeing all of his students, along with hundreds of others, that Clarke began to understand. He came to believe that the Eucharist was at the heart of their desire to learn and ability to learn. It had, he believed, illuminated their minds.[57]

In 1205, in the Chapel of San Damiano in Italy, Christ asked Saint Francis of Assisi to rebuild his Church. At first, Francis thought that this meant the literal, stone-by-stone repair of the damaged and neglected chapel. As he pondered Christ's words, however, he came

---

56. "The Mission of Franciscan University of Steubenville," http://www.franciscan.edu/about/mission-statement/#sthash.S0EDbuYO.dpuf.

57. Scott Hahn, "The New Evangelization and Franciscan University," 16 October 2013, https://www.youtube.com/watch?v=wUv1p46P3rs; Scott Hahn, interview, 11 July 2016, Steubenville, Ohio.

to see that the rebuilding he was called to was more metaphorical. Christ wanted him to love the poor, to preach the gospel, and to restore the faith of the Body of Christ, living in joyful poverty as a sign to the world. Franciscan University has inherited its namesake's vocation. It too is called to rebuild the Church. Copies of the San Damiano Cross—the rood cross before which Francis was praying when he received his commission—are found all over the campus of Franciscan University. They are a reminder that, like Saint Francis, the university lives by grace, in humility, dependent on the gifts of God, as it rebuilds Christ's Church. That is a precarious position, but a joyful one.

6

Classical Beauty

The Notre Dame School of Architecture

O NE OF THE MOST INTERESTING, accomplished, and influential professors of architecture at the University of Notre Dame in the mid-twentieth century was Paul Jacques Grillo, who came to the University of Notre Dame in 1952 and taught architecture there until the mid-1960s. Grillo, a Frenchman who had won third place at the prestigious Grand Prix de Rome of 1937, had an extensive knowledge of classical, European, and vernacular architecture. He believed that historic buildings should be studied, but never seen "as examples to be copied." The answers to the questions of the past, however fitting they once might have been, were not the answers to the questions of the present. Instead, architects should look to nature and archetypes—"elemental solutions of design evolved from the study of nature by the generations before us"—as their main sources of ideas, copying neither nature nor archetype blindly, but being inspired by them to create new forms. "We must be of our time," he argued, "and never borrow from the languages of the past."[1]

Grillo lamented that, "in the old schools," the curriculum had consisted of "putting together elements copied from history books and re-copied from magazines." The style of the architecture learned

1. Paul Jacques Grillo, *What is Design?* (Chicago: Paul Theobald and Company, 1960), 235.

159

by this method was "fake-Greek, fake-Roman, fake-Gothic," which was then "rehashed sometimes into fake-Colonial." This method of training "put architecture in a rut where it was to stay for decades," but Grillo and his generation of architects had come to a broader and, he believed, more scientific understanding of the craft.[2] Grillo advocated a sort of elegant functionalism, which he contrasted with "stylism," the addition of unnecessary decorative elements that ruined a design. For instance, in Grillo's view the Jeep was the only American automobile that had remained "true to its purpose" and not been corrupted by attempts to be fashionable.[3] Too often, he believed, through emotional associations or the simple passage of time, the public failed to think critically about famous buildings, such as the Lincoln Memorial or the United States Capitol:

> If we wake up from our routine thinking and try to find some reason for our blind admiration, we have a hard time to reconcile the rugged pioneer personality of Abraham Lincoln with the coldness of the make-believe Greek temple, or to imagine that a cross-breed between the church of St. Paul in London and the Pantheon in Paris blown up to St. Peter's size and sprinkled with Roman splendor could seriously represent the young American republic.[4]

A dispassionate analysis would reveal that these beloved monuments were actually inappropriate for their intended purposes.

Grillo contended that "art is not achieved by addition, but by a process of subtraction that we call selection or choice" and that true beauty comes from the "sveltesse" that emerges through the perfection of function and the jettisoning of non-essential features. He believed that architecture had entered a new era because "modern science and research have freed the builder of many of the limitations formerly dictated by material." No longer constrained by traditional forms or materials, the designer's imagination had been

2. Ibid., 3.
3. Ibid., 10.
4. Ibid., 16.

"unleashed." Symmetry he dismissed as unnecessary; those who insisted upon it were guilty of "engineerism" and "mathematism" and were probably lacking the sensitivity and intuition required to produce true art. Thus, Grillo called Andrea Palladio's iconic "La Rotonda" a "monsterpiece" with no discernible purpose or internal logic. "What is it? A mausoleum? A museum? A temple for some unknown God?," he asked. Rejecting the sloped roofs and other traditional features of homes in the American Midwest, Grillo designed his own home, which consisted of "two communicating areas and two adjoining trailers," with a low profile and a flat roof to reduce wind resistance and with huge picture windows to maximize views of his back yard. His other designs included a house with a "helium-filled plastic roof profiled like an airplane wing" and another in the cave-like overhang of an enormous man-made "pyramid of loose lava."[5]

In 1989 Notre Dame hired Thomas Gordon Smith as the new director of its architecture program, knowing full well that he was in many ways the antithesis of Paul Jacques Grillo. Smith had just published a book in which he called for "the revival of classical architecture as a medium for vital practice today." He called for architects to turn their backs on "the modernist mentality of alienation" and to reject the arrogance that denied "the prospect of making spiritual bonds between ourselves and historical architects, a process that has always been essential for the vitality of architecture." Instead of assuming that the contemporary period was unique and that the past was separated from the present by an unbridgeable gap, Smith argued for an embrace of "continuity" and the conscious emulation of the great works of earlier times.[6]

If Smith's words and designs were, as one critic said, "a sharp slap in the bloodless face of late-modernism," they were also a challenge to the prevailing ethos at Notre Dame.[7] Paul Jacques Grillo's seem-

---

5. Ibid., 52, 94, 130, 137, 141, 194, 199.
6. Thomas Gordon Smith, *Classical Architecture: Rule and Invention* (Layton, Utah: Gibbs M. Smith, 1988), 1.
7. Heinrich Klotz, "Preface," Smith, *Classical Architecture*, ix.

ingly absolute advocacy of functionalism and simplicity over and against tradition and decoration might have been more extreme than the views of most of his colleagues—few of them would have called Palladio's classic villa a "monsterpiece"—but they embraced moderate versions of modernism that, in the end, still elevated innovation over tradition and still produced steel and glass boxes rather than ornately detailed classical buildings. Smith was a talented architect, but in 1989 it was not obvious that he had the vision, patience, and perseverance that would be needed to change the ingrained architectural culture at Notre Dame. Every single architecture program in the United States was dedicated to modernism. Was it even possible to transform a modernist architectural program into a classical one?

Thomas Gordon Smith

As an undergraduate at the University of California at Berkeley, Smith majored in Art and wrote his thesis on John Hudson Thomas, an architect who combined various styles, including Craftsman and Prairie, in Bay Area homes built in the first half of the twentieth century.[8] "One of the reasons I felt that I was receptive as a teenager to Classicism, or continued to have a drive to resist bad context in terms of the culture, was the issue of knowing intuitively through my Catholic upbringing that there is a great deal to be learned from the past," Smith said.[9] Smith's thesis advisor, David Gebhard, was sympathetic to his interest in historical architectural forms and taught him "the difference between plagiarism and emulation."[10] On the other hand, one of his professors scoffed at such interests, wondering why he wanted to be "an applied archeologist."[11] Another professor, on seeing one of Smith's projects done in the Doric style, asked, "Who gave you permission to design a Doric

8. Smith, *Classical Architecture*, xiii.
9. Ann Carey, "Ever Ancient, Ever New," *Sursum Corda*, Summer 1998.
10. Smith, *Classical Architecture*, xiii.
11. Richard John, *Thomas Gordon Smith and the Rebirth of Classical Architecture* (London: Papadakis, 2001), 14.

house?", as if he had committed some grave transgression.[12] Smith also attended Berkeley for graduate school and received his master's degree in architecture in 1975.

As a practicing architect, his first designs were in the emerging postmodernist vein, adding classical elements to otherwise non-traditional buildings. His "Doric House," for example, featured a "grandiose classical billboard" as the front of what was otherwise "a cheap Californian bungalow."[13] At the time, Smith called his method of design "eclecticism" and said that he drew inspiration from the Renaissance and Baroque periods in particular: "I draw my sources from tradition and re-draw them to contribute new forms to tradition." He bristled at the suggestion that his work was an "antiquarian academic exercise" and said that "fluency with diverse aspects of sources" enabled him to design "expressive buildings which add to tradition, and do not merely mirror tradition."[14]

A pivotal period for him began in 1979, when he spent a year in Italy, having won a fellowship to the American Academy in Rome. Other fellows at the academy, including historians studying Francesco Borromini and Pietro da Cortona, exposed him to the depth, rigor, and beauty of the city's artistic and architectural patrimony. George Rutler, an Anglican minister who was in the process of converting to Catholicism and was studying at the Pontifical University of Saint Thomas Aquinas, worked with him on a project to design an oratory in honor of John Henry Newman, a complex building featuring Doric and Solomonic columns and extensive iconography. "The oratory was the project that allowed me to choose to depart from the typical postmodern ambivalence regarding classicism, and to emulate instead the rigorous practice of classicism incarnated in the Roman churches I was studying," Smith said.[15]

12. Gordon Bock, "Classical Architecture Contributor: Thomas Gordon Smith," *Traditional Building*, 13 December 2016, https://www.traditionalbuilding.com/features/thomas-gordon-smith.

13. John, *Thomas Gordon Smith*, 19.

14. Thomas Gordon Smith, "Re-Drawing from Classicism," *Journal of Architectural Education* 32, no. 1 (September 1978): 18.

15. Thomas Gordon Smith, "Reconnecting to Tradition," *American Arts Quarterly* (Fall 1998).

The time in Rome also deepened his Catholic faith, a process that continued throughout the coming years.

While in Rome, Smith heard that he was one of twenty architects from around the world who had been invited to create a façade for an ersatz street at the 1980 Venice Biennale, one of the most prestigious architectural gatherings in the world. Smith, unlike the other designers, took the challenge in an unabashedly traditional direction in a project that featured Doric pilasters and Solomonic columns that he fabricated himself.[16] In retrospect, it is clear that, even as many of his peers were embracing postmodernism, Smith was in the process of leaving what had been for him a way station on his journey to classicism.

In the 1980s Smith, already a prominent architect, became also a serious scholar and teacher. He immersed himself in architectural history, including that of ancient Greece and Renaissance Italy. He devoted special attention to Vitruvius, the Roman architect whose *Ten Books on Architecture* is the only surviving work written by a classical architect. He taught classical architecture, including courses such as "Rendering the Classical Orders" and "Problems in Classical Architecture as Medium for Contemporary Architecture," at the University of California at Los Angeles, the University of Illinois at Chicago, and Yale University. In Chicago he began a "Program for Vitruvian Studies" that offered lectures such as "Rule and Invention in Vitruvius."[17]

Meanwhile, the architecture program at Notre Dame was in trouble. In 1988 the national accreditation board for architecture issued a negative report that said that the school was close to being put on probationary status. The news that Notre Dame was looking for a new chairman came at a time when Smith was ready for a change. He had enjoyed his time at the University of Illinois at Chicago and had been able to teach classicism, but "the subject matter was basically inserted as an antidote to the dominant deconstruction and normative modernism" of the rest of the curriculum. "I began to

16. John, *Thomas Gordon Smith*, 40–45.
17. Ibid., 61–68.

164

yearn for a situation in which the classical language and theoretical point of view could be taught as a long and fully integrated program of study," Smith said.[18]

He saw two signs that Notre Dame might welcome a classical revision of its curriculum. He had heard that some professors already had suggested that the Notre Dame School of Architecture (NDSA) become more like Cornell University's architecture program, which, under the influence of Colin Rowe, had become interested in traditional architecture and urbanism. Secondly, NDSA's curriculum already included a compulsory year in Rome, evidence of a more than trivial interest in traditional architecture. When Smith presented his vision for a classically based curriculum, he sensed "administrative curiosity," which he attributed to Notre Dame's ongoing commitment to Catholicism—a religion based on tradition—and the larger humanistic tradition. The administrators had not envisioned a classical reformulation of the program, but they were intrigued. It seemed that even the "inherent radicalness" of his proposal appealed to the administration's desire to revitalize the school. They also appreciated Smith's academic rigor and his evident leadership qualities. "In retrospect," he later said, "I am convinced that Notre Dame's administration is the only one in the United States that would have supported the classical proposal for the School of Architecture."[19]

A Home for Tradition

Smith quickly hired four new faculty members whom he considered "well trained and committed to the cause": Michael Lykoudis, Richard Economakis, Samir Younés, and Duncan Stroik, who had been his student at Yale. This corps of likeminded professors, with support from a few older ones, such as Norman Crowe and John

18. Thomas Gordon Smith, "Reconnecting with Classicism," in *100 Years of Architecture at Notre Dame: A History of the School of Architecture, 1898–1998*, edited by Jane Devine (Notre Dame, Indiana: University of Notre Dame School of Architecture, 1999), 61.

19. Ibid., 61–62; Gordon Bock, "Classical Architecture Contributor: Thomas Gordon Smith," *Traditional Building*, 13 December 2016.

Stamper, allowed Smith's vision of a truly classical architectural education to take shape quickly.[20]

Smith and his allies were trying to create a curriculum and an educational atmosphere that they themselves had not experienced, since they, like all the members of their generation, had been educated by predominantly modernist professors in environments where modernism was assumed. Lykoudis says that he and his new colleagues at Notre Dame were "autodidacts" who had become "disenchanted with the world's built environment."[21] Together, they revamped the undergraduate curriculum to focus on classical architecture and urbanism. Smith personally taught a design course for second-year students in which they learned Doric proportions and then applied them to real world architectural situations, including a Doric redesign of the architecture building itself. For Smith, this was part of a process of "ratcheting-up expectations" so that the school would be known not only for classicism but also for excellence. The older students, who were "not interested at all" in the new direction, were allowed to finish their degrees with the same kind of modernist courses to which they had become accustomed, but new and younger students embraced the new curriculum. Smith also reworked the Rome Studies program so that it meshed with the curriculum's new focus.[22] Students who had grown up in the American suburbs often had no idea what a city was supposed to look like, how buildings were supposed to work together, and how a city could actually have a soul, a character. The Rome program was designed "to turn students on to cities" through "the sensory experience of space—noise, taste, smell" in one of the world's great cities.[23]

In their first two years and in their time in Rome, Notre Dame's students would draw and sketch, not use computers. Michael Lykoudis argues that this produced a sense of immediacy and, in the

20. John, *Thomas Gordon Smith*, 68; Smith, "Reconnecting with Classicism," 62.

21. Lewis McCrary, "Golden Age of Classicism: Notre Dame's architecture school is rebuilding the traditional city," *American Conservative*, July 2017, 48.

22. Smith, "Reconnecting with Classicism," 62–63; Bock, "Classical Architecture Contributor."

23. McCrary, "Golden Age of Classicism," 49.

end, a deeper understanding of what they were observing, in contrast to the "tabulation" that often characterized the modern approach to building. In their fourth or fifth year, students would learn to use computer drafting programs, but only after they came to an understanding and, hopefully, a deep appreciation, of Rome, classical architecture, and the skills and virtues necessary for the production of truly great places.[24] When computer drafting was introduced, it was made clear that "the computer does in fact expand the architect's traditional representational arsenal" but that, like other tools, it has "both strengths and weaknesses."[25] Even as Smith improved the graduate program and gained accreditation for its master's degree, Notre Dame's student newspaper complained about the architecture program's new "rigorous academy-like setting" and the stifling of creativity, but Smith welcomed the paper's words as evidence of his program's growing "reputation for a distinct orientation and hard work."[26]

Smith raised money that allowed for the renovation of the school's building, which previously had been the Lemonnier Library. With a major donation from William and Joanne Bond, an addition was made to one side of the building and the dilapidated interior was transformed into "a beautiful and functional setting for teaching and research." The building, which opened in 1997 and is now known as Bond Hall, also housed a library of rare architectural and design books.[27] In 1994, Smith argued for and achieved the school's status as an autonomous school, independent of the College of Engineering.[28]

---

24. Ibid.

25. Dino Marcantonio, "Exercises in Applying Knowledge," *University of Notre Dame School of Architecture Newsletter* 6, no. 10 (2004): 5.

26. Smith, "Reconnecting with Classicism," 62–63; Bock, "Classical Architecture Contributor."

27. A new NDSA building opened in 2019. Bond Hall is now used by the Graduate School.

28. John, *Thomas Gordon Smith*, 68; John Stamper, "Between Two Centuries: A History of the School, 1898–1998," in *100 Years of Architecture*, 19–21; Smith, "Reconnecting with Classicism," 63.

When Smith stepped down as chair in 1998 after nine years of leadership, the school was flourishing. John Stamper, in the official history of the school, celebrated the new emphasis on classicism:

> While pluralism has been a much talked about trend in architectural education and practice, in fact, modernism remains the dominant force in most schools. As Smith pointed out, most education and practice is based on the principle of abstraction rather than literal translation, the resulting theory and architecture invariably leading toward minimalism, fragmentation, and alienation. Believing that a pluralistic attitude should include a rational way of learning from traditional architecture, not as a point of departure for modernism, but as a basis for a continuum of tradition that relies on conviction and principle, Notre Dame's architecture program under Smith was transformed in order to offer an alternative approach to the type of education that has prevailed in other schools since the 1940s.

Stamper had come to believe that, although learning the language and methodology of classical architecture was difficult, it promised "the best possible basis" for developing each architect's creativity. He believed that the school's new emphasis on traditional drawing methods, mastery of the traditional classical orders (Tuscan, Doric, Ionic, Corinthian, Composite), and "firsthand study of ancient and Renaissance monuments" amounted to a rigorous and practical education. It did not, as its critics charged, turn its students into drones who could only copy and borrow, but rather produced imaginative graduates who understood "the timeless principles and techniques" that allowed them to be truly creative.[29]

Smith's successor, Carroll William Westfall, affirmed that the traditional focus would continue. In his view, modernism valorized change and difference, which "atomizes experience and leads to relativism." Architecture schools that embrace modernism have produced a curriculum, therefore, "which prizes only innovation." Classicism, on the other hand, embraces the "enduring" and there-

29. Stamper, "Between Two Centuries," 21.

fore "establishes links to other fields of human endeavor." Architecture programs that learn from history and tradition are both cosmopolitan and humanistic:

> These programs understand that the past informs the present, that the future is built on the basis of the current understanding of the past, that buildings are great to the extent that they make great cities and improve rather than degrade the countryside, and that cities are great to the extent that they assist in producing good citizens.

Westfall connected this embrace of the perennial to the mission of a Catholic university. The "acceptance that there is truth, that truth endures across times and within different secular and sacred traditions" was central to Catholicism, but even more to a Catholic educational institution. The architect, he believed, therefore was called to practice architecture "as a form of revealing truth" in service of a God of truth who had given human beings reason, memory, and talents. In the end, there was no one style that manifested God's grace, but the truth-seeking architect would always depend on reason, "the foundation for the study of architecture," and on tradition, which "allows the efforts of earlier colleagues to guide us in the present." Together, reason and tradition showed "where to start and how to proceed" and provided "standards of excellence."[30]

The current dean of the school, Michael Lykoudis, sounds a similar note. He argues that the school's focus on tradition is evidence of neither escapism nor antiquarianism, but rather comes from the conviction that tradition is "a prism through which to learn about and solve the problems of contemporary life." Like Smith and Westfall, Lykoudis believes in careful study of the architecture of the past and like them he emphasizes that "we still need reason to prioritize and assemble this knowledge in a useful manner, and we need virtue to direct us toward just ends." For this reason faith, too, is "a crucial

---

30. Carroll William Westfall, Foreword, *100 Years of Architecture at Notre Dame*, viii–ix; Carroll William Westfall, "What's Really Wrong With Education for Architects Today," *The Chronicle Review* 49, no. 24 (21 February 2003): B4.

aspect" of education. "Without steadfast belief in a better future," he says, "virtue and reason give way to futility and cynicism."[31]

Unlike modernist programs, which emphasize innovation and "creativity" even as they insist on being in tune with the zeitgeist of a particular age, Notre Dame unabashedly endorses and teaches sustainable, enduring, functional, and beautiful design. The last adjective is particularly important. Although modernist works are often described as "striking" they are rarely called "beautiful," even by those who approve of them; usually their architects are not even aiming for beauty. The official position of the NDSA is that "the pursuit of beauty is essential to being human" and that beauty "is what makes places sustainable and life enjoyable." The school contends that "there is beauty in the process of designing" and that consequently its students produce "hand drawings and watercolor renderings that are themselves works of art."[32] This conscious institutional pursuit of beauty and its integration into the warp and weft of the curriculum make the school unique.

If Notre Dame's new direction were merely a change to the classroom and the addition of a few new faculty members, it would be an interesting tale of an odd academic transition. Of course, the best evidence of an architecture school's transformation and of the value of that transformation is the body of work produced by the school's faculty and alumni. In NDSA's case, that body of work is impressive, beautiful, and influential. Over the last thirty years Notre Dame's growing cadre of classicist professors, students, and alumni has produced a portfolio of houses, churches, and other buildings whose description and analysis could easily fill several volumes. They have also played an important role in historic preservation and restoration. The descriptions of the endeavors of Notre Dame students and faculty that follow are meant to be evocative and illustrative, not encyclopedic.

31. Michael Lykoudis, "Our Approach," University of Notre Dame School of Architecture, https://architecture.nd.edu/about/our-approach/.

32. Ibid.

The Future of the Past

By now everyone is familiar with a certain approach to building additions to important traditional buildings. The idea is to build something blatantly out of sync with the older edifice. I.M. Pei's 1989 entrance pavilion for the Louvre is probably the most famous example. In contrast to the pillars, arcades, and ornate detail of the original museum, Pei built a stark glass and steel pyramid. In New York City, the Harvard Club took a similar approach in 2005 when it added a cement, steel, and glass wing that featured geometric shapes rather the traditional stylings of the original club building, designed by McKim, Mead & White in 1892. In both examples, the addition in no way complemented or completed the original, but rather attempted to steal the limelight in a way that diminished the original.

Notre Dame's Steven Semes, an architect who specializes in historic preservation, says that "the stark juxtaposition of an abstract image realized in industrial materials" with a classical or traditional building has become "a conventional approach to relating new and old in historic settings" but points out that such an approach has a real cost for both the historic building and its neighborhood.[33] Instead of the modernist emphasis on difference, contrast, discontinuity, and rupture, Semes calls for "the utmost caution and tact," an approach that honors buildings and their settings. He recommends instead that any changes "promote conforming and minimize nonconforming features, placing the burden of proof on those interventions that would alter or redefine the preexisting character."[34]

Modernists believe that architects must build in the style of their own time, whether or not the new work complements existing buildings in a given area. Semes responds that "daring formal experimentation, programmatic innovation, and technological progress" have their place, but they "need not be pursued in ways injurious to historic buildings and cities." In places where traditional building

33. Steven Semes, *The Future of the Past: A Conservation Ethic for Architecture, Urbanism, and Historic Preservation* (New York: Norton, 2009), 2.
34. Ibid., 243.

principles have been predominant, there should be "deference and continuity of building cultures."[35] Although dozens of universities offer classes or programs in historic preservation, they often produce graduates who lack "stylistic empathy" because their programs do not require them to understand traditional architecture at a deep level. They have not been immersed in the classical orders or traditional methods of construction and are more likely to have focused on how to preserve the growing number of aging modernist works.[36]

Before coming to Notre Dame, Semes worked in an architectural firm in which one of the partners had been given the sobriquet "Mister Preservation." Once Semes asked this supposed expert about a project that featured an unusual architrave, the beam that rests on the capitals of classical columns. The presumed expert replied, "What's an architrave?" Semes logically wondered, "How can you restore an architrave if you don't know what it is? Would you trust a dentist who gave you a blank stare when you asked him about your molars?"[37]

Notre Dame is the perfect place for a historic preservation program. Preserving important buildings and neighborhoods goes hand-in-hand with designing new classical buildings, and NDSA students do know what an architrave is. The school started offering a concentration in preservation to its bachelor's degree program in 2007 and then added a Master of Science in Historic Preservation in 2017. The value of studying historic preservation at Notre Dame is that "students will first learn how to design the kind of architecture they are being asked to preserve, giving them an understanding of our built heritage 'from the inside,' and fostering the respect for historic places that should be the starting point for preservation policies and treatments."[38] As Professor Krupali Krusche argues, "Urbanism, architecture and preservation are three fields that work

---

35. Ibid.
36. Ibid., 252.
37. Steven W. Semes, "New Preservation Program at University of Notre Dame," *Traditional Building*, 15 February 2017.
38. Ibid.

hand-in-hand. One has to learn the other two to do a good job in any one of them."[39] There are not many places other than Notre Dame where students can master the three fields.

Unlike the jarring juxtapositions favored by today's "starchitects," NDSA students have demonstrated appreciation and understanding of the specific places in which additions have been planned. For instance, in 2003, when the Corcoran Gallery of Art in Washington, DC, was considering an addition, the notorious Frank Gehry submitted a proposal that looked like a series of folded sheets of aluminum foil, intentionally clashing with the Beaux Arts style of the original, a National Historic Landmark that is also listed on the National Register of Historic Places. For her thesis project, Notre Dame senior Elizabeth Frick LaDuke also made a proposal, but one that emphasized continuity with the original. Her project, using the same colors and similar materials as the original, signals understanding and respect, whereas Gehry's "erupts in violent opposition."[40] Gehry's model attempts to dominate, to become the new center of attention. Frick LaDuke's model functions as an integral part of a more important whole.

In a similar vein, Notre Dame master's student Nana Andoh's proposed master plan for the redevelopment of a former industrial site on the Brooklyn waterfront surpasses the plan actually adopted by the city. In this case, the city's plan consists mostly of gigantic buildings on enormous plots of land, a kind of construction and development that contrasts starkly with the Brooklyn neighborhoods to the east of the development. Andoh's plan, on the other hand, consists of many smaller blocks, each with many buildings, a pattern that fits well with neighboring areas. Where the professional architect has gone for grand gestures—the kind of project that attracts publicity but tends to produce inhospitable "superblocks"—Andoh has emphasized fine-grained development that creates the kinds of neighborhoods where people want to live.[41]

39. Ibid.
40. Semes, *The Future of the Past*, 2.
41. Ibid., 253.

Saving Fenway Park

In May 1999 the owners of the Boston Red Sox proposed to close Fenway Park and to build a new $545 million stadium complex that would seat 10,000 more fans than the old park and provide parking for thousands of fans in two massive structures. The new stadium would reuse a few elements of the old park, but in general would be a modern and profitable facility, full of amenities, wider seats, and wider aisles. It would be built on land that was to be seized from local property owners through eminent domain. Baseball teams around the country had been building new stadiums, seeking to maximize income, and the Red Sox wanted to get in on the trend. At first, the proposal seemed unstoppable, "with strong initial momentum and backing from big money, big sentiment, and a phalanx of fixers." Even Red Sox all-time great Ted Williams expressed his support.[42]

But Fenway Park was not a run-of-the-mill stadium. It was an iconic park loved for its intimacy, its traditions, and its idiosyncrasies. *Sports Illustrated*'s Tom Verducci put it this way:

> When we sit in Fenway's precious few seats, and most especially the narrow, wood-slat ones behind home plate that have been there for more than 70 years, we are transported to places of history and of the heart unreachable anywhere else. The beauty of Fenway is its very irregularity, what John Updike nimbly called "a compromise between Man's Euclidean determinations and Nature's beguiling irregularities." Its angles, nooks, crannies, quirks, doorways, ladders, slats, poles and pillars seem pleasingly human and without a hint of contrivance.[43]

New York Times reporter Richard Sandomir said that Fenway was at once "stage and star." The Green Monster (the high left field wall) was its "leading man," the "quirky outfield dimensions, the fans' proximity to the players, the Citgo sign, and the hand-operated

42. Carey Goldberg, "Emotions Run High Over the Future of Fenway," *New York Times*, 4 July 1999.

43. Tom Verducci, "A National Treasure," *Sports Illustrated*, 24 November 2011: 4–9.

scoreboard" were the "supporting cast." Roger Angell, essayist and fiction editor of *The New Yorker,* went further, calling it "the best place in the world to watch baseball."[44] To destroy an edifice that the American Institute of Architects had included as one of America's 150 favorite buildings struck many fans as disgraceful, even criminal; the proposed replacement, in comparison to the original, sounded like "a chemically enhanced, replicoid-mutant new 'Fenway,' wrapped in a shopping mall."[45]

A group of fans led by lawyer Dan Wilson created an organization called Save Fenway Park (SFP) and quickly collected more than 25,000 signatures for a petition to renovate the existing stadium rather than replacing it.[46] SFP then joined with the Fenway Community Development Corporation in an attempt to develop a viable alternative for the stadium and the neighborhood. They decided to bring in Philip Bess, a professor at the Notre Dame School of Architecture who was an expert on urbanism and the role of baseball parks in cities. He would conduct a "charrette," a discussion and analysis of the situation that would result in a counter-proposal for the ballpark.[47]

Bess, probably more than anyone else in America at the time, had been thinking seriously about the role of baseball parks in the fabric of the nation's cities. His 1999 book, *City Baseball Magic,* was "a straightforward and unapologetic polemic" for the traditional urban baseball park, by which he meant not the pseudo-traditionalism of Camden Yards, the Baltimore Orioles' old-*seeming* stadium located in an entertainment zone isolated from the rest of the city, but parks like Chicago's Wrigley Field that were consonant with his "Aristotelian Catholic communitarian" philosophy of the city. At

44. Tom Huntington, "There Is No Finer Place in the World to Watch Baseball," *Smithsonian* 25, no. 7 (October 1994): 64; Richard Sandomir, "As Stage and Star, Fenway Is in Spotlight: And the Green Monster plays the leading-man role," *New York Times,* 13 July 1999.

45. Patrick Pinnell, "Fenway: A Hard-Earned Save," *The Hartford Courant,* 3 April 2005.

46. Lane Hartill, "Farewell to Fenway?," *Christian Science Monitor,* 8 July 1999.

47. Meg Vaillancourt, "Opponents offer alternative Fenway plans," *Boston Globe,* 13 August 2000.

the heart of Bess's vision of the city was the belief that "the best life for individual human beings is the disciplined life of moral and intellectual virtue lived with others in communities" and that "architecture and cities generally are physical manifestations of a culture's deepest beliefs about human nature and human aspirations." His argument for traditional urban baseball parks was thus part of a larger argument "about human nature, about cities, and about the relationship of these to human well being."[48]

Bess found the enormous stadiums that had been built in several cities during the 1990s unimpressive. Their "outrageous costs" were bad enough, but, even worse, they offered "few tangible benefits" for the taxpayers and communities that paid for them. Public officials seemed unwilling or unable to put the brakes on these extravagant projects, which featured stadiums 50 to 500 percent larger than necessary, usually built on the most expensive "downtown" real estate. This approach was evidence of "a degrading and short-sighted vision of cities as entertainment zones," in contrast to the traditional view of cities as "locations for the good life for human beings, where people are not only entertained but also live, work, shop, play, worship, and go to school."[49]

Clearly, Bess was not your average baseball fan, not even your average academic baseball fan. First, he was one of the leaders of the Congress for the New Urbanism, an organization devoted to the restoration of "urbanism," which supports traditional concepts such as mixed-use development (as opposed to single-function zoning), walkability (as opposed to automobile-dependent development), and density (as opposed to sprawl), who saw baseball parks in the context of the multi-faceted traditional city. Second, Bess was a veritable philosopher of the city who argued that cities and buildings could and should have the "ambition to unite beauty with goodness and truth." He argued strongly against the modernist notion of man as helpless in the face of irresistible impersonal forces and for the traditional view of man as "an intermediate being, simultaneously

---

48. Philip Bess, *City Baseball Magic: Plain Talk and Uncommon Sense about Cities and Baseball Parks* (Chicago: Knothole Press, 1999), ii.
49. Ibid., iii.

part of, different from, and responsible for nature."[50] In other words, he was a lover of baseball and traditional urban ballparks who had thought deeply about the nature and purpose of the city, the moral agency of human beings, and the role of ballparks in the moral and civic development of human communities.

In August 2000, Bess and six hand-picked allies, including preservationists, architects, and urban planners, began their charrette, investigating the situation and formulating a plan. For eight days the so-called "Fenway Seven" worked for eighteen hours a day in a room provided by Simmons College. Bess and his fellow experts were confident that they could provide a fresh perspective on Fenway and its future. "Up until now," said Bess, "the situation in Boston has been defined entirely in terms of what the Red Sox want—and what the Red Sox need. We would like to redefine the problem in terms of the city and the neighborhood, and to characterize our approach as an exercise in neighborliness."[51]

During the charrette, the Fenway Seven came up with ways to expand seating in the park, to solve traffic and transit problems, and to make the park generally more efficient and profitable for its owners. But they also suggested that it was inappropriate for the Red Sox to dictate terms. "We are insisting," said Bess, "that the Red Sox *be* good neighbors: that they not covet their neighbor's property, and that they not presume to divert tax money from the pockets of their fellow citizens."[52]

The Fenway Seven were criticized by Boston's sports journalists and shunned by the city's architectural community, but the group was far from discouraged. "It became clearer and clearer that saving Fenway, and getting both the Red Sox and the neighborhood what they needed, was eminently feasible," says Patrick Pinnell, a Connecticut architect who was one of the Seven. "The then-owners of the team really were overlooking all kinds of spaces and possibilities within the stadium complex—and not only things useful to a reno-

50. Philip Bess, "Building on Truth," *First Things*, no. 249 (January 2015): 47–53.
51. Philip Bess, *Till We Have Built Jerusalem: Architecture, Urbanism, and the Sacred* (Wilmington: ISI Books, 2006), 291.
52. Ibid., 292.

vated park, but how the process of renovation could be managed, inside and outside the park."[53]

On 12 August, the Fenway Seven shared their plan with the press and one hundred of their closest supporters. Pinnell summarizes their proposal as follows:

> Need more seats? Instead of knocking the place down and starting over, why not add seats in small groups here and there around the park? Some, atop the famed Green Monster left field wall, could be the best seats in baseball. Others set on left and right field rooftops, while less spectacular, could still have angles, distances and sightlines better than any newer ballpark's. Better concessions operations could be gained by reconfiguring areas behind the right field wall, better subway access could be had by opening a second entrance to the Kenmore Square MTA station—and so on. By acting with a finer-grained, incremental vision within and around the existing structure of Fenway, the Sox could in fact get just about everything they wanted, and at half to two-thirds the expense of a new stadium.[54]

For Bess, the heart of the issue was that "the best ballparks in the country are neighborhood ballparks." Fenway could be rehabilitated, remain a neighborhood ballpark, and still offer new revenue streams to its owners.[55]

At first, the Red Sox were unmoved. "Our architects and engineers have thoroughly studied the option of rebuilding in place, and have concluded it is not physically or economically feasible," said Red Sox spokesman James Healy. The team was convinced that the alternatives proposed in the charrette simply would not meet its "needs" for amenities and public subsidies to compete with other teams that already had those advantages.[56] But the charrette's ideas

---

53. Pinnell, "Fenway: A Hard-Earned Save."

54. Ibid.

55. Meg Vaillancourt, "Opponents offer alternative Fenway plans," *Boston Globe*, 13 August 2000.

56. Ibid.

slowly gained currency in Boston. Momentum for a new stadium began to fade.

In December 2001 a new ownership group took over the team. The new owners implemented much of the Fenway Seven's plan and in 2003 they invited the Seven to dinner and a game, which they enjoyed from the very seats on top of the Green Monster that they had proposed.[57] In 2012, at its one hundredth anniversary, Fenway Park was looking like "a restored oil painting." It had new amenities, but its intimacy and tradition were what made it truly impressive.[58] The park's survival and ongoing popularity is a testimony to the integration of reason, faith, and architectural tradition that the Notre Dame School of Architecture has developed over the past thirty years and is now sharing with the world.

Our Lady of Guadalupe Seminary

The Priestly Fraternity of Saint Peter, a society of priests who celebrate the traditional Latin Mass, turned to Thomas Gordon Smith to design their seminary in Denton, Nebraska. The fraternity, which was recognized by Pope John Paul II in 1988 as a "Society of Apostolic Life of Pontifical Right," is the most prominent traditionalist body inside the Catholic Church.[59] Its 330 priests, serving in 146 dioceses around the world, celebrate the pre-Vatican II form of the Mass with great reverence and, as much as any other group in the Church, strive to honor the ancient traditions of the Faith in liturgy, theology, and morality. It was natural for the Fraternity, although it was newly established and therefore not wealthy, to want its new seminary to reflect its foundational respect for tradition. The new chapel, library, dormitory, administrative building, classrooms, and refectory should embody the Fraternity's vision and mission.

---

57. Pinnell, "Fenway: A Hard-Earned Save."

58. Verducci, "A National Treasure."

59. The Society of Saint Pius X, from which the fraternity arose, has an ambiguous canonical status, despite progress toward regularization during the pontificates of Benedict XVI and Francis. The founder of the society, Marcel Lefebvre, and the other episcopal members of the society were excommunicated in 1988, but in 2009 Benedict XVI lifted the excommunications.

Smith designed a complex of Romanesque buildings that consists of a chapel, consecrated in 2010, and an adjoining quadrangle for the other buildings. The materials used for the exterior include cedar posts, limestone, and bricks in red, rose, and yellow.[60] The Romanesque style, with its "expanses of unadorned walls and restrained use of ornament" allowed Smith to express "strength and grandeur with a relatively modest expenditure."[61] He positioned the complex "on the spur of a hill with wings nestled into adjacent ravines" to give the effect of a set of buildings "that appears to have always existed in this location."[62]

Architectural historian Denis McNamara says that the design of the seminary "makes clear the hierarchical priorities of the community." The chapel "steps forward as the public face of the complex, indicating the public nature of the chapel and the importance of the worship within" and its entrance "maintains a tranquil unity of design that gives no hint of self-conscious eclecticism." The thick walls of the chapel produce "a sense of heft which reads as convincingly traditional and avoids the modernist tendency to make tight-looking walls with the depth of only a single brick." The interior of the chapel has an "austere masculine sophistication." The placement of all windows above eye level provides light while simultaneously giving "a sense of enclosure from the fallen world." The other buildings have different heights and rooflines and the "functional wings of the complex put on no airs, being indicated simply by rows of repeating windows in blocks of varying brick and different levels of detail." Even in the less ornate areas, Smith's "synthetic creativity" is evident, for instance, in the use of "extremely simple elements" to produce "a heroic motif."[63]

McNamara concludes that the building of the seminary marks "a climactic moment in the renewal of Catholic liturgical architecture." The seminary is "something rare in architecture," an architec-

60. John, *Thomas Gordon Smith*, 126.

61. Denis McNamara, "Lively Mental Energy: Thomas Gordon Smith and the Our Lady of Guadalupe Seminary," *Sacred Architecture* 18 (2010): 20.

62. Ibid.

63. Ibid., 20–22.

tural complex that is "at once vital, creative, and new, yet as ancient as it is new." It reflects "apostolic simplicity enriched with communal, ecclesial, and celebratory touches all in the right places."[64] In designing a seminary that reflected the dynamism of Catholic tradition, Notre Dame's guiding light had demonstrated the ongoing potential of classicism in contemporary America.

Our Lady of the Most Holy Trinity Chapel, Thomas Aquinas College

In 2012, actor Anthony Hopkins was driving through the hills of southern California on Highway 150 when a striking tower caught his eye. He pulled off the highway and found that the tower belonged to the chapel of Thomas Aquinas College, of which he said "I've never seen such beautiful place in my life."[65] Our Lady of the Most Holy Trinity Chapel had been consecrated just three years before. It had been designed by Duncan Stroik, one of Thomas Gordon Smith's early hires at NDSA. Stroik, who had become a leading voice for traditional architecture and an advocate in particular of traditional church architecture, had designed impressive churches before, but there is no doubt that the chapel is his masterpiece.

Thomas Aquinas College is a Catholic college in Santa Paula, California, that has a Great Books curriculum for all of its students. It was founded in 1971 as a response to the drastic decline in Catholic higher education in the post-Vatican II era, when openness, secular standards, and Rahnerian theology were replacing the Western canon, Catholic tradition, and Thomism. The college has a become a bastion of traditional learning and orthodox Catholicism, one of the few colleges in the United States where students can be confident of encountering believing Catholic faculty members, and one of just a handful of places where the Western canon defines the curriculum.

Thomas Dillon, the president of the college from 1991 until his

---

64. Ibid.
65. "Sir Anthony Hopkins Talks to the Students of Thomas Aquinas College," 3 April 2012, https://www.youtube.com/watch?v=N2IWo8L1gLY.

death in 2009, was a master fundraiser who had overseen much of
the building of Thomas Aquinas's campus, including a library, a science building, five dormitories, and an administration building. He
had wanted, as his last project, to build a chapel. After Duncan
Stroik beat out his mentor Thomas Gordon Smith and other classical architects in a design competition, Dillon took Stroik around
California and Italy to research the best examples he could find.
Together, the two men strove to make every element of the church
excellent. Stroik says that Dillon "wanted to be convinced through
words, drawings, and precedent that every design decision was correct." In fact, Dillon wanted to measure the quality of the new
chapel against the greatest works of the past. Comparison to the
classic churches of the Renaissance "inspired higher quality in
design and materials—mahogany, marble, bronze, and limestone,"
which meant that Dillon needed to raise more money than originally planned. For instance, Stroik originally planned the columns
of the nave to be made of plaster, but was later persuaded to make
them of limestone, and then again to make them of botticino marble. "Their significant increase in cost was difficult to stomach," says
Stroik, "yet when the building was complete everyone saw how right
he was to advocate for them."[66]

The chapel that Stroik ended up designing is a "harmonious
fusion" of the California Mission style that predominates at the college and in traditional churches of southern California, with the
more ornate style of Renaissance master architect Filippo Brunelles-
chi.[67] Its placement, nestled into surrounding hills and at the head
of the college quadrangle, makes it clearly the most important
building on campus, "both physically and symbolically."[68] Except
for the terracotta-tiled roofs, white and off-white shades predomi-
nate inside and outside of the cruciform building, which has a 135-
foot bell tower and a dome over the altar. Stroik says the chapel

66. Duncan Stroik, "Ad Maiorem Dei Gloriam et Beatae Mariae Virginis,"
Sacred Architecture 15 (2009): 2.
67. Catesby Leigh, "A Return to Grace," *Wall Street Journal*, 18 March 2010.
68. Duncan Stroik, "Thomas Aquinas College's New Chapel: Interview with
Duncan Stroik," *Zenit*, 24 April 2009.

"begins as an early Christian basilica" and then "develops spatially and architecturally in light of the last 1,500 years." He describes the architecture as "cerebral," in that it reflects the thought of college namesake Thomas Aquinas, and "much of the symbolism inside and out refers to the life of Mary as she lived in communion with the Trinity."[69]

Stroik's work caught the attention not only of Anthony Hopkins but also of architects and scholars around the world. Architectural historian Denis McNamara calls the chapel an example of "theology in built form." He sees the influence of Mission, basilica, and Renaissance works, but remarks that "no other building in history has looked exactly like this." The chapel "cites the past and addresses the needs of its own time, all the while expressing the fundamentally heavenly origin of all church buildings as images of the Heavenly Jerusalem." "Simply put," says McNamara, "no classical Catholic church building of this quality has been built since the Second Vatican Council." The chapel is so successful that "the compelling power of Truth takes the architectural form of Beauty, and the result is joy."[70]

The progressive religious architecture journal *Faith & Form* tended to avoid even reviewing traditionalist projects, but it could not ignore the new chapel at Thomas Aquinas. Admitting that new traditional churches were usually considered "at best, outliers and, at worst, retrograde and liturgically incorrect," reviewer George Knight said that the chapel was one of the rare traditional projects that deserved serious consideration "because of its quality and character and because of what possibilities it reveals." After detailing the chapel's many design decisions, some of which he finds formulaic, Knight concluded with words of real praise:

> It is rare to see traditional design executed with such finesse and capability. Throughout the chapel one sees examples of an architectural language commanded by a designer who can satisfy its

69. Ibid.

70. Denis McNamara, "Consecration of Thomas Aquinas College Chapel of Our Lady of the Most Holy Trinity," *Adoremus* XV, no. 2 (April 2009).

rigor while offering delightful and meaningful spaces for its users. Whether at the juncture of varied scales of vaulting; the intersection of column capitals; the integration of varied orders; or the profiles of entablatures, bases, and balusters, the Thomas Aquinas College chapel evidences competency and resolution that are rare. . . . What is perhaps more intriguing is the testimony it provides to the idea that classical architecture is vibrant, relevant, and (most surprisingly) achievable. One of the common explanations provided to those who had resisted admonitions that our culture should not re-adopt traditional building was that it was beyond the reach of possibility; that its trades, designers, and craftsmen were all but gone; that, even if they were available, they would be financially impossible for any client to afford.[71]

In other words, the chapel breaks stereotypes and speaks for itself. It invites daily communicants, casual visitors, and even convinced modernists to consider the power of beauty and tradition.

Conclusion

By the mid-1990s Notre Dame's new emphasis was attracting national and international attention. An article in the *New York Times* took note of a new wave of classical and traditionalist architects, whom it called "young old fogies," coming out of "the now-classicist Notre Dame School of Architecture," which was the "Athens of the new movement." Although the *Times* quoted critics who called the new classicists "bizarrely backwards" Luddites with "no new ideas," the article itself seemed more intrigued than dismissive and admitted, "at their best, the new classicists seek to combine graceful proportions and ornamentation with affordable materials and an almost Shakerlike simplicity."[72]

Liturgical design consultant Michael DeSanctis was less impressed. In an essay that indicted Smith and Duncan Stroik for

71. George C. Knight, "Style as Substance," *Faith & Form 43*, no. 2 (2010).
72. Patricia Leigh Brown, "Architecture's Young Old Fogies," *New York Times*, 9 February 1995.

"paranoia and self-righteousness," "noisy posturing," and a lack of intellectual rigor, DeSanctis argued that American Catholics could no longer accept the kind of church buildings that Notre Dame's architects wanted to build. Over the past few decades, Americans had been shaped by "the modernist eye for practicality," which had given them "strong, handsomely appointed buildings with decent restrooms, coatrooms, diaper-changing rooms; proper planning-and-primping-and-feasting-and-mourning rooms, all conceived with the same care as the room reserved for divine worship."[73] Despite his strong words, DeSanctis was making the case for the importance of Notre Dame's new approach. His emphasis on the practical, the mundane, and the functional; his use of "handsomely appointed," rather than "beautifully adorned"; and his admission that the restrooms and coatrooms had been designed with the same care as the sanctuary: his own words pointed to a domestication and horizontalization of architecture that could not help but produce drab and pedestrian structures.

A decade after its first report, the *Times* had become even more accepting of the movement, profiling Thomas Gordon Smith with evident sympathy and characterizing his designs as displaying "the irony-free rigor of an ancient." This time the article quoted various luminaries from the worlds of art and architecture, all of whom had positive words for Smith, Notre Dame, and the new classicists. Robert A.M. Stern, dean of Yale's school of architecture, called Smith's designs "free and fresh."[74] In 2004 the school was ranked in the top ten in the United States by the *Almanac of Architecture & Design*.[75]

By 2017, it was clear that Smith and Notre Dame had in fact started a new movement. David Brussat, writing in a magazine, *Traditional Building*, whose very existence was evidence for his thesis,

73. Michael DeSanctis, "Notre Dame's Neo-Classicists Yearn to Build Grand Old Churches," *National Catholic Reporter*, 21 April 2000.

74. Deborah Baldwin, "Giving Neo-Classical a Little More Neo: An Architect Who Quietly Battles Trends Finds That He Nearly Is One," *New York Times*, 11 March 2004; see also James Parker, "A Requiem for Postmodernism—Wither Now?," *Southern Baptist Journal of Theology* 5, no. 2 (Summer 2001): 55.

75. "Ranked Among the Top Ten," *University of Notre Dame School of Architecture Newsletter* 6, no. 10 (2004): 1.

asserted that Smith "led a revolution at the University of Notre Dame's School of Architecture" that contributed to a "classical revival" by "producing architects capable of traditional design at the highest level of classical virtuosity."[76] *The American Conservative* was speaking of a "golden age of classicism" at Notre Dame, not only because of the many successful projects completed by the faculty and alumni of the school, but even more because of the countercultural ethos of "virtue and care for place" based on "designing buildings that respect their surroundings and community, including their future inhabitants."[77] Although Notre Dame was no longer alone—architecture programs at Catholic University, the College of Charleston, and the University of Colorado at Denver have attempted to turn toward tradition—the arrival of other classical programs was in itself evidence of Notre Dame's influence.

That Smith prevailed in turning the NDSA into a school devoted to the classical tradition is testimony to four interrelated factors: 1) Smith's qualities of architectural brilliance, wisdom, and leadership; 2) the support of the Notre Dame administration for a potentially controversial change of direction in one of its professional schools; 3) the coherence, beauty, and utility of classical architecture and urbanism; and 4) the exhaustion of modernism, even at its moment of seeming triumph, and hence the opening for an alternative vision. In short, Thomas Gordon Smith was the right man, with the right philosophy, at the right time, and in the right place. Smith, a few brave administrators, a handful of visionary professors, and a steady stream of talented students rejected DeSanctis's "handsomely appointed" functionalism and Grillo's minimalist "sveltesse." Instead, they embraced tradition and dared to reach for beauty.

76. David Brussat, "Assertively Classical: Thomas Gordon Smith at Notre Dame," *Traditional Building*, 13 February 2017.
77. McCrary, "Golden Age of Classicism," 49–50.

7

Hope for the City

Joe Riley and the Revival of Charleston

I N 2011, *Condé Nast Traveler* presented the city of Charleston, South Carolina, with an award for being the top tourist destination in the United States, beating out New York, Chicago, and number one for the previous eighteen years, San Francisco. Charleston won the same award for the next three years, until the magazine created new categories that split larger and smaller cities. Charleston has won its category ever since and would probably continue to beat its larger rivals if it was still allowed to compete with them.[1]

The South Carolina city is home to its share of luxurious hotels and gourmet restaurants, and it has an aquarium, a retired aircraft carrier, a minor league ballpark, and various museums, but every city on *Condé Nast's* lists offers similar amenities. What sets Charleston apart is its walkable streets, its well-preserved historic buildings, its distinctive palate of paint and brick, its mysterious alleyways, its dignified waterfront parks—the impression it offers of being a place, a specific place, shaped by history, tradition, custom, and culture. In 2015 the *New York Times* put it this way: "The elegant buildings from different eras strut across Charleston's downtown neighborhoods like notes on a major scale: the Gothic churches, the Greek Revival storefronts, the homes in vivid pastels exuding

---

1. Emily Williams, "Condé Nast names Charleston top U.S. city for 8th consecutive year," *The Post and Courier,* 9 October 2018; Brian Hicks, *The Mayor: Joe Riley and the Rise of Charleston* (Charleston: Evening Post Books, 2015), 321.

Queen Anne grace, Georgian symmetry and Italianate grandeur."[2] Unlike much of North America, Charleston is not a conglomeration of randomly assembled buildings, parking lots, and streets. The fabric of the city shows the unmistakable signs of care and planning. "At its finest," says novelist Pat Conroy, "the city looks as though it were imagined by a committee of Anglicans appointed by a tasteful deity."[3]

Recent visitors to Charleston might assume that the city has always been tasteful, attractive, and well cared for, but it only gradually become a magnet for national and international travelers, starting in the late 1970s under the leadership of Mayor Joe Riley. A leading colonial port city and still the sixth largest American city in the 1820s, it became the "cultural center of the South" in the early nineteenth century, but struggled and declined in the aftermath of the Civil War. By the 1960s, many of its antebellum houses were in bad shape and the center of the city was full of "aging, decrepit buildings and failing businesses."[4] Future mayor Joe Riley's childhood friend Michael Duffy described the old city this way: "Joe Riley and I grew up in Charleston when it was literally too poor to paint and too proud to whitewash. We had two hotels and three restaurants, the economy was the shipyard, the state port, and a little bit of tourism."[5] Charleston generally avoided the violent confrontations that characterized the African American civil rights movement of the time in states like Alabama and Mississippi, but the city's legacy as the initiator of the Civil War and, before that, as the major slave port of the thirteen colonies and the early republic had not been transcended. Blacks were still second-class citizens and there was no sign that their condition would improve in the immediate future. Anyone who had suggested that soon Charleston would become a model for the rest of the country would have been

2. Richard Fausset, "In Stately Old Charleston, the New Buildings on the Block Are Struggling to Fit In," *New York Times*, 24 January 2015.

3. Pat Conroy, Foreword, Hicks, *The Mayor*, 9.

4. Hicks, *The Mayor*, 29; Douglas W. Rae, *City: Urbanism and Its End* (New Haven: Yale University Press, 2003), 42.

5. Rob Price, "Life of a Legend: Mayor Joe Riley," WCBD News, 9 July 2015, http://counton2.com/2015/07/09/life-of-a-legend-mayor-joe-riley/.

suspected of mockery. Much of the credit for Charleston's revival goes to Mayor Riley (b. 1943), who was elected in 1975 and reelected nine times before his retirement in 2016. He worked unflaggingly on racial injustice, decaying infrastructure, and a host of other problems for forty years. When he left office Charleston was not perfect—no city ever is—but it had been transformed and revived.

From Boy Mayor to Charleston Institution

After serving three terms as a state representative, Joe Riley decided to run for mayor of Charleston. He had grown up in Charleston as part of a prominent, politically and socially involved family. His father, Joseph Riley, Sr., ran the Joseph P. Riley Real Estate and Insurance Company, and often invited politicians such as Governor Jimmy Byrnes and future US Senator Fritz Hollings (1922–2019) to the family home. After attending Catholic elementary school and high school, Riley went to the Citadel, South Carolina's military college, and then law school at the University of South Carolina. In 1967 Riley opened a small law firm and was elected to the state legislature. Although he was seen as a rising star in the state Democratic party, Riley decided not run for re-election in 1974, due mainly to the stress of spending time away from his wife Charlotte and their two young sons while the legislature was in session in Columbia. The plan was to practice law full time with his friend and partner Capers Barr. However, in early 1975, four-term Charleston mayor Palmer Gaillard announced that he would not seek re-election. Democratic leaders, almost immediately, courted Riley to run for the position. At thirty-two years of age, Riley was young, but he already had a reputation as an economically moderate, racially progressive leader. After an intense campaign, Riley soundly defeated preservationist and fiscal conservative Nancy Hawk. Although he had told his wife that he wanted to serve only one term and had assumed that he would soon return to his law firm, Riley was re-elected in 1979, and eight times thereafter.

It is no exaggeration to say that contemporary Charleston is the city that Joe Riley built during his forty years as mayor, from 15 December 1975, to 11 January 2016. His influence on the city came in three main areas: racial reconciliation, economic development, and the enhancement of the public realm. In a sense, he threaded the needle: he managed to seek progress in a way that respected tradition and to honor tradition in a way that did not impede legitimate cultural, political, and economic development. More than any other mayor of a major American city during the late twentieth and early twenty-first centuries, Riley had a vision of the goodness and possibilities of urban life that proved widely attractive and actually came to fruition.

Racial Reconciliation

Charleston had a central role in the slave trade and in the Civil War. Almost 50 percent of the enslaved Africans who were brought to the United States passed through Charleston, which was a major port and trading center in the colonial period and the early Republic. In fact, roughly 80 percent of the contemporary African American population is probably descended from ancestors who first came to America through the port of Charleston.[6] Of course, after South Carolina's secession from the United States in December 1860, the first shots of the Civil War were fired at Fort Sumter in Charleston Harbor in 1861.

While Riley grew up in Charleston in the 1940s and 1950s, African Americans were enduring social discrimination and political disfranchisement, and the few white South Carolinians who tried to stand up for them, such as federal judge Julius Waties Waring, were ostracized. In 1963 Riley watched Martin Luther King, Jr., deliver his "I Have a Dream" speech at the Lincoln Memorial on television. The speech was a pivotal moment for Riley and in later years he said that it changed his life.[7] Although he already had been coming to his own reevaluation of the southern tradition, especially through a history class he had taken at the Citadel, King's words crystallized

6. "Slavery in The Lowcountry," International African American Museum, https://iaamuseum.org/history/slavery-in-charleston-and-the-lowcountry/. Accessed 30 May 2020.

7. Hicks, *The Mayor*, 37, 58, 65–66.

for Riley the need to reject boldly, openly, and firmly the racial prej-
udice that often figured as a central part of that tradition. "I became
more and more aware of the injustices that African Americans had
been subjected to, and how wrong that was for them and our country," he said.[8] He seldom spoke publically of his faith, but it seems
clear that Riley's Catholicism also influenced his racial attitudes. As
he said in 2015, "It's not possible to separate" faith and politics
because "faith permeates you, your spirit, your perspective."[9] No
one can accuse Joe Riley of hating tradition *per se* or wanting some
sort of wholesale rejection of the past—his name has become syn-
onymous with preserving the historic buildings and southern
charm of Charleston, after all—but it is important to see that his
love of tradition did not prevent him from evaluating the customs
of the South Carolina low country and fearlessly jettisoning what
was wrong and unjust.

During Riley's time in the state legislature, he tried to make the
Democratic delegation more diverse, supporting African American
candidates such as Herbert Fielding, who was successfully elected in
1970 as the first black state representative since Reconstruction. He
spoke up for striking Charleston hospital workers, mostly African
American, comparing their struggle to that of homerun king Hank
Aaron and saying that they were fighting for basic civil rights, since
they were being paid below the national minimum wage.[10]

In the legislature, Riley had just one vote, but once he was mayor,
he had more ability to effect change. Even his supporters had little
idea how committed Riley was to changing the racial situation in
his city. It soon became clear that Riley was "far more liberal on
racial issues than any of them expected, perhaps more of a racial
liberal than any white Charleston politician had been since Reconstruction."[11] He began challenging the *status quo* on his first day.

8. Richard Fausset, "Charleston Mayor, Champion for Integration, Prepares to
Bow Out," *New York Times*, 15 November 2015.

9. Amy Wise Taylor, "Mayor Riley: Building Interracial Bridges," *The Catholic
Miscellany*, 20 July 2015.

10. Hicks, *The Mayor*, 27–41, 65–66, 78.

11. Steve Estes, *Charleston in Black and White* (Chapel Hill: University of North
Carolina Press, 2015), 35.

Riley's inauguration on 15 December 1975, featured two black men in prominent positions. The opening prayer was offered by Ward Nichols, a bishop of the African Methodist Episcopal Church. Black pastor Robert Woods administered the oath of office. Then a choir sang "Lift Every Voice and Sing," a popular hymn in black churches that is sometimes called the "Black National Anthem." The band from Charleston's mostly African American high school performed. Riley quoted Martin Luther King in his acceptance speech and said "Fundamentally, we are but one people." He rejected segregation and called for more African Americans in important municipal positions.[12]

Once in office, Riley established an African American history trail and worked to make the police department more responsive to community concerns, especially in predominantly African American neighborhoods. He installed a picture of Martin Luther King in city hall and established a Martin Luther King week to be celebrated in Charleston every January. By the late 1970s disgruntled white critics were calling Riley "LBJ," not in reference to the former president, but as the initials for "Little Black Joe." They thought he was focusing too much on blacks and neglecting his white constituents. They were also scandalized by the permission he had given for the installation of a painting of Denmark Vesey, who had led an unsuccessful 1822 slave rebellion in Charleston, in a municipal auditorium.[13] "If black leaders in Charleston had searched for a thousand years they could not have found a local black whose portrait would have been more offensive to many white people," said one local journalist.[14]

Irish Americans were shocked when Riley refused to attend the Saint Patrick's Day banquet of the Hibernian Society because the organization had not extended an invitation to Lonnie Hamilton, the African American chair of the Charleston County Council, even though it normally invited all top municipal and county officials to

---

12. Hicks, *The Mayor*, 114–15; Estes, *Charleston in Black and White*, 52.
13. Hicks, *The Mayor*, 117–18, 128–29.
14. Estes, *Charleston in Black and White*, 55–56.

the event. A year later Riley forced the issue by bringing a leading black politician as his guest at the banquet.[15]

Riley's second inauguration, in 1980, featured Charleston native Septima Clark, one of the great, but sometimes underappreciated, leaders of the civil rights movement. Two years later he hired Reuben Clark as Charleston's first African American chief of police, a bold step in a city that had not hired any full-time black police officers between 1896 and 1950, and which used the handful of black officers hired since 1950 almost exclusively in black neighborhoods. In 1987 Riley worked to save the "Old Slave Mart," a former slave auction site that had long been a privately owned museum, the city's only museum that focused on African American history. Although Riley's great-grandfather had been a Confederate soldier and Riley himself had graduated from the Citadel, which still flew a Confederate flag, in 1987 Riley also took on the "third rail" of South Carolina politics: the Confederate flag that flew over the Statehouse in Columbia. He called the flag "yet another barrier to black and white Southerners achieving social and economic progress together" in an op-ed piece. In retaliation for Riley's outspokenness on the flag issue, the Ku Klux Klan asked for permission to march through Charleston. Constitutionally, he could not deny them a permit, but he scheduled the march for a hot day in August and had his black police chief personally supervise the march.[16]

Critics sometimes implied that Riley was just giving lip service to racial issues, making grand gestures but doing little of substance. In reality, he tried to do what he had promised in his inaugural address. When one of the white men who led one of the city's departments retired, he always tried to find an African American or a woman for the job. "By the early 1990s, there were about a dozen black department heads and an equal number of women running major city departments, from the police to public works," says historian Steve Estes. "In fact, women and minorities outnumbered white men in comparable positions."[17]

15. Hicks, *The Mayor*, 117–18, 128–29, 140–41.
16. Ibid., 157, 172–74, 195–98; Estes, *Charleston in Black and White*, 66.
17. Estes, *Charleston in Black and White*, 55.

In 2000, with the Statehouse still flying the Confederate flag, Riley organized the "Get in Step with South Carolina" march, which traveled the 120 miles from Charleston to the Statehouse in Columbia in five days. Riley received death threats and had to wear a bulletproof vest during the walk, but he suffered from nothing worse than blisters and attracted national attention, as he had hoped. Carolina celebrities such as novelist Pat Conroy, singer Darius Rucker, and football coach Lou Holtz supported the march, as did prominent state politicians. When the tired marchers arrived at the Statehouse, Riley and other speakers urged the state's legislators to step up and remove the flag. A few days later they did exactly that, removing the Confederate flag from the Statehouse dome and three other spots and also scheduling a state Martin Luther King holiday. The only blemish on the march's accomplishment was that a Confederate flag continued to fly at a military monument near the Statehouse.[18]

In 2015, as Riley faced his last two years in office—he had decided that ten terms were enough—he was as active as ever. Although he had several important projects that he was still working on, the most ambitious was the International African American Museum. Riley envisioned a large $75 million facility on the exact spot, Gadsden Wharf, where many enslaved Africans arrived in America, a place that historian Henry Louis Gates once called "ground zero for the African American experience." The museum would call attention "to this powerful place and to the stories of the people who came ashore here—their countries of origin, the trajectory of their lives and the lives of their descendants in America, their courageous battles for freedom, and the indelible marks of culture, tradition, and language that continue to enhance and define our country." Riley successfully lobbied the state for $50 million and began raising the remaining $25 million from private donors.[19]

On 17 June 2015, tragedy struck. A white supremacist massacred nine people at Mother Emanuel African Methodist Episcopal Church, trying to start a race war. Knowing that the city needed to

18. Hicks, *The Mayor*, 17–24, 283–86.
19. Ibid., 329.

grieve, Riley reserved the amphitheater at the College of Charleston and organized a prayer service. More than 4500 people heard Riley say that white supremacy was a sin. "Our hearts are broken. We have an anguish like we have never had before. In our broken hearts we realize we love each other more," he said.[20] In court, the daughter of one of the victims addressed the killer: "I will never be able to talk to her ever again. But I forgive you. And have mercy on your soul."[21] From any other white mayor Riley's words might have sounded hollow and in most other cities words of anger would have come before the words of forgiveness pronounced by the victim's daughter. But Joe Riley had won the right to speak that way. From his first day in office, at political and social cost to himself, he had sought the good of Charleston's African American community. And Charleston, still not perfect, had made genuine strides in terms of racial justice during his four decades in office.

Governor Nikki Haley soon invited Riley and former Governor David Beasley to join with her in revisiting the issue of the remaining Confederate flag at the military memorial near the Statehouse. After they agreed, Haley called for the legislature to remove the flag. A few weeks later, both houses voted to do so.[22] In many ways, it was Joe Riley's victory. He had started the process with his article in 1987, continued it with his march in 2000, and finished it with his support in 2015.

Sharing the Vision, 1975–1995

Joe Riley took office at a time when many Americans were convinced that cities were irredeemable. Many others who would not go quite that far still viewed cities through the lens of seemingly intractable problems like poverty, violence, crime, and homelessness. Some cities might be centers of the arts, culture, and commerce, but these attractions tended to be overshadowed by the

20. Ibid.
21. Nikita Stewart and Richard Pérez-Peña, "'I Will Never Be Able to Hold Her Again. But I Forgive You': Raw Emotion as Victims' Kin Address Charleston Suspect," *New York Times*, 20 June 2015.
22. Hicks, *The Mayor*, 346–47.

negative side of the equation. Many Americans chose to live in the suburbs even if they worked in the city. In this way, they could take advantage of a remaining strength of the city, employment, while avoiding its negative sides. Children could grow up away from urban problems in a "safe" environment. The rings of suburbs that surrounded the country's cities continued to expand, concentric circles of new developments, each one a longer commute from the center city. Some cities responded by trying to be more like the suburbs, "ill-advisedly struggling for relevance by shoe-horning in suburban amenities—like high-speed arterials, strip malls, and acres of surface parking."[23]

Joe Riley did not share the suspicion and rejection of cities that characterized the 1970s and he did not believe that cities should try to become more suburban. There were several reasons for his contrarian stance, but the most simple and perhaps the most basic was that he had grown up on the streets of Charleston. In a succession of homes, small and large, rented and owned, he and his parents and three sisters always lived in downtown Charleston. As a boy, Riley walked and biked all over the city with his neighbors and friends. In those days, the 1940s and 1950s, the city was genteel but shabby. It had preserved many older buildings, but many of them were in disrepair. With both of his parents involved in the community, including with business, political, religious, and charitable organizations and with his father's friends often coming to the family home, young Joe Riley received the opposite lesson from the dominant narrative of the city.[24] In later years, when Riley was reading about city life and urban planning from authors like Jane Jacobs, Andres Duany, and Holly Whyte, he realized that his greatest teacher had been Charleston itself: "I grew up in Charleston, and it was teaching me when I didn't know I was being taught."[25]

Where millions of Americans in the post-World War II era

23. Wayne Curtis, "How Mayor Joe Riley Shaped Charleston," *Architect Magazine*, 3 November 2015, https://www.architectmagazine.com/design/how-mayor-joe-riley-shaped-charleston_0.

24. Hicks, *The Mayor*, 42–63; Joe Riley, interview, 12 September 2019.

25. Peter Lyden, "Charleston: An Architectural Legacy, Part II. An Interview with Mayor Joe Riley," *The Classicist*, 23 February 2016.

believed that the future lay in suburbia because it promised safety, health, and comfort, Riley saw the city as a normal place for human living, a site of human community, even as the privileged place for human flourishing. "I always believed human nature was not going to reject urban experience, but rather embrace it because of its diversity and dynamism," he said.[26] For Riley the solution to the urban problems of the 1970s was not moving out of the city. The solution was to revive the city, to help it live up to its potential. Believing that an urban revival was possible was one thing, but, of course, the next issue was how to do it.

Some of the steps that Riley took were standard actions for cities across the nation. To make the streets safer, he put more police on the street, paid for with a small tax increase. To build up the tax base and make room for expansion, he lobbied for the annexation of adjacent areas, which he was able to accomplish in most cases. When the closure of a Navy base threatened the loss of thousands of jobs, Riley worked with state and federal politicians to mitigate the damage and to recruit replacement employers. When Hurricane Hugo hit in 1989, the mayor was a steady leader and the city's dogged advocate during the process of rebuilding and seeking federal aid.[27] These actions were necessary and important, but they did not separate Riley from many other American mayors who were trying to lead their cities into prosperity.

What did separate Riley and Charleston from the pack was a commitment to beauty, accessibility, and excellence in the public realm.[28] In his office the mayor prominently displayed the Greek Oath:

> We will never bring disgrace on this our City by an act of dishonesty or cowardice. We will fight for the ideals and the Sacred Things of the City both alone and with many. We will revere and obey the City's laws, and will do our best to incite a like reverence and respect in those above us who are prone to annul them or set them at naught. We will strive unceasingly to quicken the

26. Stephanie Hunt, "Oh Joe! One Year to Go," *Charleston Magazine*, November 2014.

27. Hicks, *The Mayor*, 119, 124–25, 139, 154, 157, 209–36, 238–39, 240–3, 252–53.

28. Hunt, "Oh Joe."

public's sense of civic duty. Thus in all these ways, we will transmit this City not only, not less, but greater and more beautiful than it was transmitted to us.[29]

Riley seems to have had this commitment when he arrived in office, but it was amplified and deepened by trips to Europe and Taiwan, by reading Jane Jacobs, and by meeting Holly Whyte and Andres Duany.[30] The German Marshall Fund gave Riley a fellowship to study urban development in England and Germany in 1979. "I was young in this job and didn't know exactly what I was looking for, but in those cities I saw the value of the public realm, the parks and boulevards, places where people shared things together," he said.[31] By the end of the trip Riley had come to a pivotal insight: "I realized I was seeing cities where the public realm was accorded the highest priority, and that the citizens revered that."[32]

He came to believe, more and more deeply, that the public parts of a city, such as parks, municipal buildings, squares, museums, and the downtown area needed special care because they "belong to everyone and they matter to everyone."[33] Streets in residential areas do serve a public purpose, in that anyone can drive or walk on them, but their primary beneficiaries are those who live there. On the other hand, downtowns and other key elements of the public realm have a much broader constituency—and therefore deserve special attention. "Often architecture is thought elitist, that you've got to be schooled or have a special interest, but not long after I was elected, I'd see visitors in town. They looked like they were retired blue-collar workers, and you'd see them admiring buildings. Beauty

29. Steve Ramos, "The Week of Duany," *Buildings Are Cool* (blog post), 16 March 2015.
30. Jane Jacobs, *The Death and Life of Great American Cities* (New York: Random House, 1961); William Hollingsworth Whyte, *The Last Landscape* (Garden City, NY: Doubleday, 1968); Andres Duany, Elizabeth Plater-Zyberk, and Jeff Speck, *Suburban Nation: The Rise of Sprawl and the Decline of the American Dream* (New York: North Point Press, 2000).
31. Hunt, "Oh Joe."
32. Curtis, "How Mayor Joe Riley Shaped Charleston."
33. "5 Questions for Joe Riley," AARP Livable Communities, www.aarp.org/livable-communities.

has no economic litmus test. It's a basic human need and instinct," Riley said.[34] His concern for beauty is thus related to his concern for justice because a beautiful public realm is a gift to all, black and white, rich and poor.

One of the places where Riley tried to make a big change was the development that came to be called Charleston Place. He wanted a vibrant and productive downtown area, but in the late 1970s historic King Street, which should have been the commercial heart of the city, had a "five block vacant eyesore" that was home to prostitution and drug dealing.[35] The city had commissioned a study of the downtown area that recommended a new hotel complex for the blighted spot. Riley agreed: "It was a logical decision. The site we chose, located on two important corners downtown, had the most catalytic potential if done right. The main challenge was not to compromise on any aspect of the project. It needed critical mass; it needed to be scaled and designed correctly; and it needed a lot of energy. What downtowns need is the life that occupants and visitors give them."[36]

Initially a builder proposed a "boxy, fourteen-story hotel with enclosed commercial complex, a 700-car parking garage, and exhibition space with its windowless exterior walls." The vocal and active local preservationist community—Charleston was the first South Carolina city with zoning regulations and the first in the nation with a comprehensive historic preservation ordinance, both adopted in 1931—was outraged, and Riley was not happy either. The last thing he wanted was a modernist behemoth that ignored its surroundings. The city found new developers with more respect for the surroundings. They proposed "an eight-story tower, which was discretely set back behind four-story buildings with retail fronting the streets, some featuring façades salvaged from 19-century buildings."[37] While Riley was much happier with the new proposal, he felt that the brick the developers wanted to use "wasn't quite at

---

34. Curtis, "How Mayor Joe Riley Shaped Charleston."
35. Hunt, "Oh Joe."
36. Lyden, "Charleston: An Architectural Legacy, Part II."
37. Curtis, "How Mayor Joe Riley Shaped Charleston."

home here." He personally drove them around the downtown area "to let them see some late nineteenth and early twentieth-century buildings to help them understand the city's design palette." The field trip worked: the developers chose a classic red brick that complemented neighboring buildings.[38] After completion in 1986, the new complex slowly brought life and respectability back to the downtown area, providing an upscale hotel, various shops, and hundreds of jobs in a package that even most preservationists had to admit fit well with its surroundings. Today it is hard to imagine that King Street was ever in trouble.

A second major improvement of the public realm was Waterfront Park. A developer was planning to build a massive complex of condominiums and stores on a thirteen-acre plot on the Ashley River. Riley objected to seeing the downtown area's last large piece of undeveloped waterfront land used for private purposes. In 1979 he secured grants from the Parklands Foundation and the federal government that enabled the city to buy the property so that it could be turned into a public park.[39] To say that Riley supervised the development of the park would be an understatement. Officially, the park was designed by Sasaki Associates, but Riley was involved in every detail. He asked for benches with especially deep seats, to enable slouching, and he wanted them placed at the correct distance from the wall along the river so that those sitting on the benches could put their feet on the wall. He pondered the height of the walls and eventually decided on fourteen inches. "We studied that. We wanted a place that once they got here, a parent could let the child's hand go," he said. He also analyzed forty different kinds of gravel for the paths, specifying that its size should enable easy walking in a variety of footgear and that its color should reflect "Charleston's palette."[40] He also made sure that the park was beautiful, despite the great expense:

---

38. Lyden, "Charleston: An Architectural Legacy, Part II."
39. Hicks, *The Mayor*, 154–55.
40. Curtis, "How Mayor Joe Riley Shaped Charleston."

It's used by all kinds of people, from the poorest to the most affluent. You know why? We made it beautiful. We used beautiful materials, which I learned during my visit to Europe is so important. When we received the bids, they were over our budget, and the contractor said: "Don't worry Joe, I can get it down. We'll just take the gold plate out." And I said, we're not taking any gold plate out—I'll find the money. The quality of that place, a public space, and its design and execution became a reference point for future projects. If it's in this city, it's got to be done right.[41]

This is the opposite of the usual contemporary American approach, which saves opulence for the private realm and justifies mediocrity in the public realm as "saving money" or "being prudent."

As is probably becoming clear, Riley had a vision of how Charleston should look, even of how Charleston should feel. Part of this involved the colors and styles that fit harmoniously with previously existing architecture, but his vision was not merely aesthetic; he had a sense of the meaning and message of buildings and places. He knew what messages should be sent, and what messages should be avoided. In one instance, an investor wanted to build a Hard Rock Café in a central downtown location. Riley told him, "We don't need a Hard Rock Café in Charleston. That's not Charleston."[42] The point was not that Riley was against rock music but that a chain restaurant found in vacation spots around the nation was not the best use of prime Charleston real estate.

In another instance, the College of Charleston was planning to buy the Francis Marion Hotel to turn it into a dormitory. Built in 1924 on the corner of King Street and Calhoun Street, it had once been the most luxurious hotel in the state. From one perspective the college's proposal was attractive, in that a run-down and no longer popular hotel would be refurbished by the college, but Riley opposed the plan. "This building at this critical intersection—a three year-old would look at that building and say 'That is a hotel,'"

41. Lyden, "Charleston: An Architectural Legacy, Part II."
42. Jack Hitt, "Mr. Mayor: The Exit Interview," *Garden and Gun*, October 2015.

he said. Any onlooker, he believed, could see that what had once been a grand hotel was reduced to a lesser purpose. "This is a visible light blinking in your downtown that now says, this used to be a great corner in a great city, but now it's slipped and the best that they can do is a dorm," he said. It took a great deal of effort, including a $12 million grant from the National Trust for Historic Preservation, to put the hotel back on track, but in 1996 the twelve-story hotel reopened and has been one of the pillars of downtown Charleston ever since.[43] The point was not that a dormitory was bad, but that it was not the best use of an iconic building.

On a vacation in North Carolina, Riley was impressed by the Highlands Biological Station and Nature Center, an award-winning museum and research center that focused on the flora and fauna of the Carolina mountains. Riley realized that a similar center devoted to the animals and plants of coastal South Carolina could be attractive to tourists and locals. In 1983 he proposed a combination aquarium and science museum. In 1988 the South Carolina legislature authorized $9.5 million in bonds for the proposed facility and Charleston voters approved a similar amount. The South Carolina Aquarium, which eventually cost $69 million, opened in 2000 and immediately became a major tourist attraction, with half a million visitors in its first five months.[44] Today it is one of the leading aquariums in the United States. In 2017, for example, it opened a sea turtle rehabilitation center, hosted a conference on plastic pollution for 535 experts and activists from around the world, and launched a distance learning program that used videoconferencing to reach over 21,000 students in South Carolina and other states.[45]

Another goal of Riley's was to improve the cultural life of Charleston. Even before he was mayor he had worked to bring the Spoleto Festival to the city. Italian composer Gian Carlo Menotti, a Pulitzer prize winner remembered today for *Amahl and the Night Visitors,* had started a music and art festival in the village of Spoleto in the hills of central Italy. Menotti, who had written several

43. Hitt, "Mr. Mayor."
44. Hicks, *The Mayor,* 179, 204–5, 286–87.
45. South Carolina Aquarium, "2017 Annual Report."

English-language operas in the 1940s and 1950s, was working with the National Endowment for the Arts to find a city in the United States that could offer an American version of the Spoleto Festival. Charleston had beaten out Savannah and other cities for the honor, with the first festival scheduled for the summer of 1977, but in 1976 the festival's organizers warned Riley that Menotti was untrustworthy and that Charleston simply was not ready to host such a large, complex, and expensive gathering. Riley calmed the organizers and negotiated with Menotti—who in fact did prove to be undependable and difficult—because he thought that Charleston would benefit culturally, economically, and psychologically from the festival.[46] He stuck to his guns because, he said, "It forced the city to accept the responsibility for putting on something world class." It was part of his overall attempt to raise people's sights: "You need a city to commit to excellence, and the arts expose you to that."[47] "Whether it's their voice, or the violin, or their brushes or their typewriter," he said, "these creative people are doing the best they can to excel. When you expose a community to that, then it makes the citizens of a community less apt to accept mediocrity in whatever they do. Whether it's their personal lives, whether it's in the community initiatives or nonprofits, or whether it's in education or whatever, the arts expose people to the beautiful search for excellence."[48]

The 1977 Spoleto Festival did not attract as many tourists as expected, but it was covered by *Time*, *Newsweek*, and the *New York Times* and most of the events were well attended. Over the succeeding years the festival grew dramatically and became everything that the mayor had hoped. It hosted Renée Fleming, Emanuel Ax, Joshua Bell, Yo-Yo Ma, the Emerson String Quartet and Jean-Yves Thibaudet early in their careers and offered premieres and specially commissioned works by Tennessee Williams, Arthur Miller, Martha

46. Hicks, *The Mayor*, 120–23, 126–27.
47. Frank Bruni, "Is Joe Riley of Charleston the Most Loved Politician in America?" *New York Times*, 5 July 2014.
48. Joe Riley, "Taking the Long View: Mayor Joe Riley and Charleston's Revitalization," National Endowment for the Arts, https://www.arts.gov/stories/video/taking-long-view-mayor-joe-riley-and-charlestons-revitalization.

Clarke, Laurie Anderson, Philip Glass, Urban Bush Women, and many other artists and composers.[49]

A danger in bringing something like Spoleto to Charleston was that it would attract only the wealthy and the elite. Riley therefore went out of his way to sponsor smaller scale events—Piccolo Spoleto, that is "Small Spoleto"—and a number of free events. One of the largest of these was a free symphony concert on the steps of the old Custom House, overlooking Waterfront Park.

In 1999 Riley received the Local Arts Leadership Award from Americans for the Arts, largely because of his sponsorship of Spoleto, which was by that point recognized as having produced an "artistic renaissance" in Charleston and to have generated "over $1 billion" in economic development.[50] For Riley, though, the arts still transcended tourism and economics. In 2013 he was again connecting the arts with the deeper emotional health of the city: "When we are exposed to the beauty and the quest for excellence, we can't be comfortable with just getting by. Whether it's in the public spaces or buildings we create, whether it's about how we lead our life individually or civically, [art] challenges us to excel."[51]

A Parting Gift

In 2015, in his last year of office, Riley and the Historic Charleston Foundation invited architect and urbanist Andres Duany and his firm, Duany Plater-Zyberk (DPZ), to Charleston for a "charrette" (public consultation and study) and report on Charleston's architecture, more specifically on the mediocrity of much recent Charleston architecture and its failure to relate harmoniously to its surroundings. During a week in March, Duany and his associates analyzed twenty-two new buildings, including the Holiday Inn on

49. "About," Spoleto Festival USA, https://spoletousa.org/about/.

50. "Mayor Joseph P. Riley," Local Leadership in the Arts, Americans for the Arts, https://www.americansforthearts.org/by-program/promotion-and-recognitio n/awards-for-arts-achievement/annual-awards/public-leadership-in-the-arts/may or-joseph-p-riley-jr-d-charleston-sc.

51. Hunt, "Oh Joe."

Meeting Street and Memminger School on Beaufain Street, and met with the Board of Architectural Review, city planning staff, architects, developers, neighborhood representatives, contractors, builders, preservationists, and members of the public.[52]

In some of the public meetings Duany took a combative stance, asking why so many new buildings looked like they could have been built in Atlanta or Charlotte and denouncing the modernist Clemson school of architecture. He said the city's architects not only did not understand the place where they were working, but even had "contempt" for the city's residents and wanted "to be liberated from the historic constraints." They needed to develop a much better understanding of the "Charleston Brand" and the city's vernacular styles of building.[53] He challenged them to embrace their locale and develop its native genius, not ape the styles of other cities: "Charleston cannot be a net importer of architectural ideas. Charleston has to model its own genetic material, which is considerable and sophisticated. And Charleston has to become an exporter of architectural ideas. The world is fascinated by Charleston. Charleston is the greatest influence of my own work." The heart of the matter was that the city's architects "are not loving Charleston" and "they're trying to make it something else."[54] He rebuked preservationists for opposing almost every form of development except for "geriatric monoculture" that disregarded the needs of families and young people. He criticized the fire marshal for allowing gigantic new fire trucks to determine the size of streets, rather than finding trucks that fit the streets that already existed. He rebuked the police chief for seeing bicycles as a problem and called Clemson University a parasite on the city.[55]

Duany and his colleagues noticed that "most of the new work is good enough urbanistically and architecturally" but they judged it "good enough for other cities, not for Charleston." For instance, the

52. DPZ Partners, "Revised B.A.R. Process for New Construction and Large Projects," 9 September 2015.

53. Ramos, "The Week of Duany."

54. Robert Behre, "An Rx for what ails Charleston," *Charleston Post and Courier*, 12 March 2015.

55. Ramos, "The Week of Duany."

Horizon building, which was approved by the Board of Architectural Review "after six months of reviews, without apparent enthusiasm by anyone present, including its architects," was a busy combination of brick and glass, with towers at each corner, and an enormous dark-colored web-like carapace on its front. In five hours, one of Duany's associates produced an alternative, brick with cream-colored detailing and no strange exterior paraphernalia.[56] The DPZ version was so obviously preferable that it produced "a series of sighs in the crowd similar to what you hear at the grand finale of a fireworks show."[57] The lesson was not that Duany's firm was superior, but that the process of review tended to produce mediocrity. The report held up the restored Francis Marion Hotel and the Mills House Hotel as models of excellence that showed that even large buildings could be at once beautiful and respectful of their surroundings. In contrast, new office buildings at 174 Meeting Street and 158 Meeting Street failed simultaneously to mesh with their surroundings and to offer any hint of distinction.[58]

As might have been expected, many architects were aghast. The director of Clemson's architecture center said Duany's criticisms were unfair and based on a lack of understanding of Clemson and the city's community of architects.[59] Architect Jonathan Thompson said that Duany's knowledge of Charleston seemed to be "superficial" and that he had insulted the city's architects with "reckless criticisms" and "verbal abuse." He believed Duany was insisting that the city should allow only one architectural style, a suggestion he considered "absurd and dictatorial."[60]

The final report was not as harsh as Duany had been in person, but it was still critical of recent planning and architecture. It noted that, in general, urban quality was based on "walkability, a mixture of uses, and the character of public space," often buttressed by "a coherent, consistent architectural style." In Charleston, the key ele-

---

56. DPZ Partners, "Revised B.A.R. Process."
57. Ramos, "The Week of Duany."
58. DPZ Partners, "Revised B.A.R. Process."
59. Behre, "An Rx for what ails Charleston."
60. Jonathan Thompson, "Superficial perspective gets Charleston wrong," *Charleston Post and Courier*, 20 March 2015.

ment was not so much a specific style, but a "very special building type" known as the Charleston Single House, "a long, thin building that is narrow to the street front and includes a modest private side yard." The report concluded that "it is this building type, more than it is the harmonious repetition of one particular style, that makes Charleston unique."[61]

The Charleston Single House, because it is adaptable from residential to commercial buildings and from small to large buildings, should therefore serve as the basic model for Charleston architecture. For example, for shops, "the Single Houses can maintain the narrow facade, by eliminating the gardens and sometimes retaining an adapted piazza that provides a passage to the rear." The Single House could also be scaled up for much larger buildings, still "maintaining the narrow front to the street and side yard to the south," as evidenced by the Mills House Hotel. Acceptable, but not ideal, was breaking the large building "into smaller forms, which replicate the rhythm of a row of Single Houses," but it was simply not acceptable to build "monolithic structures without internal divisions." These monoliths were fine in most cities, but "in the historic heart of Charleston, however, buildings of this character will degrade the character of the city."[62]

Why did Riley invite the combative and opinionated Duany at a time when the mayor had only months left in office? As Riley must have known would happen, Duany stirred up a controversy that blew back on the city government and on Riley himself at a point in his career when Riley simply did not have the ability to fix the problems that Duany was identifying. The invitation to Duany had created anger and criticism and could not benefit Riley politically or practically. Even if Riley agreed with everything in the DPZ report, which came out in September 2015, he had to leave office in January 2016. What was the point? Why not leave office quietly?

To answer these questions it is important to understand that Riley cared more about Charleston than about his own reputation. Knowing well that Duany would ruffle the feathers of architects,

61. DPZ Partners, "Revised B.A.R. Process."
62. Ibid.

preservationists, and government officials, Riley invited a report on key issues of architecture and urbanism that, he knew, would continue to be issues for Charleston long after he had left office. In fact, he was allowing his successor, whoever that might be, to point to the report, without having been responsible for it. In other words, the "week of Duany" was Riley's way of putting important issues on the agenda of government officials, preservationists, architects, and others concerned with the city's built environment. He knew that he was leaving and could no longer provide the careful attention to the urban fabric that he had given for the previous forty years. He knew that his friend and fellow New Urbanist Andres Duany would see the city clearly and insightfully and would not be afraid to speak honestly, pointedly, and forthrightly. In a sense, the DPZ visit was Riley's parting gift to the city. Think about your buildings and your streets, he was saying. Do not take them for granted. Build with excellence. Build to last. Build something your children and grandchildren will be proud of.

Conclusion

Riley's forty years as mayor of Charleston and his success in ten municipal elections can obscure the degree of opposition that he faced at every step of his career. He was challenged by some Democrats for being too conservative and by others for focusing too much on racial reconciliation. He was criticized by African Americans for not hiring enough African Americans. He was blamed for gentrification and the rising cost of living in Charleston. He was denounced for the congestion caused by cruise ship passengers. He was attacked by preservationists for almost every new building or facility that he championed. He was attacked for bringing the outspoken Duany to town.

Riley persevered because he had a vision of what a city could be. He knew that Charleston could be more just and more beautiful, a better place for both residents and guests. This vision is illustrated by Riley's account of an epileptic shoe-shine man whom Riley saw several times in the downtown area:

I said, "I saw you at the park the other morning."
And he said, "Yeah, Joe."
I said, "Do you go often?" It hadn't been open that long.
And he said, "I go every morning."
And I said, "Why?"
He said, "Because it's so beautiful."

Riley reflects on this incident that, "so often we tend to think of beauty in the arts erroneously as something that the more educated we are, the more apt we are to appreciate them. But it's not the case." The incident has stayed with Riley ever since. He says, "that just reinforced me in all of my work since then." It highlighted for him the importance of "the arts, a good urban design, insisting on beauty, great public spaces and more." Providing these things is not extravagance, but rather "a gift to every citizen in every walk of life, everyone."[63]

A just and compassionate city offers beauty to its people, Riley believes:

> You know, every human being needs beauty, and every human being might see it differently, but they need it. And then they come together and experience it. And the beauty can be in the beauty of a park, it can be in the beauty of a building, it can be in the beauty of a choir. When they're experiencing that together, then it's just so much more reinforced. We're sharing this, we share the moment.[64]

To offer people beauty is to take them seriously. Of course they need food and clothing. But to give them beauty is to acknowledge their higher nature.

---

63. Riley, "Taking the Long View."
64. Ibid.

Conclusion

S AINT JOHN HENRY NEWMAN describes a situation similar to our own, when, after the fall of the Roman Empire, Saint Benedict established monasteries in the ruins of a once great civilization:

> He found the world, physical and social, in ruins, and his mission was to restore it in the way, not of science, but of nature, not as if setting about to do it, not professing to do it by any set time or by any rare specific or by any series of strokes, but so quietly, patiently, gradually, that often, till the work was done, it was not known to be doing. It was a restoration, rather than a visitation, correction, or conversion. The new world which he helped to create was a growth rather than a structure. Silent men were observed about the country, or discovered in the forest, digging, clearing, and building; and other silent men, not seen, were sitting in the cold cloister, tiring their eyes, and keeping their attention on the stretch, while they painfully deciphered and copied and re-copied the manuscripts which they had saved. There was no one that "contended, or cried out," or drew attention to what was going on; but by degrees the woody swamp became a hermitage, a religious house, a farm, an abbey, a village, a seminary, a school of learning, and a city. Roads and bridges connected it with other abbeys and cities, which had similarly grown up; and what the haughty Alaric or fierce Attila had broken to pieces, these patient meditative men had brought together and made to live again.[1]

As in the days of Benedict, the great project of today is not criticism but construction. For decades, gifted thinkers have been pointing to

---

1. John Henry Newman, "The Mission of St. Benedict," *Rise and Progress of Universities and Benedictine Essays* (Notre Dame, Indiana: University of Notre Dame Press, 2001), 410–11.

the flaws in modernity. One can find shelves of books that provide detailed critiques of every aspect of modern politics, modern economics, and modern culture, and that expose the philosophical errors that make modern pathologies inevitable. These are good and worthy treatises from which I and countless others have profited, but now the day is late and the time for analysis is over. Now is the time for building.

The examples in this book are meant to inspire. They cannot be imitated precisely, for people's gifts and dispositions differ, as do their situations, histories, and resources, but the spirit and courage of the men and women in these pages can be embraced. Let me close with a few reflections on what we have seen in these stories. Some of what follows I had in mind from the start of this project, but much of it came to me only after reflecting on what I had written.

The Vitality of Tradition

First of all, I hope you sensed the sheer *adventure* of these stories, not despite their all having something to do with a restoration of tradition or a reaffirmation of orthodoxy but for the very reason of their connection to tradition and orthodoxy. G. K. Chesterton made the point more than a century ago, but the idea that orthodoxy is the true adventure bears repeating because it is continually undermined by the nostrums of popular culture, which glamorizes rebellion and novelty and denigrates tradition.[2] Heresy and accommodation are boring, stale, and sterile because they are not based on truth and therefore cannot grow and reproduce; they can only tear down. Rejection of the past and of tradition initially seems liberating, but ends with entrapment in the present. Severing ties to the past unmoors the present, makes it meaningless. If you want meaning in your life, the last thing you should do is disconnect yourself from your people, your place, and your history, much less the spiritual traditions of the Church founded by Christ himself. If you want meaning, embrace tradition; if you want life, submit yourself to the truth.

2. Gilbert Keith Chesterton, *Orthodoxy* (Garden City, NY: Image Books, 1959).

Frederick Hart, for example, became one of the truly distinctive artists of his day by honoring tradition, not by rejecting it. He was by no means an unquestioning imitator of the past, but his love of the great figurative sculptural tradition enabled him to learn from what had gone before, following in the footsteps of the great sculptors of the past, while simultaneously producing works like Daughters of Odessa that spoke powerfully to the issues of his day. In the same vein, the Dominicans of the Province of St. Joseph have prospered not by rejecting their traditions, but by embracing them. The seemingly run-of-the-mill "Western Civ" curriculum of the Integrated Humanities Program went off like a bomb at the University of Kansas. All that was needed was a few professors to take those traditional readings seriously. The orthodoxy of Franciscan University of Steubenville makes that small campus burn like a fire in the night.

Beauty

My second point is the priority of beauty. When I started this project I planned to focus each chapter on one of the transcendentals: truth, or goodness, or beauty. As I wrote, however, I had one realization that led to a second. First, the convertibility of the transcendentals (the idea that the true is also good and beautiful and the good is also beautiful and true, and so on), which had been merely notional for me, became more and more evident. It became difficult for me to say that the Dominicans were about truth, without also mentioning the goodness of their actions, or to focus on the beauty of Frederick Hart's work without pointing to the goodness and truth that flowed from it. In all of the examples, truth, goodness, and beauty were so intertwined that I gave up pretending that each chapter could focus on one transcendental. I saw that all seven chapters would incorporate all three transcendentals. At the same time, paradoxically, I came to my second realization: I was writing more about beauty than I had planned.

The example that opened my eyes to the surprising upsurge of beauty on my pages was the chapter on the Sisters of Life. Here was an order of women devoted to saving human lives, which, in my initial plan, seemed like a clear example of pursuing the good.

When I wrote the chapter, however, I found myself beginning with Heather King's story of being struck by "the light those sisters threw off" and titling it "Brilliant Innocence," a reference to the splendor—that is, the beauty—of holiness. My best attempt to introduce the Sisters of Life turned not to the category of goodness, but, almost against my inclinations, to the category of beauty. It was as if there was something deep and mysterious that made beauty the best way to express the essence of the Sisters of Life.

With the help of James Matthew Wilson's *The Vision of the Soul*, I came to see that the mysterious pull of beauty was not just some personal eccentricity on my part. As Wilson says, "when truth presents itself to the mind's eye, it does so as Beauty."[3] It does so because beauty is the splendor of all the transcendentals:

> Far from being an incidental quality or perfection of material things, beauty in its purest sense designates a finality at which the human intellect arrives when it fulfills itself, when it is most fully saturated in reality. This is not to collapse truth into beauty, for truth loses nothing of its integrity when we know it so well that we see it. Rather, we see the truth, love it as good, and finally perceive it as a reality unto itself, a form, that stands in relation to all other things and speaks of their harmonious existence as created. Beauty is this total showing forth of form and splendor, distinct from truth because we may encounter it as an existence, as being, before we recognize it as true, but also distinct from truth and goodness, because in its vision these things are finally held together within the form, within the fullness of being.[4]

In other words, "Beauty comes first and also last in our experience."[5] Beauty pulls us in and, after contemplation, becomes in the end both more real and more intense. This priority and finality of beauty is not a psychological quirk, but rather a reflection of a fundamental reality: "the world is itself ordered by and to Beauty."[6]

---

3. Wilson, *Vision of the Soul*, 82.
4. Ibid., 85.
5. Ibid.
6. Ibid.

The implausibility of that last statement to the vast majority of contemporary Americans highlights both the massive mystification successfully perpetrated by modernity—our fellow citizens have come to believe that they live in a vast, neutral, empty cosmos—and the great necessity of rebuilding a culture that does not merely embrace beauty but sees beauty as built into the very fabric of existence. Thus, it is fitting that the teachers of truth and the doers of good in these pages appear beautiful. It is fitting to come to truth through beauty and it is fitting to see the good, in the end, as beauty. It may come as a surprise to this nation of pragmatists, but the most "realistic" life, the life based on the most rock solid foundation, is the life devoted to beauty.

Institutionalization

A third issue in these stories is institutionalization. When something goes well, whether it is an artistic endeavor or an academic pursuit, the natural consequence is the desire to institutionalize it, that is, to make it last. Since we love the good, we want the good to continue. Such a desire is natural and praiseworthy, but it always comes with temptations. I am influenced here by Ivan Illich, who describes two kinds of institutions, the manipulative and the convivial.[7] The manipulative institution attempts to guarantee results and, in doing so, gradually becomes coercive and counter-productive. The classic example is the mandatory public school system, which, starting with the noble intention to impart an education, ends up with a compulsory twelve-year conveyor belt that has come to seem more and more like a prison system and that produces people who have credentials but little love for learning, knowledge, or truth. The convivial institution, on the other hand, is humble and modest, providing a framework that serves the desired end, but never presumes to guarantee it. The convivial institution has few

---

7. Ivan Illich, *Celebration of Awareness: A Call for Institutional Revolution* (Garden City, NY: Doubleday, 1970); Ivan Illich, *Deschooling Society* (New York: Harper & Row, 1971); Ivan Illich, *Tools for Conviviality* (New York: Harper & Row, 1973).

rules, little bureaucracy, and a high degree of freedom, because it is devoted to serving persons, not producing results.

The Dominicans are a good example of institutionalization done right. Their religious order has survived for 800 years because it has a strong identity, a living tradition, and a high degree of flexibility. It has firm rules but not too many of them; it has good leaders and administrators, but most friars are able to devote themselves to scholarship, teaching, and preaching, rather than to administration. On the other hand, the most conspicuous failure of the Dominicans of the Province of St. Joseph is Providence College, an institution that has adopted the characteristics of the modern administrative university. It is full of offices, agencies, departments, supervisors, and administrators; it produces plans and statements in an amount and of a quality similar to its secular competitors. Its logic has become manipulative, oriented more toward preserving the institution, than toward contemplation and truth. It is almost impossible to imagine the college producing a new Albert the Great or Thomas Aquinas.

For those of you working in good institutions, it is necessary to be vigilant. Never trust in administrative procedures to accomplish what human persons are called to do. Only human beings can love. Only human beings can forgive. Teaching is personal. Learning, although *possible* in isolation, occurs best in the context of friendship and community. As a rule, resist the temptation to add another layer of bureaucracy; better yet, if at all possible, *eliminate* a layer of bureaucracy. If you have a choice, hire the artist or the doctor, not the administrator.

These chapters have also demonstrated that failing institutions are not lost causes: Michael Scanlan renewed Franciscan University; Thomas Gordon Smith turned the Notre Dame School of Architecture around; Joe Riley revitalized Charleston. Such reversals are rare because once an institution becomes large and manipulative, the logic that dominates decision-making is no longer about education, or music, or justice, but rather about institutional survival. The stakeholders imbibe the warped logic of institutional preservation to such an extent that they can no longer see what the institution was founded for in the first place. Thus, the best opportunity for institutional reorientation is a time of crisis. When the institution's future is doubtful, a moment of clarity comes for even the most "institutionalized" bureaucrats. When they see that the current trend is leading toward institutional demise, they often admit that a change of course might offer the best chance for survival.

Franciscan University, for example, was at such a low point that it was trying to sell its buildings. Charleston was grubby and racially divided. Notre Dame's architecture school was at risk of losing accreditation. In these crises, Scanlan, Riley, and Smith had room to operate that they never would have had in more functional institutions. Their vision and commitment to reform, which would have caused intractable bureaucratic resistance in normal circumstances, could be seen as a potential lifeline. Consequently, for those of you in failing institutions, this may be the time to present your daring plan. If things are going from bad to worse, you might feel that it is time to jump ship—and it may be! But be open to the possibility that this crisis is providential, a time for reform and rebuilding.

Religious Orders

It was not my intention to make this a book about religious orders for the simple reason that religious orders are not a large part of daily life for most Americans. They seem odd enough that a Dominican friar strolling around a secular college campus inevitably receives strange looks and, from the bold, questions like "what are you?" It did not occur to me, when I started this project, to think of it as mostly about religious orders, but as I look back at my seven chapters, I see that five of them feature religious orders as the protagonists or in strong supporting roles. The Sisters of Life and the Dominicans *are* religious orders. Notre Dame is a university of the Congregation of Holy Cross, while Franciscan University is run by the TOR Franciscan friars. The Integrated Humanities Program had a strong Benedictine influence and some of its alumni became monks.

In retrospect, there is good reason for a book about seeking the true, the good, and the beautiful to give a great deal of attention to religious orders. In addition to being dedicated primarily to our God, who is Truth, Goodness, and Beauty personified, orders have charisms and missions oriented toward specific goods, such as preaching the truth or serving the poor. Religious orders, then, are convivial institutions dedicated to the kind of activity that I am calling for in this book. They teach, preach, heal, and serve because they have members who have dedicated themselves to God and to their specific task.

One implication of this acknowledgment of the central role of religious orders in seeking the true, the good, and the beautiful in America is that you should consider joining a religious order. There may be a group of men and women out there who have exactly the charism you need and are already doing the job you are called to do. If readers of this book start joining the Dominicans, the Franciscans, the Sisters of Life, the Congregation of Holy Cross, the Benedictines, and other orders, I will be overjoyed.

There is another option, an option that might seem strange, even radical. God could be calling some of you to start new religious orders. I am convinced that our sad world is crying out for new religious movements that will bring orthodoxy and tradition to bear upon the problems of our day. It may be that your growing call to religious life is actually a call to found a new religious order or to join someone who is about to do so. As the culture continues to decline, God will not leave us alone. As Cardinal O'Connor said, "God raises up religious communities to address the needs of the time." New saints and new founders will emerge to start new movements. I hope you are one of them.

Many of you are neither interested in joining a religious order nor called to do so. Perhaps, like me, you are happily married with children and a mortgage. But even those of us who will never join an order can still work with religious orders and benefit from their work. Just as Thomas Gordon Smith worked with members of the Congregation of Holy Cross to reform the architecture school at the order's university, you can work with a religious order to accomplish your true, good, and beautiful task. Many young people who will never take vows still benefit enormously and bring blessings to others by supporting, publicizing, and participating in the works of the Dominicans, whether at the House of Studies, at a Dominican parish, or in a chapter of the Thomistic Institute. In a similar way, dozens, maybe hundreds, of lay Catholics are working with the TOR Franciscans to serve the students in Steubenville. Religious orders are worth seeking out. It might even be worth moving to a city or a neighborhood specifically to be in their vicinity.

I should provide a caveat about religious orders. Many of today's orders have sold their birthright for a mess of pottage. Instead of the pure, orthodox doctrine to which Catholics have a right, these orders provide either an ambiguous message or actual heresy. Please do not assume that a religious order is a good one simply because it exists. It is a sad necessity of today's world that orders must be approached with caution. But one of the great joys of today's world is that vibrant, orthodox orders continue to exist and continue to bring truth, good, and beauty to the world around them.

Clear Creek Abbey

To conclude, I would like to tell the story of Clear Creek Abbey in Oklahoma, which is a continuation of the story of the Integrated Humanities Program, and also brings together several of the threads in the other six chapters. The Clear Creek story begins with Philip Anderson. After growing up in a Unitarian family, Anderson came to the University of Kansas in 1971, where he decided to participate in the Integrated Humanities Program: "I entered the program with no spiritual direction about anything in life. My personal life was out of hand. We really believed that the cultural leaders of the time, like Bob Dylan, had something."[8]

When he encountered John Senior's confident assertions and integrated view of truth, initially Anderson was offended and confused, but he gradually came to believe in truth, then in God, and then in Catholicism. He was one of six IHP students who traveled with Senior to Fontgombault Abbey in France in July 1972, and, after graduation and a stint in the Marines, he and two other students began as novices at the abbey. Although some monks left,

8. Mason Beecroft, "Let Them Be Born in Wonder: Catholic Legacy from the Humanities Program at University of Kansas Endures," *Eastern Oklahoma Catholic* (June 2013), 13.

Anderson came to love the silence, the prayer, and the simple beauty of the Benedictine life. He stayed at Fontgombault, lived the hidden life of a monk during the 1980s and 1990s, and became the abbot of one of Fontgombault's daughterhouses.

Meanwhile, Fontgombault and the Solesmes family of twenty-nine Benedictine monasteries and convents prospered, attracting vocations from around the world. The abbot of Fontgombault had long been thinking of establishing a new monastery in the United States and by the late 1990s he had several American and Canadian monks who could serve as the nucleus of a new foundation. In 1999, he sent Anderson and twelve other monks, including another IHP graduate and six other Americans, to Cherokee County, Oklahoma, to establish a new Benedictine monastery, now known as Our Lady of Clear Creek Abbey.[9] Today Anderson is the abbot of a monastery of 57 monks.[10] Senior's dream of a new monasticism in America once seemed unrealistic, but it has come to pass with one of his old students as the new abbot.[11]

Clear Creek Abbey is a blessing to many people who are not monks. Families have moved to the vicinity of the abbey so that they can participate in its liturgy. Like the monasteries of the Middle Ages, the abbey has become a center of culture and spiritual life. It has also become a place of pilgrimage, as Catholics from all over the United States come to stay with the monks, to worship with them, and to be reminded of the simplicity and beauty of God.

The abbey is a sign of the continued vitality of tradition and orthodoxy. Here is a religious order that traces its roots back to the beginning of the Middle Ages, starting anew in Oklahoma. Here are American young men seeking a life of prayer and simplicity, pledging themselves to the countercultural values of poverty, chastity, and obedience. Here are buildings emerging in the wilderness, just

9. Ibid.
10. "One day with the Lord is as a thousand years.—A Score of Years: 2000–2020," *Our Lady of Clear Creek Abbey*, 13 September 2020, https://clearcreekmonks.org/one-day-with-the-lord-is-as-a-thousand-years-a-score-of-years-2000-2020/.
11. One of the monks, former IHP student Francis Bethel, sees the abbey as "in many ways ... the outcome of a quest that had begun in the 1970s" in the IHP: Bethel, *John Senior*, 1.

as they did in Europe 1500 years ago. Here is a convivial institution, the Benedictine monastery, that has survived for more than a millennium and continues to offer its fruits to the world around it. Here is a religious order whose rule is the very model of convivial institutionalization: short, specific, and focused.

Clear Creek also shows the hidden depths of divine providence. The connection to John Senior and the IHP has already been mentioned. But the abbey's buildings were designed by Thomas Gordon Smith, who treasured this project and found that working with the monks deepened his faith. Much of the abbey's sculpture was carved by Thomas Gordon Smith's son Andrew Wilson Smith. The story of Clear Creek was told to the author by Innocent Smith, OP, a friar of the Dominicans of the Province of St. Joseph who is the son of Thomas Gordon Smith and the brother of Andrew Wilson Smith.

Sometimes, I think, we fear that if we truly pursue the true, the good, and the beautiful, in the way that God is calling us, we will end up alone and rejected, doing something peculiar that no one will ever appreciate. One of the messages of Clear Creek is that God weaves together seemingly disparate threads to create something beyond the capabilities of any of the individual participants. In this case, Thomas Gordon Smith pursued his vocation to design beautiful buildings and to teach others to do the same; his children grew up to appreciate the true, the good, and the beautiful. The father's design would one day be adorned by the son's sculpture and then relayed to this writer by another son dedicated to the truth.

While Thomas Gordon Smith was embracing classicism, raising his family, and growing in his Catholic faith, John Senior was instilling in his students a love for truth and beauty that, decades later, came to fruition in France and then at Clear Creek. In retrospect, it seems clear that the life of a Benedictine monk is in fact one of the best ways to live out the Integrated Humanities Program's vision of poetic knowledge. Daily life slowly ingrains prayer and chant into the consciousness of the monks. Just as the IHP students memorized poems, the monks eventually memorize much of the liturgy. They "know" the prayers and chants not just in being able to repeat the words but in the manner of knowing a friend. Their lives become lives of prayer and chant. In a way, they *live* the prayers and chants.

The agricultural and other work that they do is different from prayer, but serves as a complement, not an encumbrance. Work, especially manual labor, is an encounter with the real. Just as Professor Dennis Quinn once asked television-befuddled freshmen to gaze at the stars, the Rule of Saint Benedict asks the monk to put his hand to the plow. The reality of dirt and seed and plow, the reality of human muscle and human sweat, the reality of heat and rain: these are all in their own ways as mysterious and wonder-full as the stars. The Benedictine life is one of encountering wholes and receiving their goodness. The Benedictine monk receives the liturgy and treasures it; he does hard physical labor, knowing, in humility, the goodness of service and the goodness of God's gift of the earth. There is, then, a great resonance between the Benedictine life and the poetic knowledge of the IHP.[12] One might even say that the Integrated Humanities Program was the perfect preparation for the Rule of Saint Benedict and that the Rule of Saint Benedict was the fitting consummation of the Integrated Humanities Program. We rarely see the master plan, but we have to trust that God has one. Our seemingly insignificant individual initiative could be a small part of a much larger scheme.

Thus, in the Kingdom of God, failure is a relative term. In 1980, it looked like John Senior and the IHP had failed. The program was ignominiously rejected by the University of Kansas and had lasted only a decade, but the lives of those who participated in the IHP were indelibly changed by their time in the program. Their conversions to Catholicism, their religious vocations, their solid marriages, and their continued friendships suggest that the program was gloriously successful. What Senior, Quinn, and Nelick did in Kansas had lasting results, results that include the ongoing blessing to the Church and the world that is Clear Creek Abbey.

The Benedictine consummation of the Integrated Humanities Program and its interweaving with the story of the Notre Dame School of Architecture should give us great hope. Because we are followers of the Resurrected Christ, we can take big risks. Or perhaps it would be better to say that we can take what *appear* to be big

---

12. Taylor, *Poetic Knowledge*, 34–35.

risks. First of all, with God on our side, the tiny mustard seed of faith can result in the growth of a large and sturdy tree. Second, the deeds we are called to do are worthwhile, regardless of the results. That is, the good, the true, and the beautiful are still good, true, and beautiful, even if they "fail," even if no one else ever sees them.

Inevitably, "failure" came to the Benedictines of the early Middle Ages. Some new invader came to destroy what the monks had built. When this happened they did not give up:

> nothing was left to them but to begin all over again; but this they did without grudging, so promptly, cheerfully, and tranquilly, as if it were by some law of nature that the restoration came, and they were like the flowers and shrubs and fruit trees which they reared, and which, when ill-treated, do not take vengeance, or remember evil, but give forth fresh branches, leaves, or blossoms, perhaps in greater profusion, and with richer quality, for the very reason that the old were rudely broken off.[13]

As with the Benedictines of long ago, our call today is to build something good and true and beautiful. We do not know what the results will be, but we know that nothing in the Kingdom of God is wasted.

---

13. Newman, "The Mission of St. Benedict," 411.

Made in the USA
Monee, IL
30 August 2021